A Ramble Around Blessington Lakes

The Aimless Meanderings of an
Amateur Photographer

Paula O'Sullivan

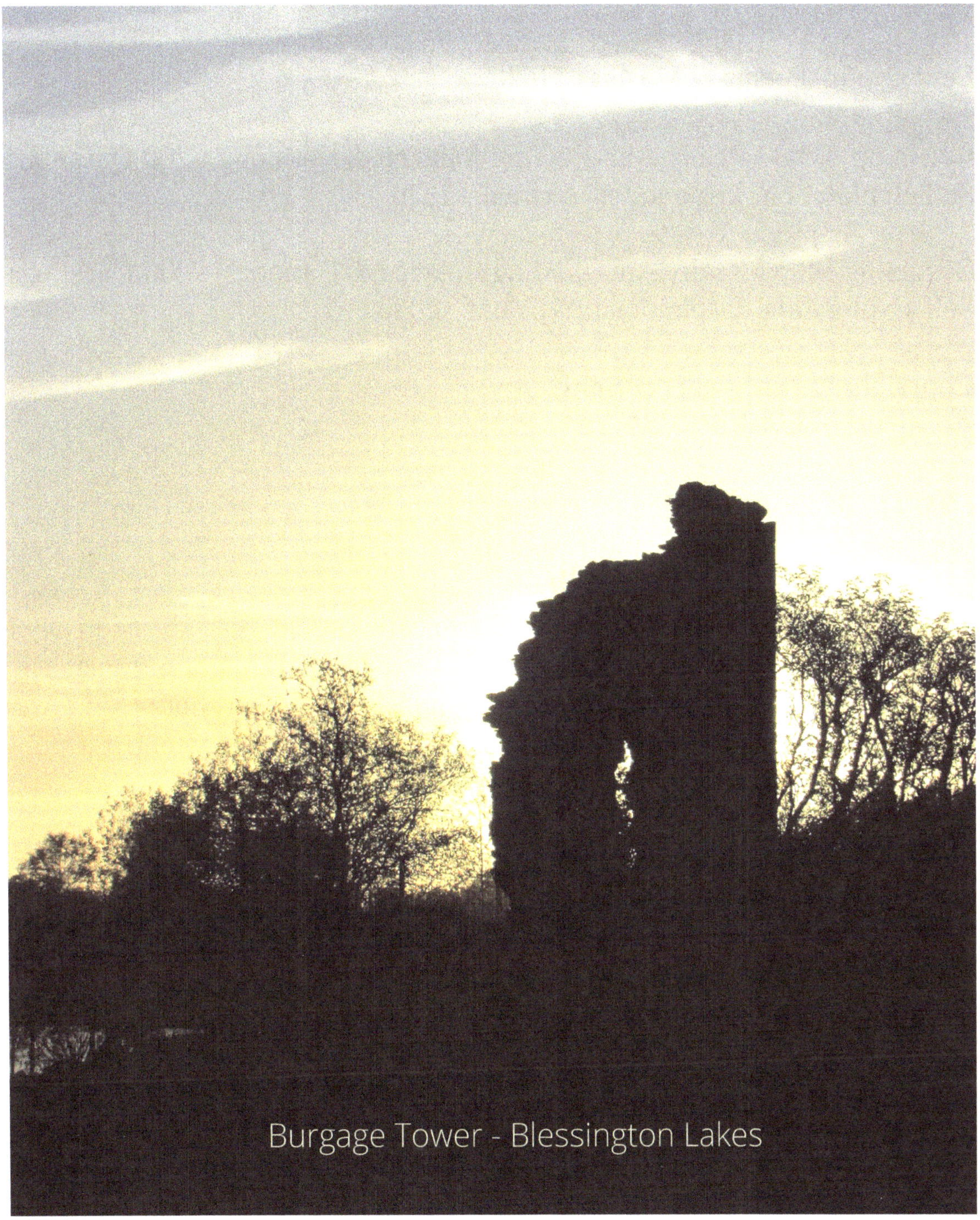

Burgage Tower - Blessington Lakes

Other books by this author

Different Perspectives for a Different World–Essays for Life
- 2013

Different Perspectives for a Different World–Essays for Life
– Revised Edition-2017

Same Shit Different Day–Breaking the Patterns that Make us Miserable-A Metaphysical Approach to Wellbeing-2019

Let Love In–Poems & Musings-2020

Becoming Who I Really Am -Finding Balance & Harmony - 200 Questions for Self-Exploration -Inspirational Journal - 2020

Becoming Who I Really Am -Finding Balance & Harmony - 200 Questions for Self-Exploration -Inspirational Wisdom - 2020

Copyright © 2021 Paula O'Sullivan
All rights reserved.

ISBN: 9798476176350
Imprint : Independently Published

All rights reserved. No part of this book may be copied, reproduced in any form on by an electronic or mechanical means, including information storage and retrieval systems, without prior permission from the author, nor be otherwise circulated in any form of binding or cover other than that in which it is published and without a similar condition including this condition being imposed on the subsequent purchaser.

This book is available in print at most online retailers.

You may contact the author at

E-mail paulaosullivan1@gmail.com
Facebook Paula O'Sullivan's Author Page
Website www.paulaosullivanscreations.com
Blog www.paulaosullivan.wordpress.com

CONTENTS

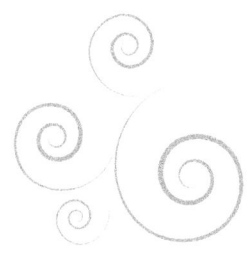

4   JUST A BLOW IN!

7   BLESSINGTON

13   BLESSINGTON LAKES

15   MY MEANDERINGS

24   ST. MARKS CROSS

25   BURGAGE TOWER

30   BLESSINGTON GREENWAY

48   VIKINGS!

54   FLOODS!

57   RUSSELLSTOWN

66   RUSSBOROUGH HOUSE

77   VALLEYMOUNT

85   BRIDGES

90   WINTERY DAYS

103   ARTWORK VS PHOTOGRAPHY

115   RECOMMENDED READING

JUST A BLOW IN!

I moved to Blessington in 2007, hailing originally from Dublin. We had been frantically trying to move home and were trying to purchase a property in Dublin. Nothing was going right and after the third attempt, I suggested we take some time out and take a day trip to Blessington.

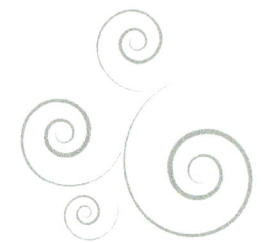

I had just a few memories of visiting over the years. When I was a child my parents had brought us up once or twice for a picnic by the Lakes. My only memories were fear. There was a sunken village under the waters, I was told, and if I tried to paddle, the piranhas would get me!

I once got the bus up in the 1980's when I was 15, with a friend. We were going to the An Oige Youth Hostel named Baltyboys. We underestimated the walk and it was late, raining and very dark by the time we arrived. The place was teaming with Boy Scouts.

They were in frisky form. I'd no sooner sat on the window ledge, because there was no room anywhere else to sit, when the lights went out. Suddenly someone lunged at me ! My elbow hit the window which cracked a little, and I screamed! A leader came into the room wanting to know why the lights were out and why was there a crack in the window. We left the next day!

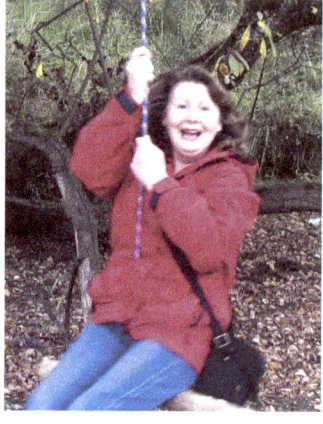

When I was 18, a boyfriend and I once came up for a hike and a few pints in the West Wicklow House. We reluctantly staggered onto the last bus as we didn't have enough money to try and get somewhere to stay the night.

I went to wedding reception of two friends in the Downshire Arms in the early 90's I think.

After that I came to visit the odd time on a Sunday in '97 / 98. I used to come up with my husband to buy plants from the garden centre, and then we'd have a look around the open air market that used to be there.

Things had changed a bit since we'd last been here in 1998. There were a few new housing estates that had sprung up, and before I knew it we were viewing them. Of course it took another few attempts before we eventually got a house.

We were only in our house a year when I separated from my husband. He eventually left the area, I decided to stay, it felt like home and I liked the people here.

I've met some really amazing people in Blessington, and I've enjoyed the sense of community that I didn't find in other places that I've lived in over the years.

I had an oul digital camera but I always said I'd like to get a proper camera. Of course I couldn't afford one, so I got a little bridge camera instead and that was the beginning of my meanderings around the lakes in 2014. I eventually bought a DSLR, but I found it tiresome changing the different lens, and it was awkward carrying it, so I went back to using my lightweight bridge camera.

A selection of the photos that I took over the years since then are included in this book, alongside my artwork and my ramblings about my experiences and some historical facts too!

Some of the photos and artwork from this book have found their way onto various cards, keyrings, postcards, coasters, framed prints and so on as I make my work widely available at affordable prices. They can be found for sale at The Blessington Tourist Office, Co. Wicklow, Ireland. Once monthly on the fourth Sunday at The Valleymount Country Market, Co. Wicklow, and my artwork is in The Craft Corner, Donard, Co. Wicklow. Check my website for updated details, www.paulaosullivanscreations.com

I hope you find it interesting.

Paula O'Sullivan 2021 xxx

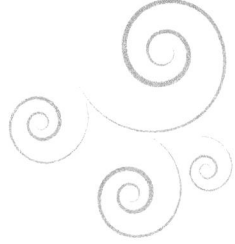

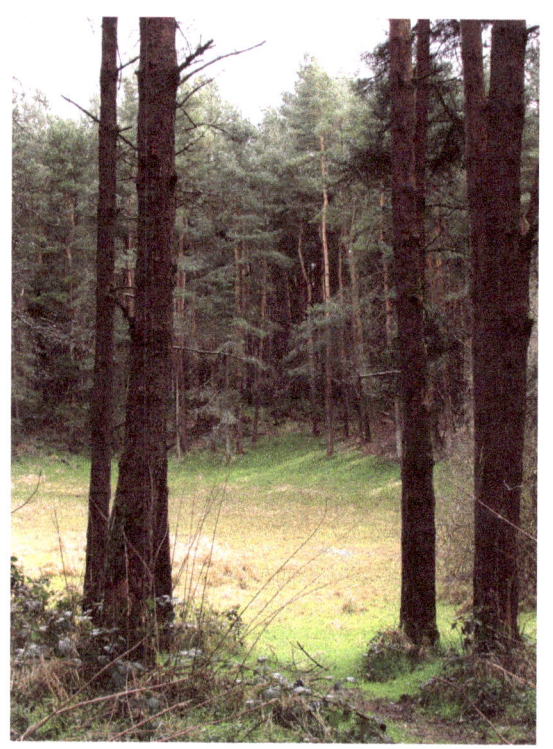
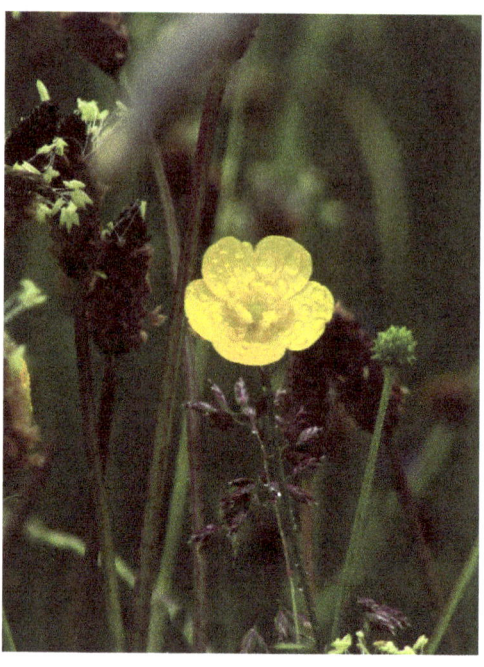

In the Meadows near the lakes

Blessington Greenway is an amazing series of walkways

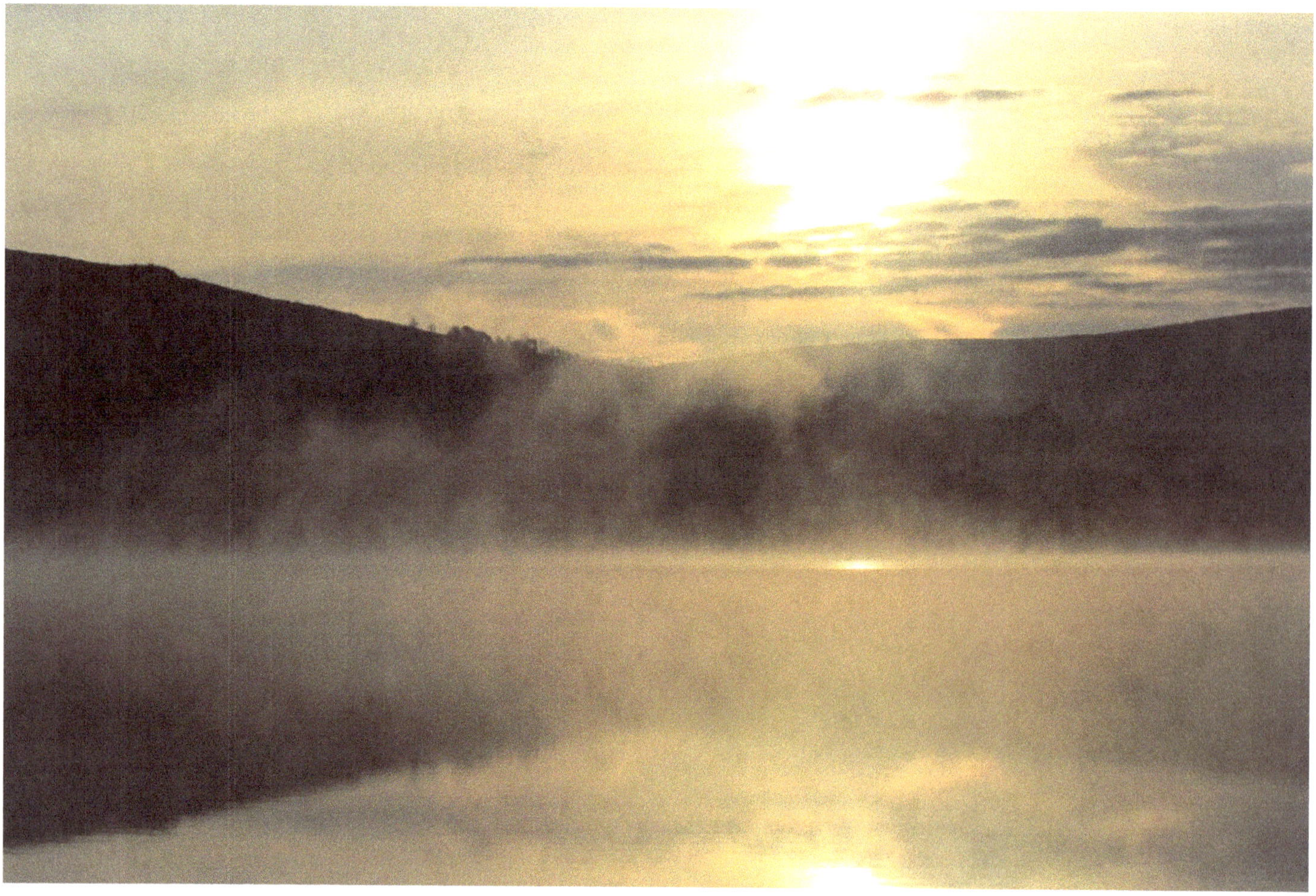

Blessington Lakes is stunning on a sunny misty morning.

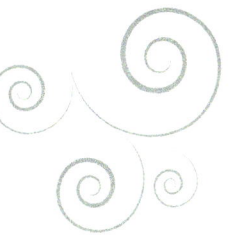

BLESSINGTON
Baile Coimin

The area has been known by the name of Blessington since approximately 1669. Apparently it had also been called Munfine in Medieval times. Then Comenstowne c.1640 connected with Archbishop John Comyn who lived in the area around the 12th century. Then it was known as Ballecomine c.1660. Archbishop Michael Doyle was granted local townlands in 1667. It was suggested by King Charles II that Blessington should be a free borough extending 200 acres every way from the middle of the town.

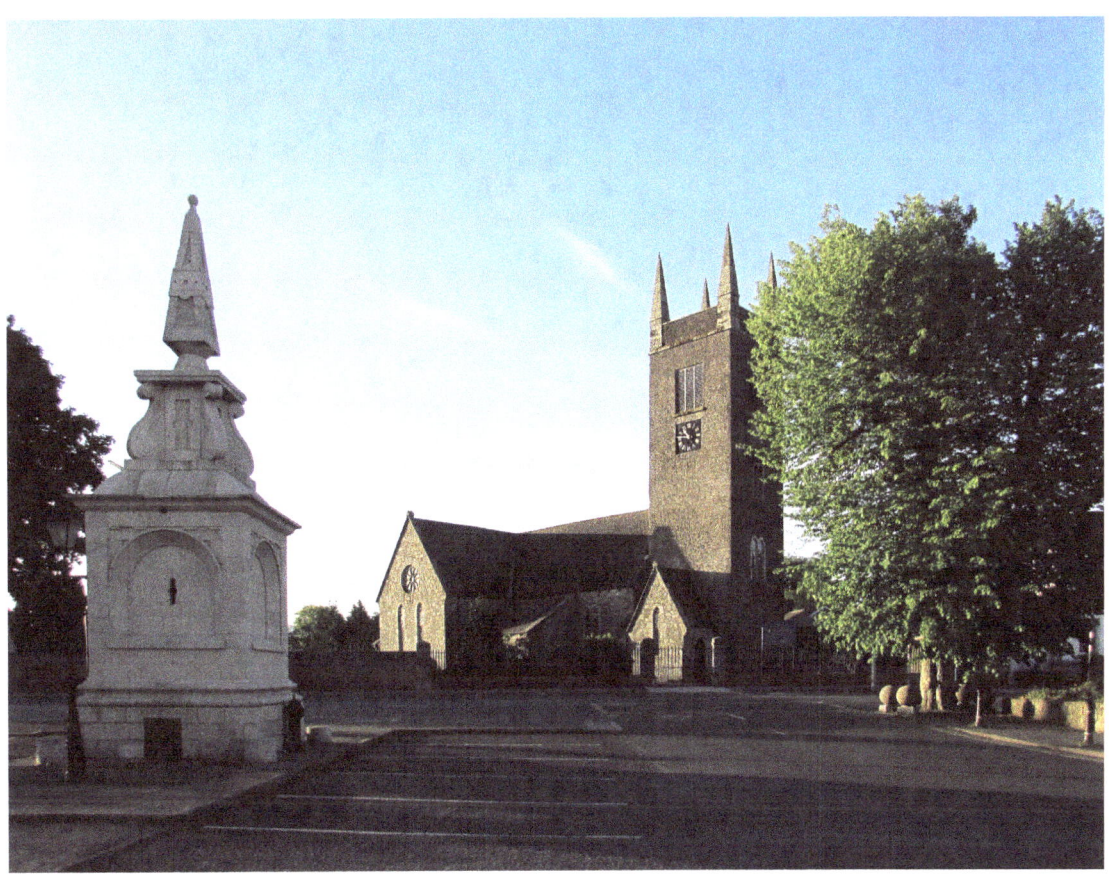

Downshire Monument, St. Mary's Church and The Four Stone Tree on Blessington Main Street.

St. Mary's Church of Ireland was planned by Archbishop Doyle, it was consecrated on 24th August 1683. He provided the bells which are still in use, and a set of Communion plate.

When we moved to Blessington we didn't know many people, but that soon changed as we started attending Morning Service in St. Mary's Church and our children started in Blessington No 1 School (named that because it was originally built as the first girls school in the area in 1820 and was situated on the Kilbride Road) The school later began catering for both girls and boys and then moved to Main Street and then to its current location in Blessington Demesne.

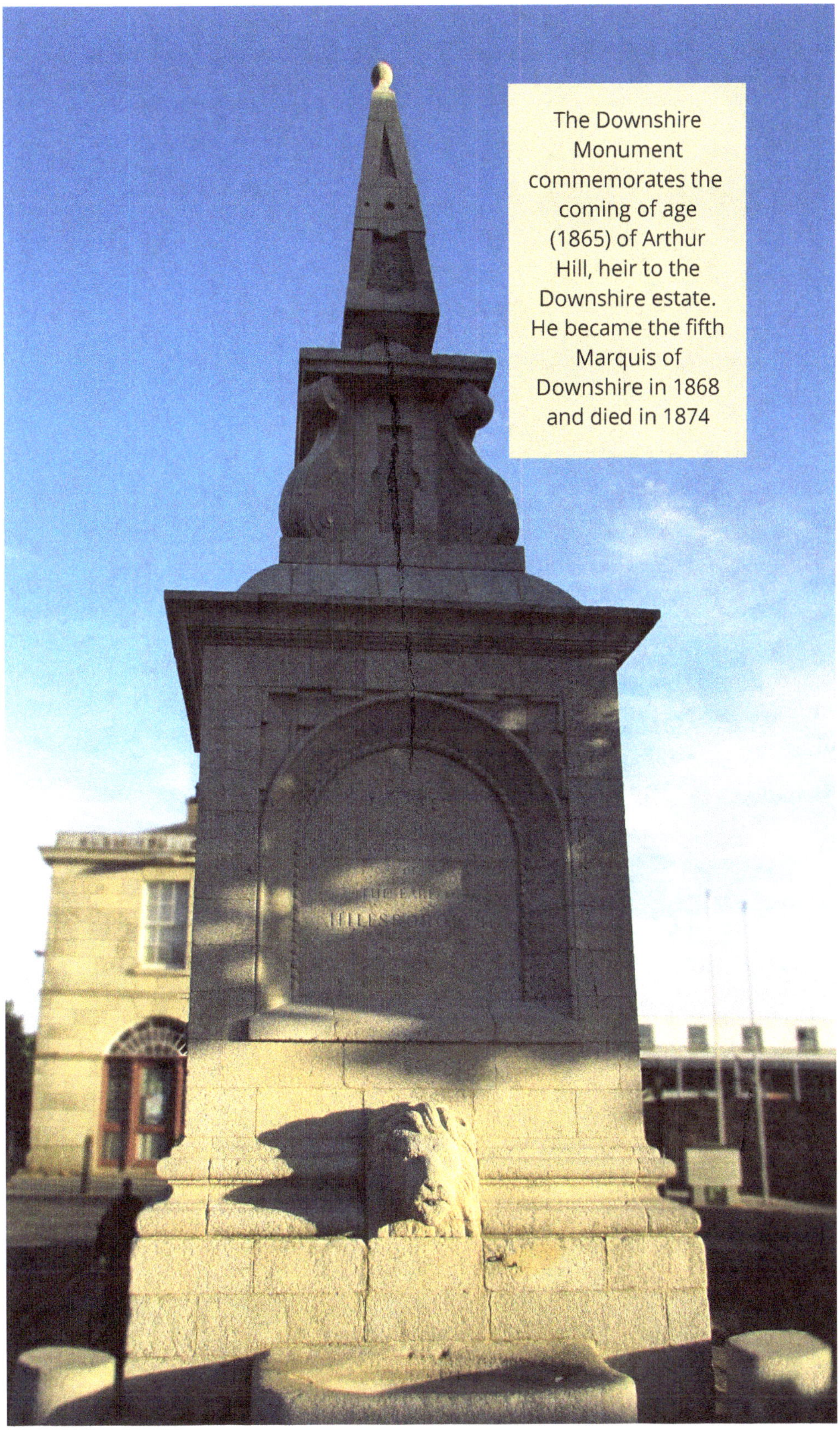

The Downshire Monument commemorates the coming of age (1865) of Arthur Hill, heir to the Downshire estate. He became the fifth Marquis of Downshire in 1868 and died in 1874

Downshire Monument in front of Credit Union House on Main Street Blessington

The inscription reads: Erected on the coming of age of The Earl of Hillsborough 24th Dec 1865

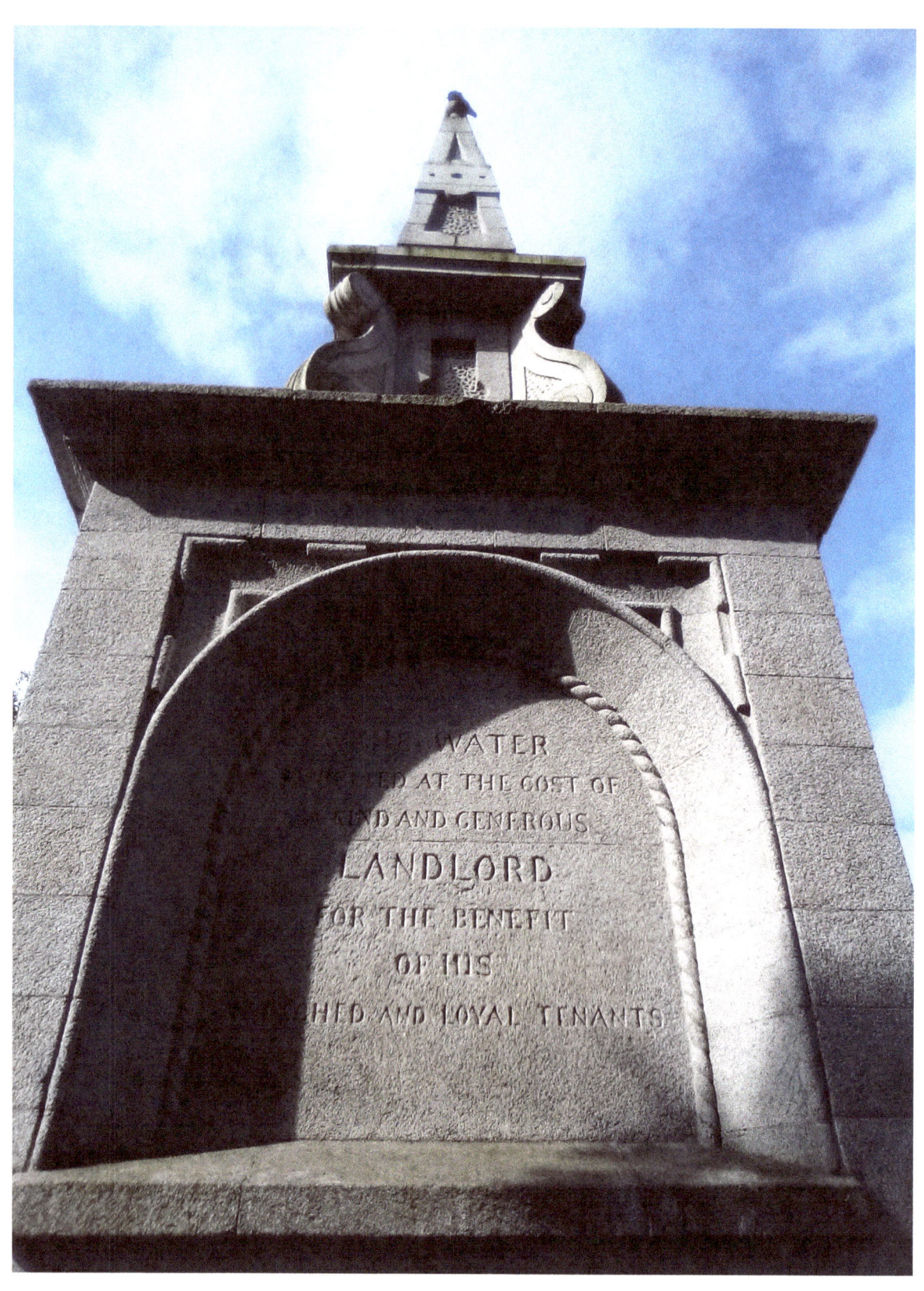

The inscription reads: The water supplied at the cost of a kind and generous landlord, for the benefit of his attached and loyal tenants.

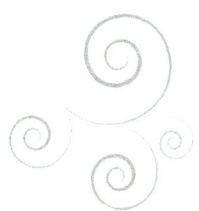
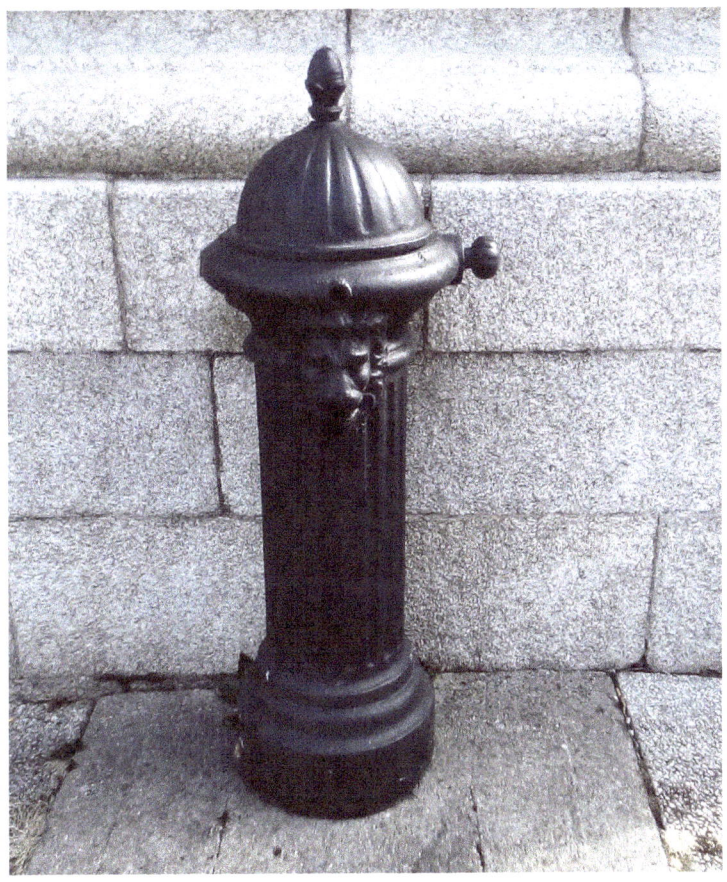
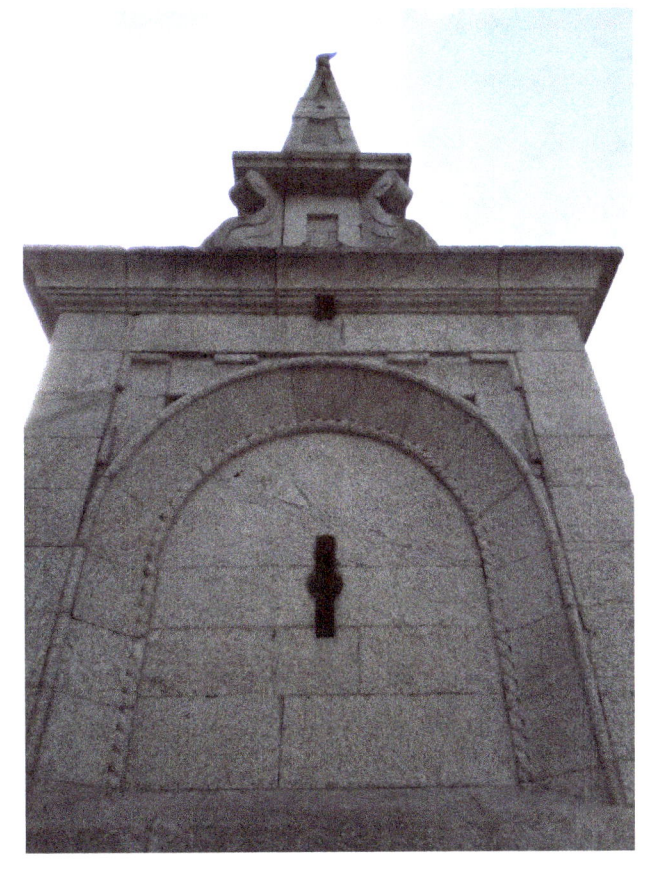
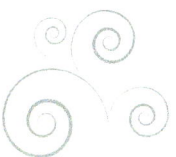

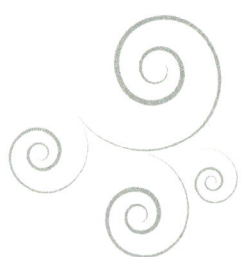

Credit Union House - as it is now called, was originally built as a Market House and Courthouse in the 1820's. It was used as a Market up to the mid 1900's by local farmers, who would meet up to sell their grain and animals. It has been used as a financial institution since 1988.

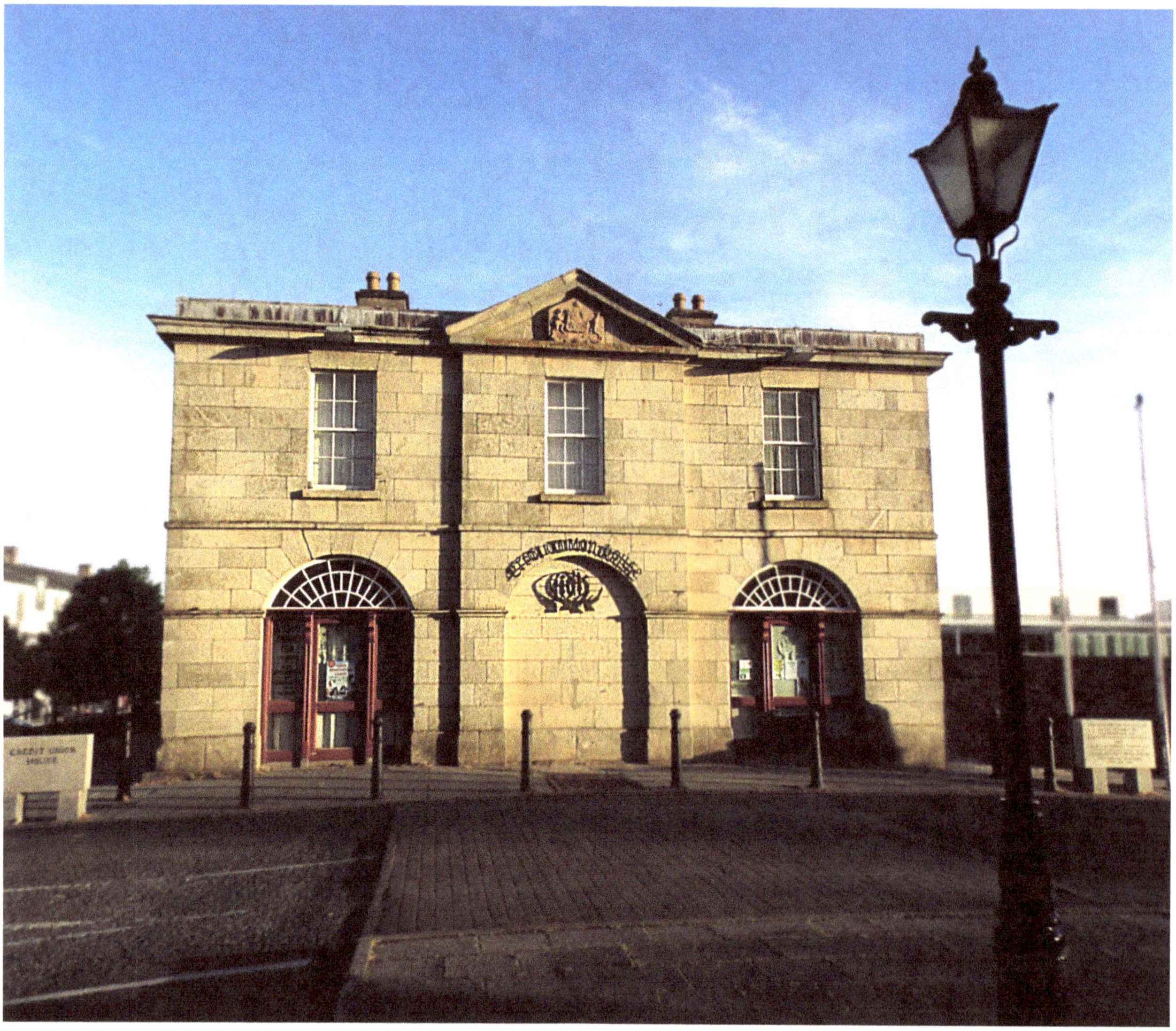

Credit Union House on Main Street Blessington

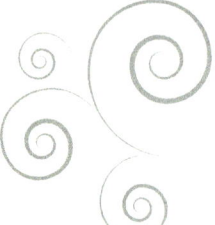

BLESSINGTON LAKES

Blessington Lakes viewed from the N81

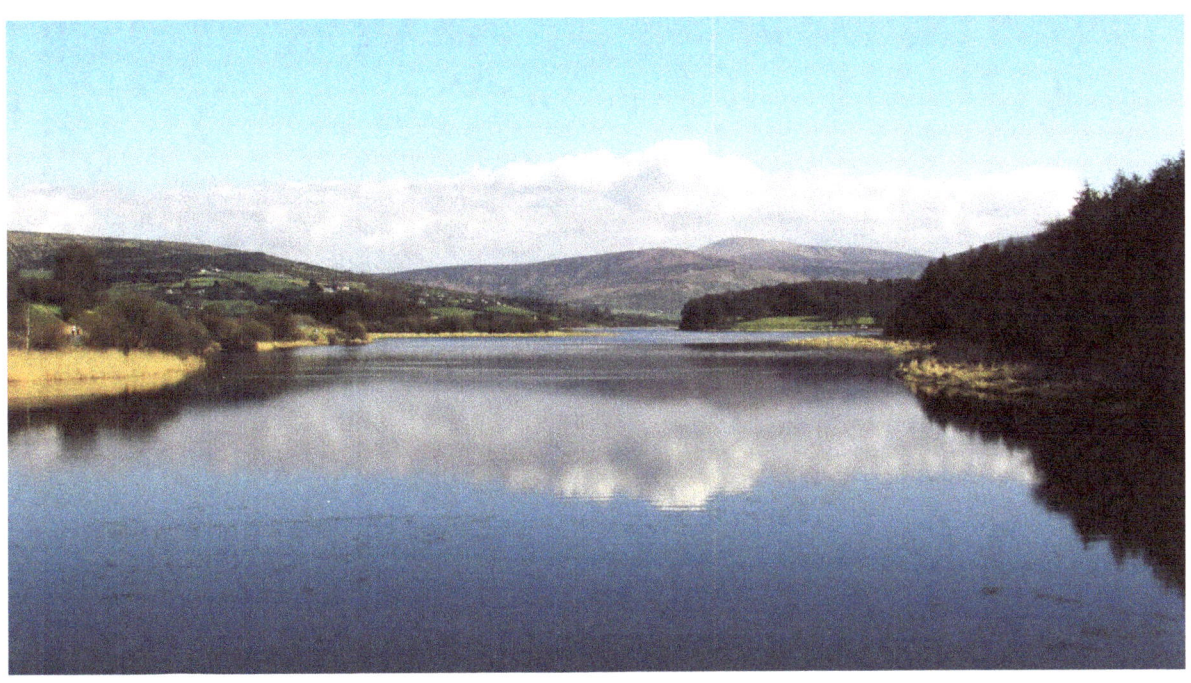

Blessington Lakes viewed from Burgage shoreline - a man watching his dog have a swim

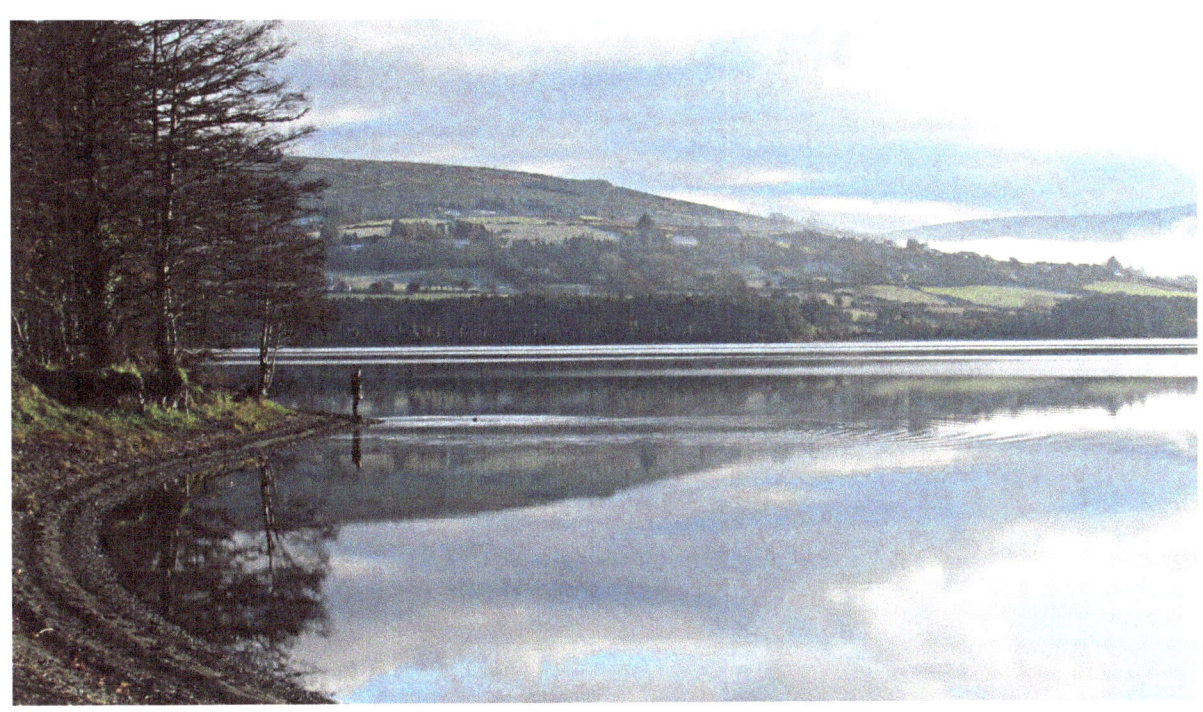

If I saw a bit of mist, I was down to the lakes with the camera, if time allowed. There were a few mornings when I was questioning my sanity. I would get to the shore and there would be a wall of fog, nothing to see, but I would wait for a while in the eerie silence until the sun came out. Then I was clicking like mad!

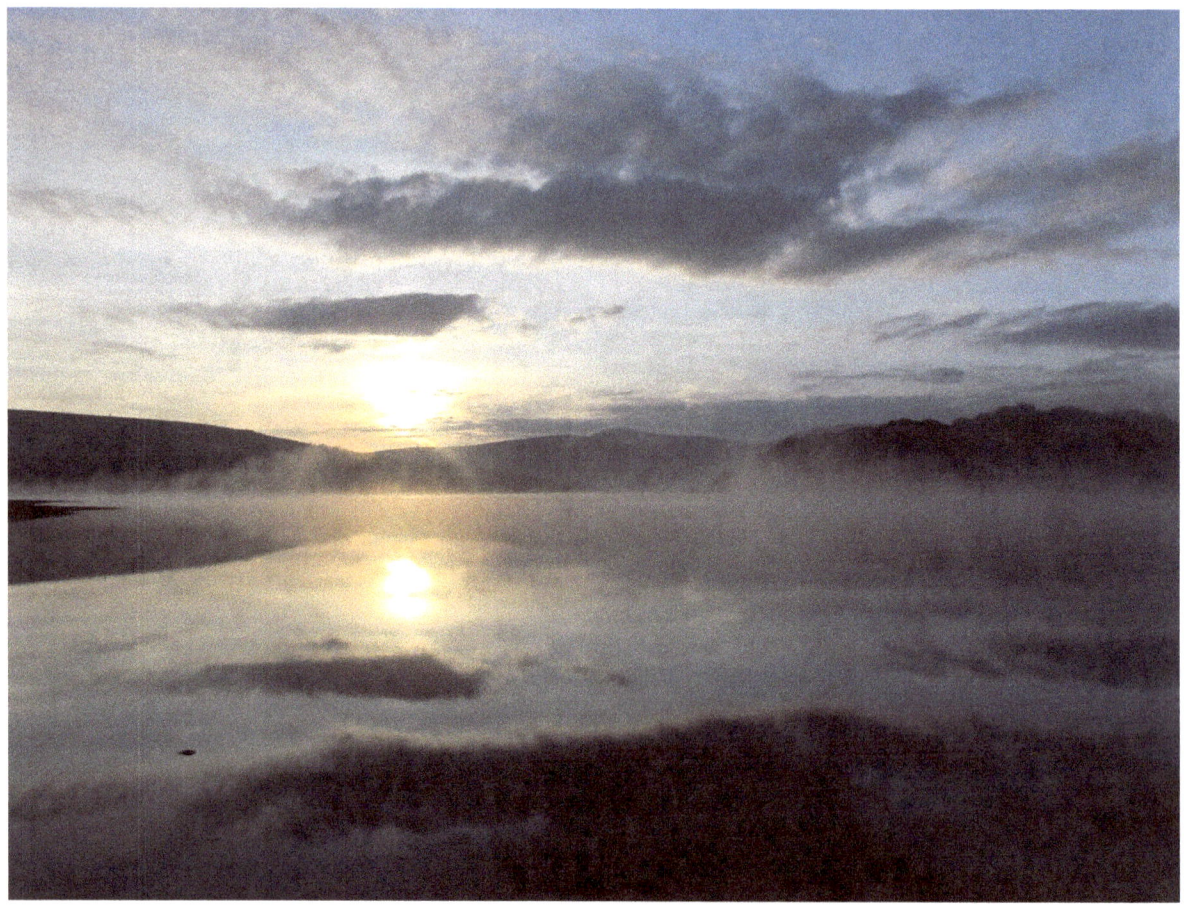

Blessington Lakes taken from the Burgage Shoreline on a marvellous misty morning

Blessington Lakes are manmade and have been in existence as we see them today, since the 1940's. It was decided to create a Liffey Reservoir Scheme, with details included from Dublin Corporation and the E.S.B. and a bill was presented to the Dail by Sean Lemass in 1936. Several townlands were affected and one called Ballinahown was completely covered. Approximately 50 farms, 55 homes and 12 labourers cottages were affected with the flooding of the area, including bog land that was necessary for turf for local families. In total about over 5,500 acres was used for the project. Many families were not adequately compensated for their loss of land and property.

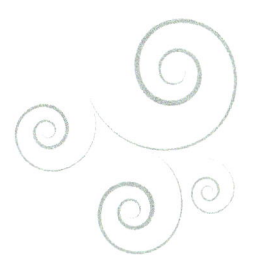

My Meanderings

Of course I didn't know any of this history, except that there might be a village under the waters, which gave me the creeps for some reason when I thought of it. However in 2014, as I mentioned at the beginning of the book, I finally decided to get myself a little oul camera. It was just a Canon Powershot with a built in zoom, and that's when my ramblings around the Lakes began in earnest.

All my life I had lived in a state of fear. I had grown up in Dublin and I wasn't used to going off into the wilderness on my own, the thought of it terrified me. However there were these amazing Lakes and Woodlands so close by, and some wonderfully accessible pathways. I had joined some facebook groups called Blessington Lake Views and then later the Blessington Lakes Photography Group, and I was so inspired by what I saw, that eventually I took my courage in my hands and set out exploring this beautiful area. Rain or shine, wind or snow, I was out and about, I couldn't get enough of it. It was like a second chance for a childhood for me, I just felt so free and happy.

I just love days when the sun is shining and the Lakes are reflective.

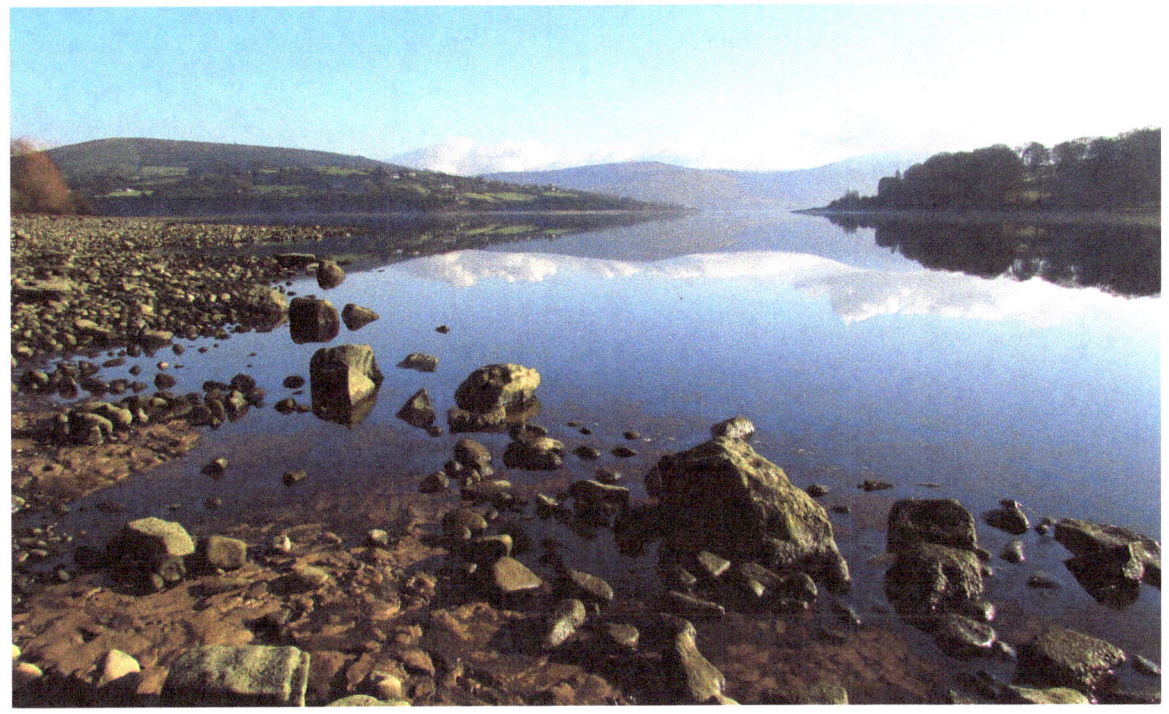

Burgage shoreline facing Lacken and Ballyknockan

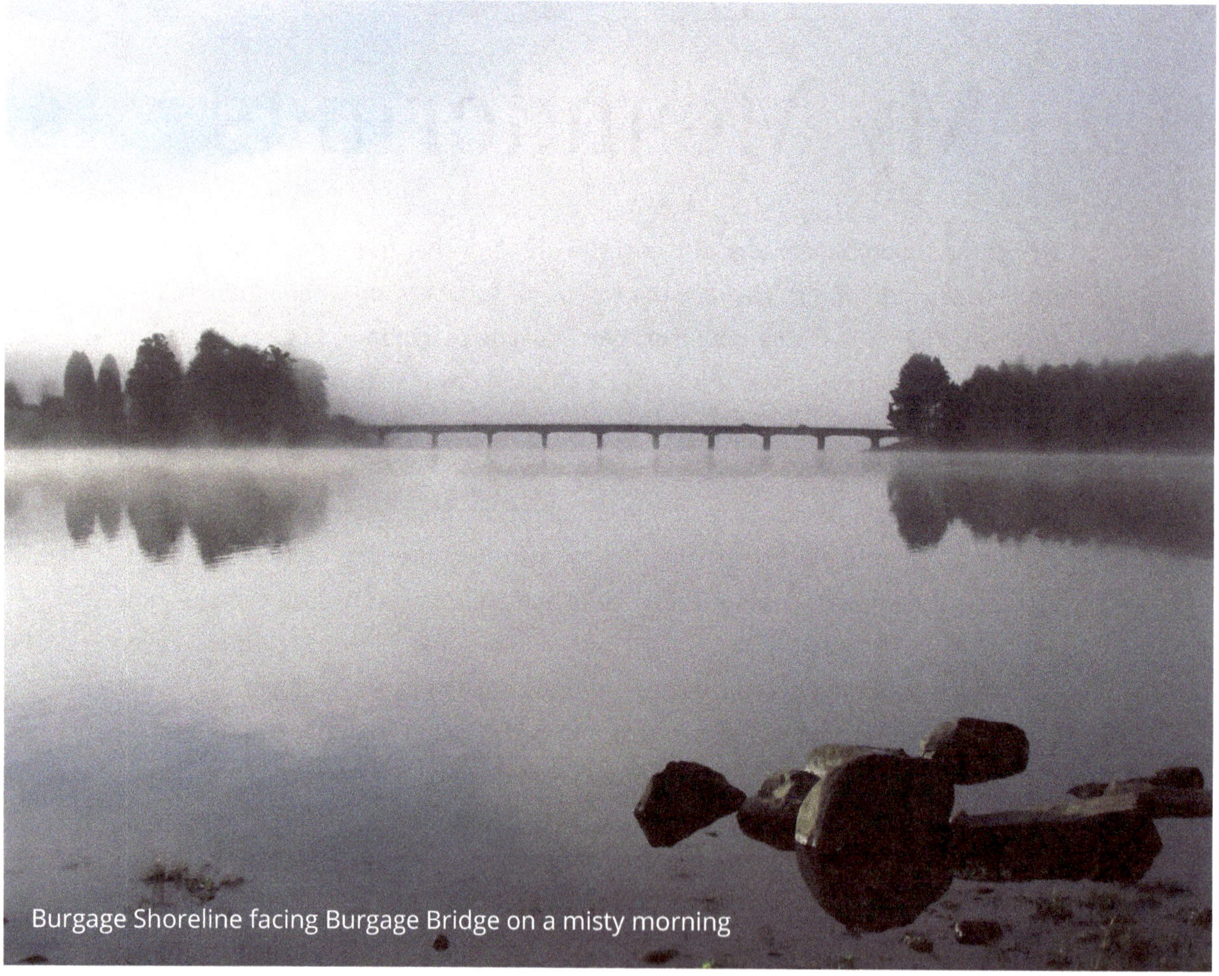

Burgage Shoreline facing Burgage Bridge on a misty morning

Burgage shoreline was the nearest to where I lived, so I was very lucky that the Lakes could be walked to so easily. Plus I had a choice. I could walk through the grounds of The Avon as it is now called and be onto the Greenway and at the lakes in about 10 minutes, or I could walk down a country laneway near Burgage Cemetery and be on a different part of the Greenway in 15 minutes. This way led to other options like Russborough too. It was really exciting and there was no end of photographic opportunities!

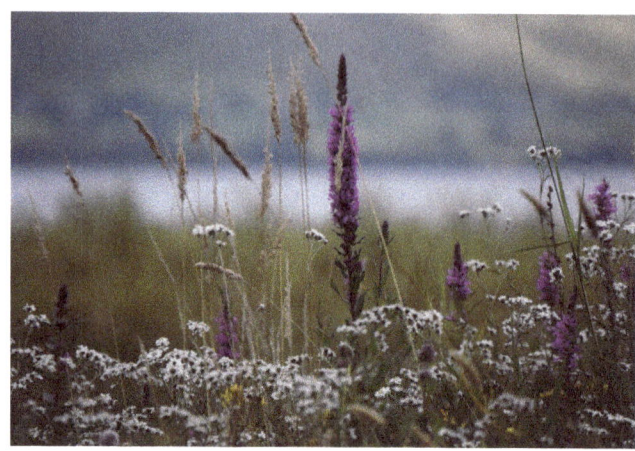

Beautiful wildflowers between the Avon and Burgage Shoreline

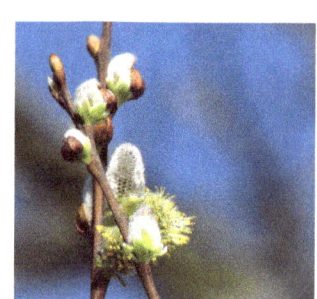

Spring buds

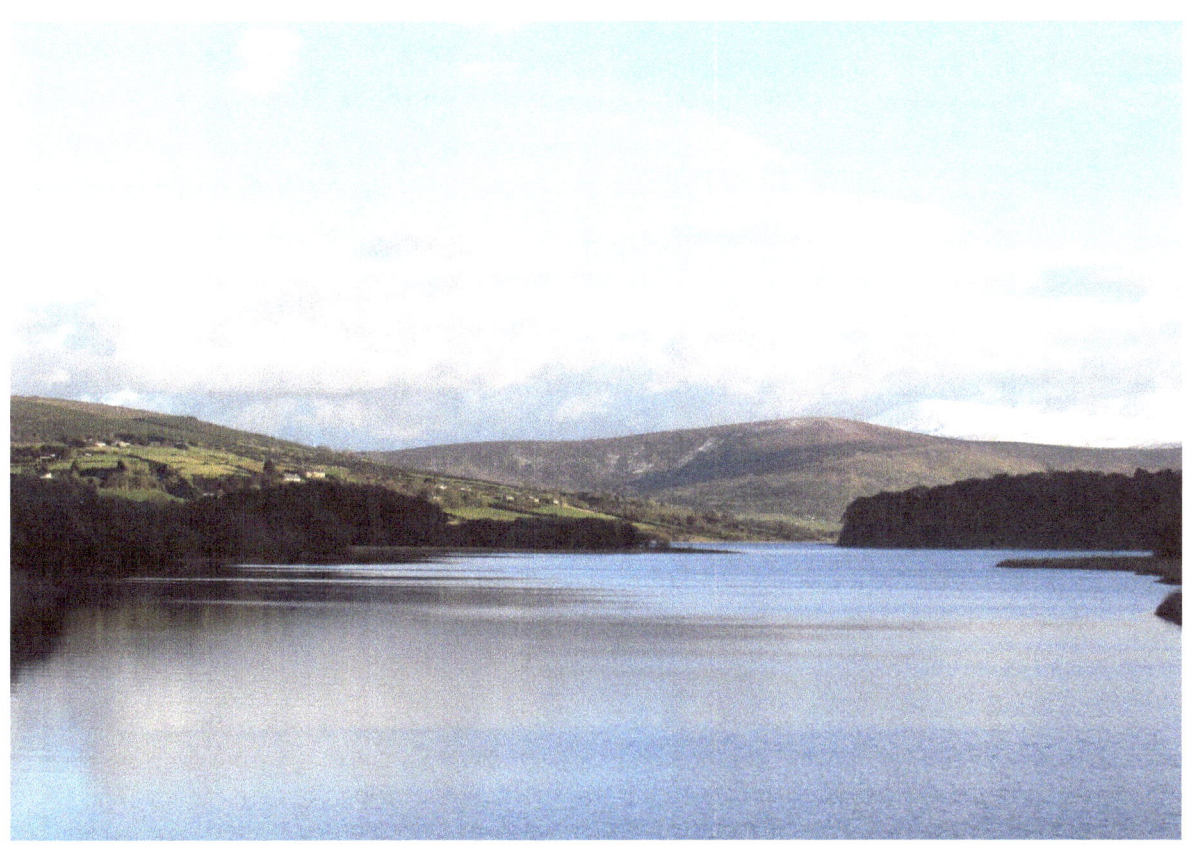

The Lakes taken from the N81 part of the Greenway

Whether sunny or grey the Lakes are always beautiful - view from Lackan Shore -
Yes I got home before the rain got me!

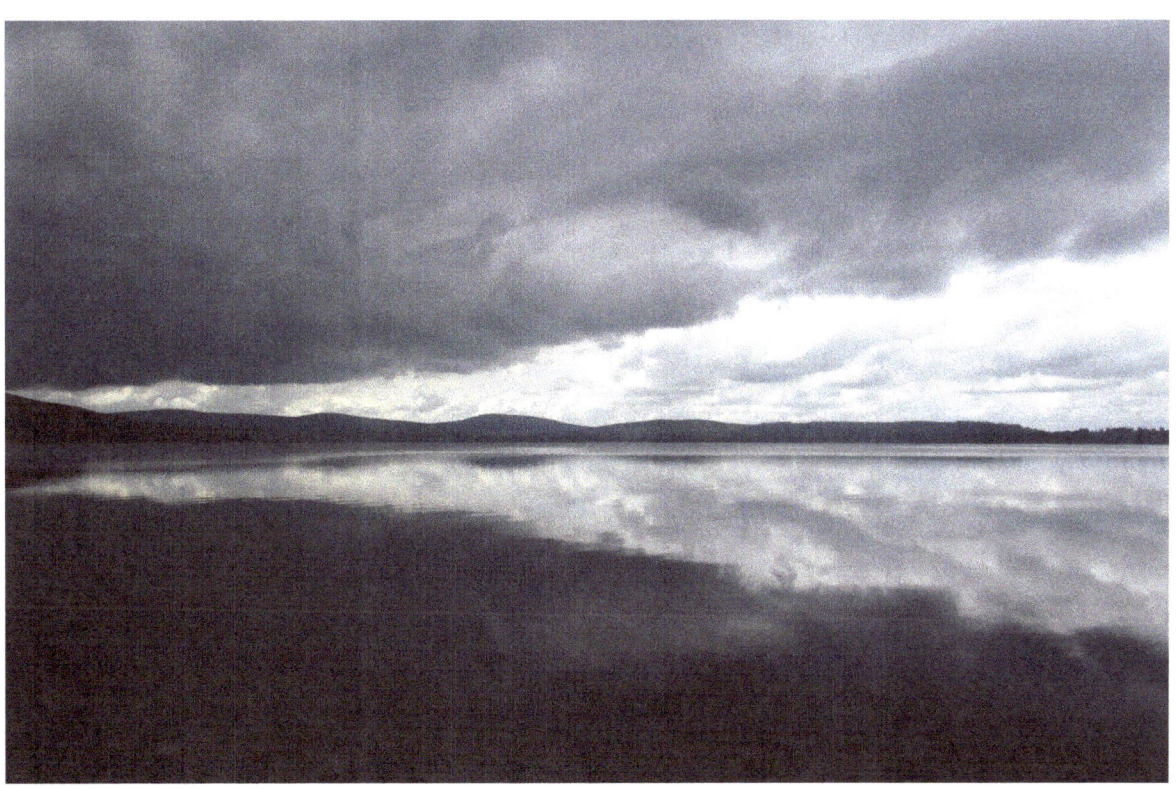

I've had so much fun exploring the Lakes, over the past few years and interacting with group members on Facebook Blessington Lake Views and Blessington Photography Group. They were always posting new photos and then I'd try to find the same spot to get my take on it. Or they would have taken a fabulous sunrise or sunset, and we would be all asking questions and sharing info. Also you were never quite sure who was watching you through their lens!

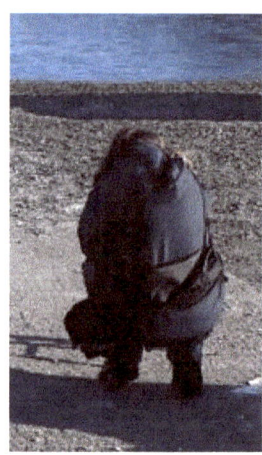

Me with my little shorty tripod, secretly photographed by Tom Costello at Russellstown

Not long after I'd started taking photos in 2014, and after a while of taking more than a few blurry shots, I decided to invest in a tripod. It was a grand little tripod, it seemed to be kinda short, and even though my 50 year old creaky knees at the time, were complaining as I contorted myself into the unusual positions required to get those amazing shots from a lower perspective, I was quite content to bide my time until I would invest in a taller one.

All this changed one day when I went out for a photo shoot with Mary Kavanagh, from our local photography club. Mary hadn't got a tripod of her own with her, and I offered her a loan of mine, so that she could get a close up of some interesting flora without camera shake. 'Doesn't it go any higher?' she asked, 'My back wouldn't be able for this', she said. She vowed she would get a taller one, and mentally so did I.

The following week we met again, Mary was proudly sporting her new tripod. We spent an hour and a half taking pictures, she with her taller one and me with shorty. As we made our way back towards the car, I noticed her folding up her tripod and clicking it in place, and that was when I discovered that my tripod was exactly the same as hers. 'Oh look Mary' I said, unclicking the catch as a long tripod leg was released from its prison, 'We have the same tripod, and I never knew!' I couldn't stop laughing as I unclicked all the catches excitedly to reveal a tall tripod! That's amateurs for ya!

Now how many of us are like this tripod? We go through our lives not really knowing what we can do until we observe someone else doing something. For me in my life experience, the catch that needed to be discovered and opened was a belief. I believed I couldn't. It really was that simple, all my life, I said repeatedly to everything, 'I can't'. Two very simple words that made my life a misery. But back in 2009, I decided to take the 't' off the word can't. I then wrote I CAN, on some bits of post it notes, and put them everywhere. Every time my little mind said 'I can't', I would find a post it, to remind me of what I wanted to achieve.

It's amazing what a difference dropping a letter makes. Suddenly I was filled with fear, if I could do everything that I always said I would do, but had been using the excuse of 'I can't', now I was accountable for myself. Now I would have to do those things, no more excuses. It was a revelation, albeit a scary one. This also gave me an opportunity though, to go past the fear that I had, and see that yes I could now do things, that I couldn't before, but did I really want to do them? Aha... what a moment of freedom that was. It was then that I started to enjoy my life, as I decided to focus on the things I did really want to do, and then to put some effort into finding out how to do them, and to practice often so as to gain confidence. It was then I discovered my hidden ability and you can too... but only if you want to.

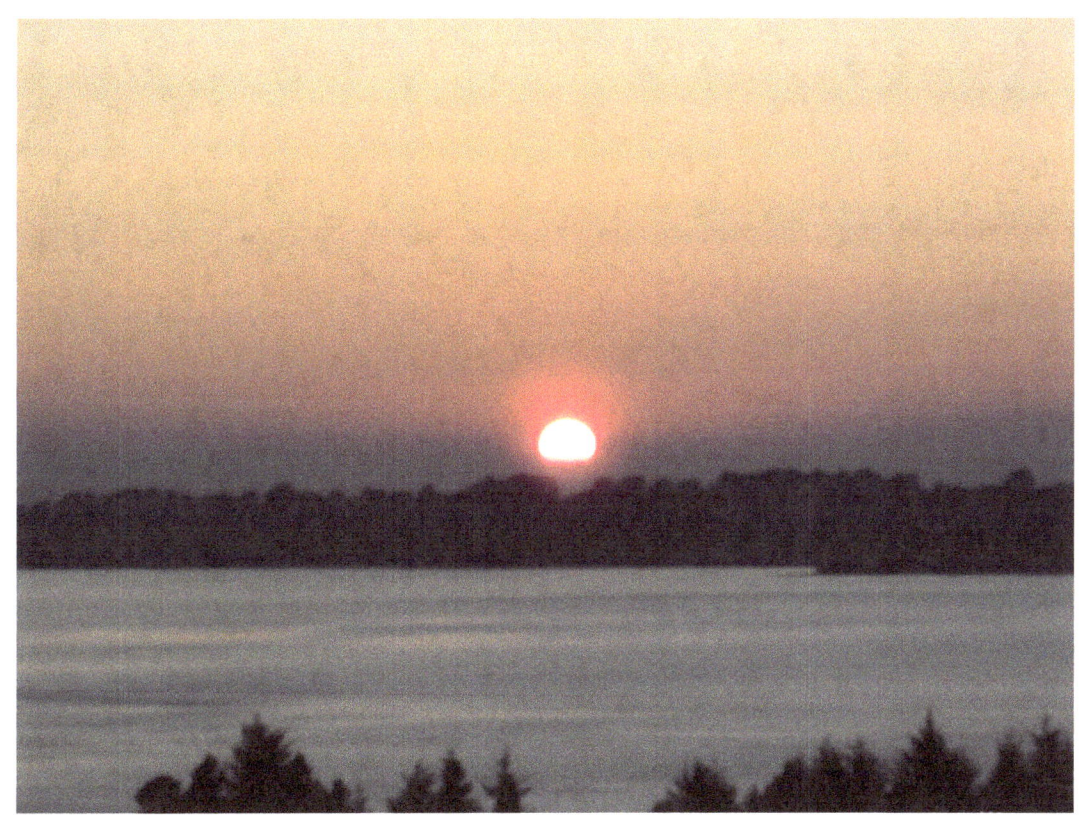

Sunset taken from Lackan

Sunset taken from Burgage Bridge

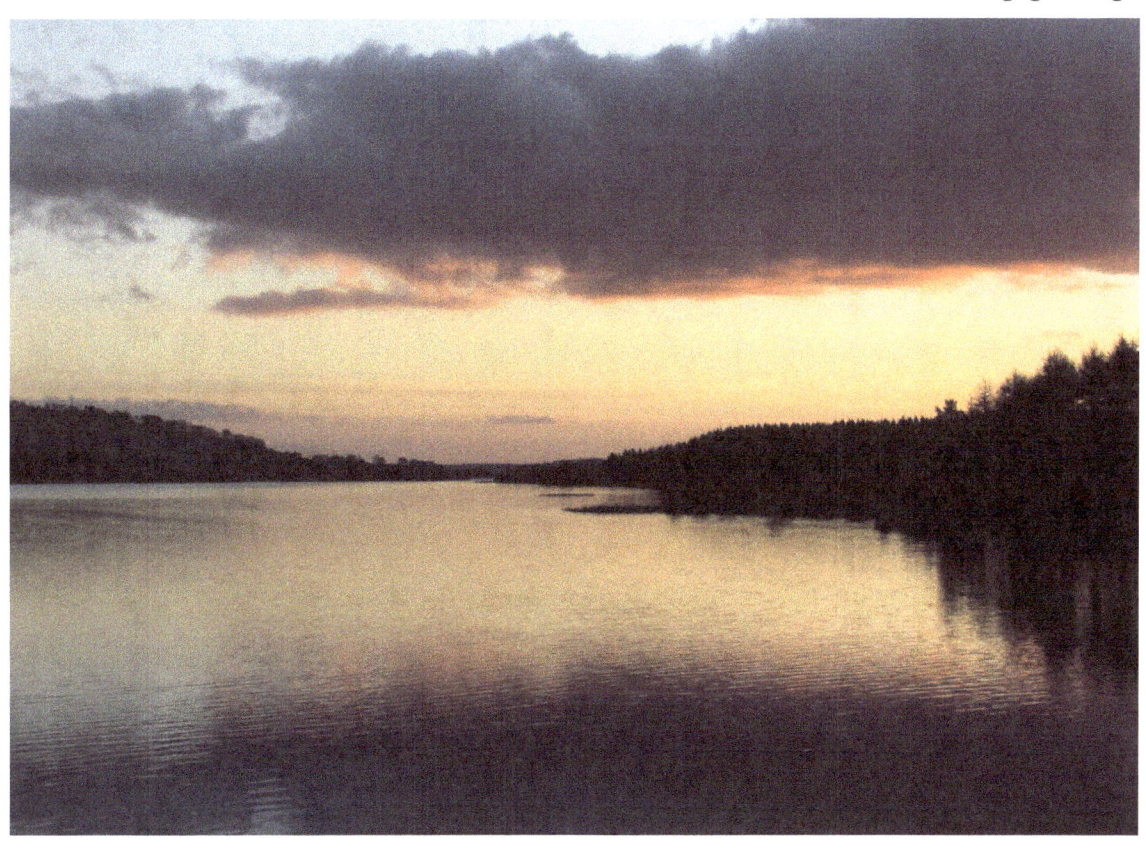

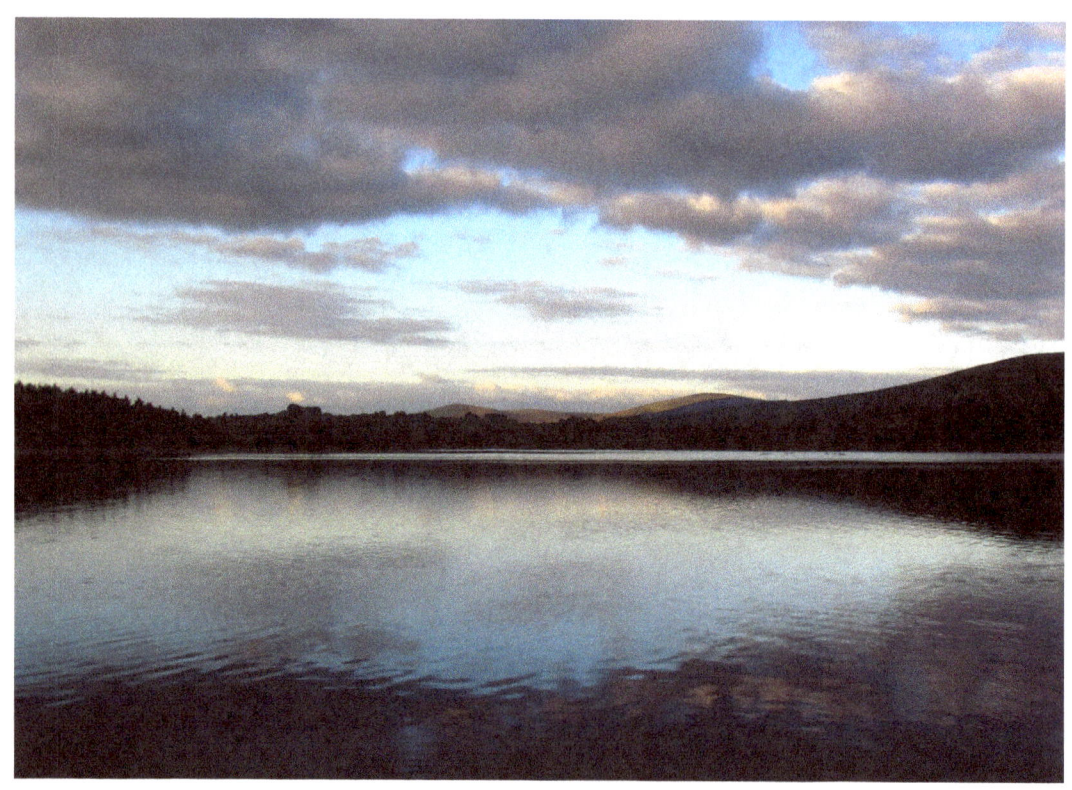
Evening light on Blessington Lakes taken from just off the Valleymount Road near the Avon to Russborough part of Greenway

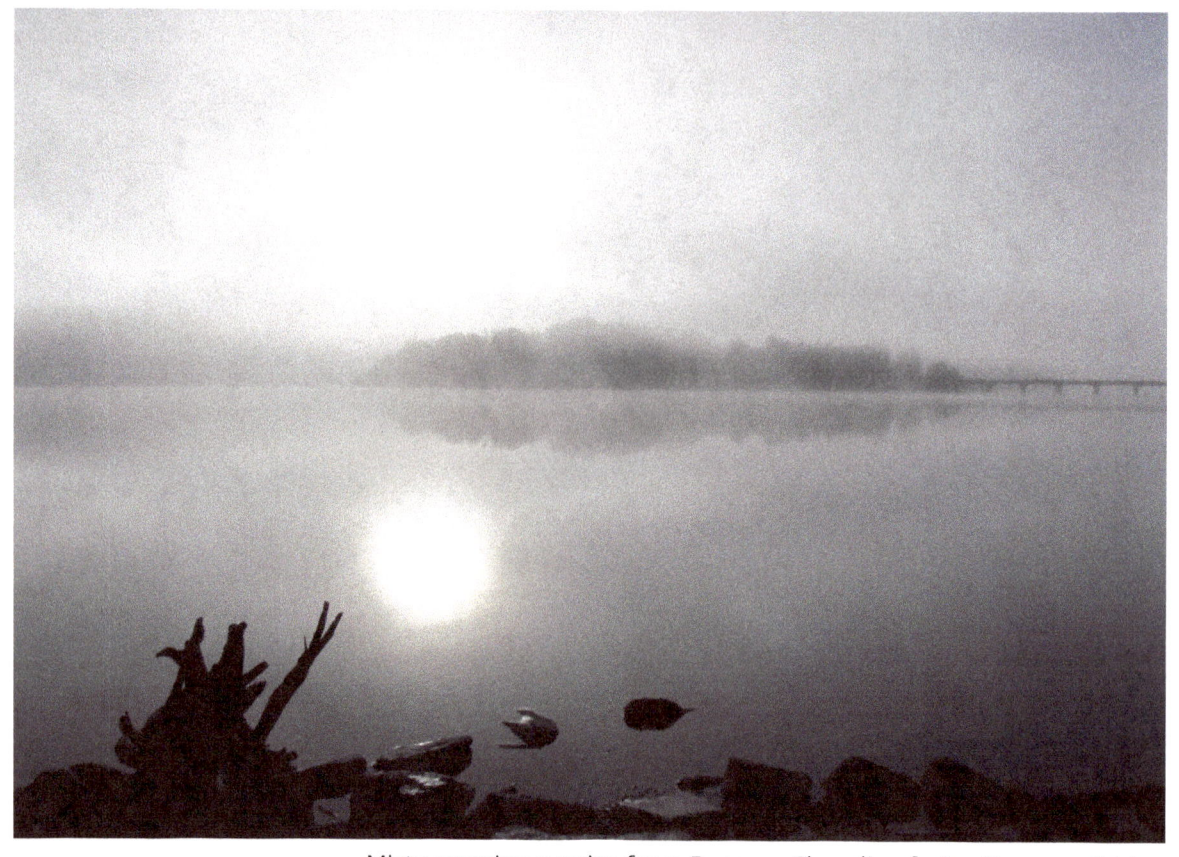
Misty morning sunrise from Burgage Shoreline facing Burgage Bridge

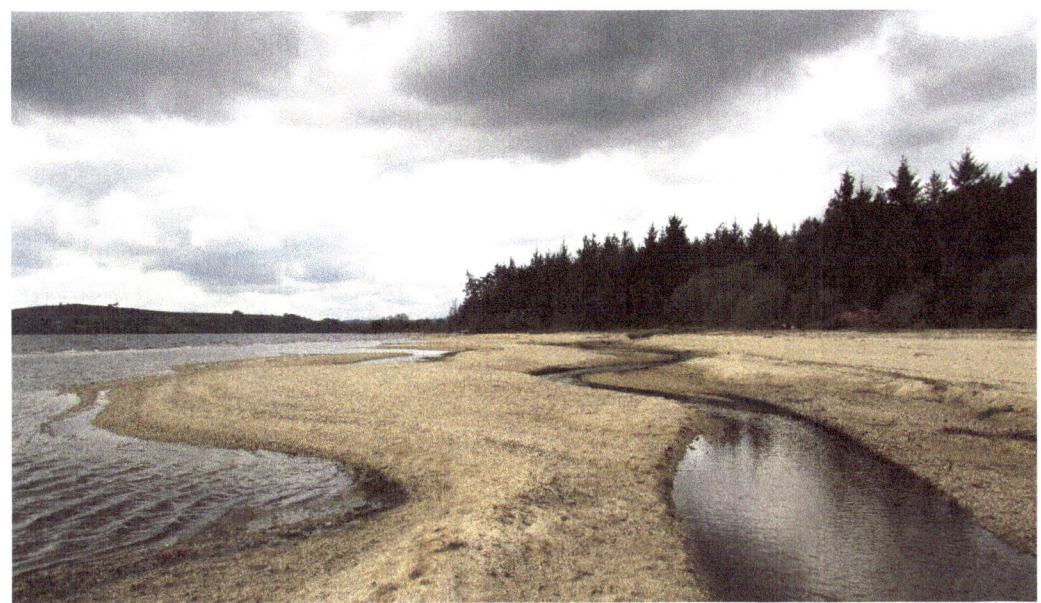

Lackan Shoreline worth getting lost on for a while

I just couldn't get enough of the Lakes. I would drop my son off at school and I would head out for some snaps. I'd take hundreds on a day, and then only use a few! One day I was so absorbed taking snaps on Lackan strand, that when I checked the time I realized that I'd better be heading back to collect my son. The problem was I had travelled so far I couldn't see the exit point to get back to my car. I walked back and forth trying to work it out and trying not to allow a sense of panic that was threatening to ruin what had been a lovely photo shoot. As I was considering climbing up an embankment into a farmers field to head in the general direction, which I really didn't want to do, the exit point came into view and I was saved. I was much more careful about taking note of landmarks after that!

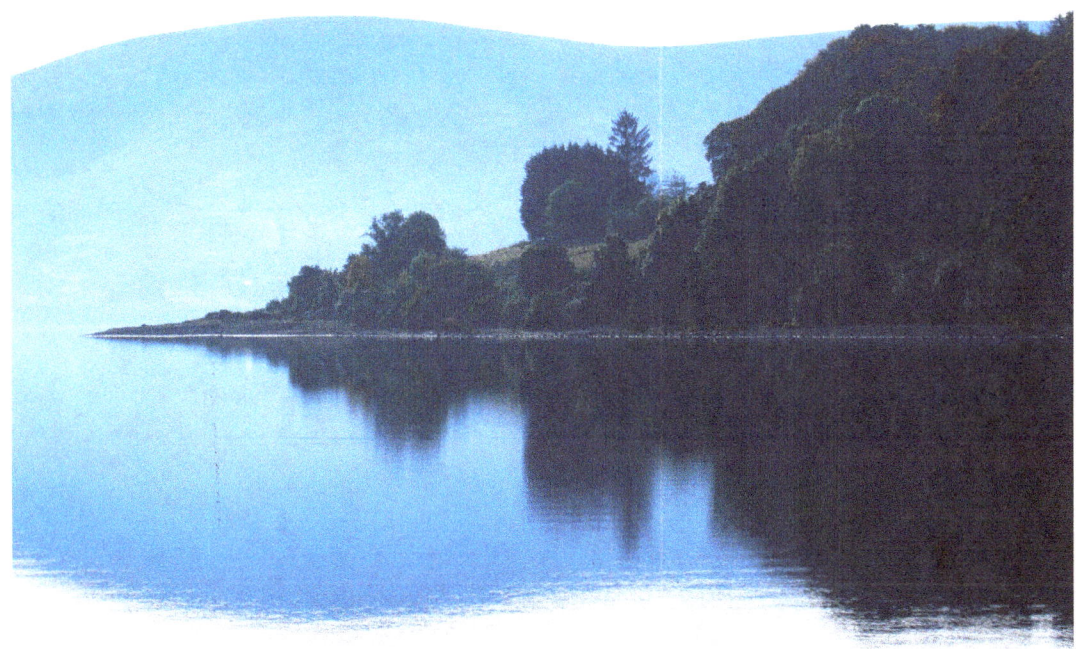

I zoomed in from Burgage Shoreline to get this shot of Baltyboys area

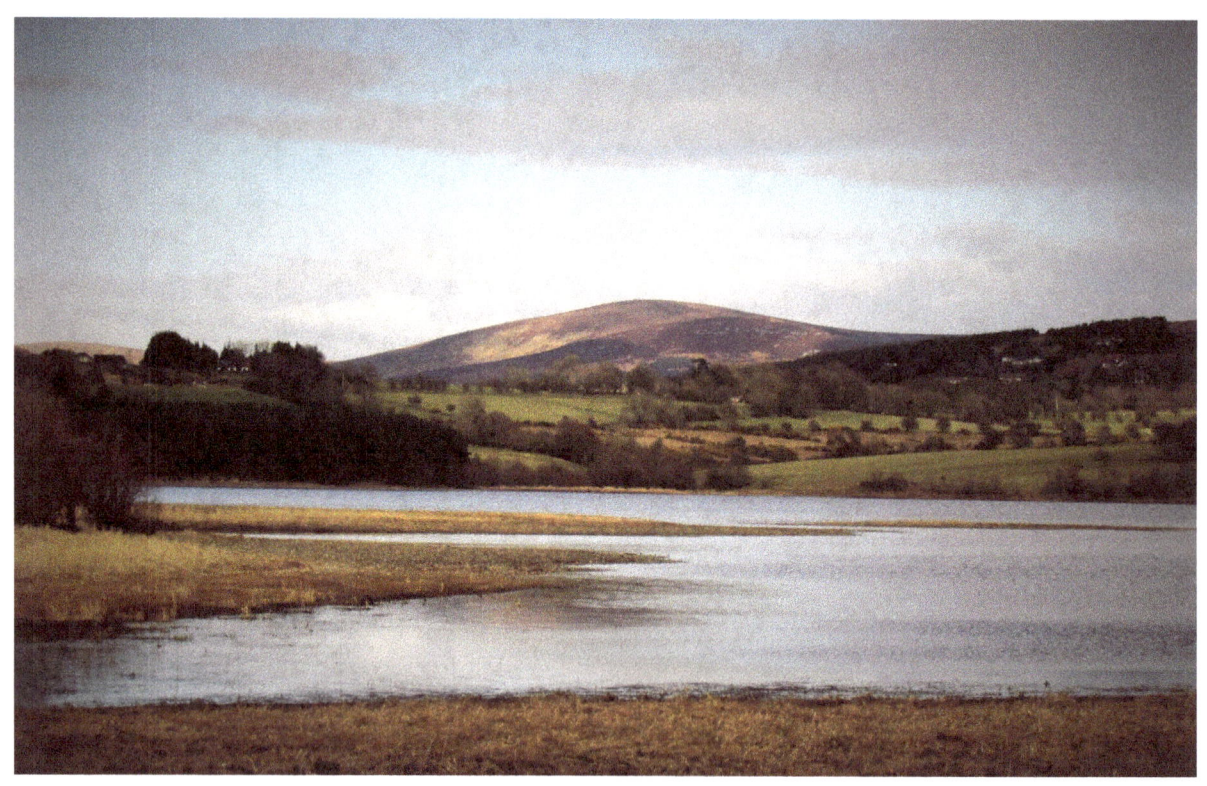

Taken on the Greenway from The Avon to Burgage

Looking over towards Ballyknockan from Baltyboys shoreline

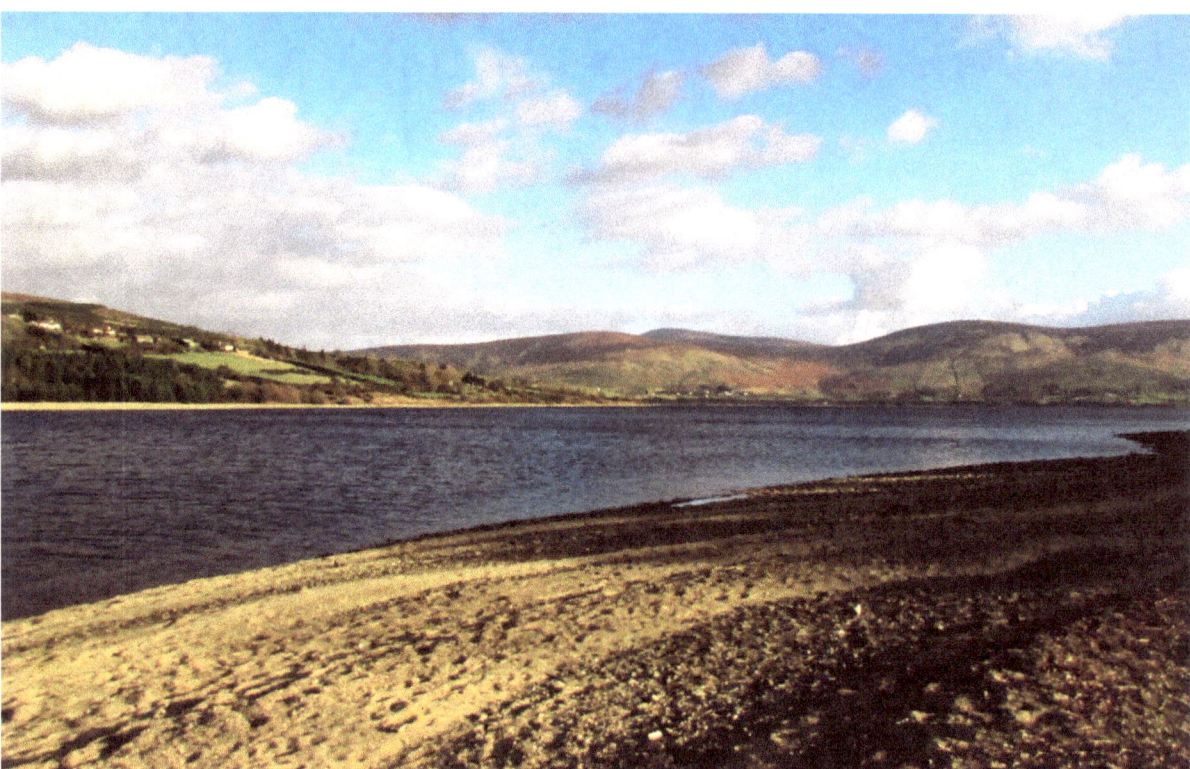

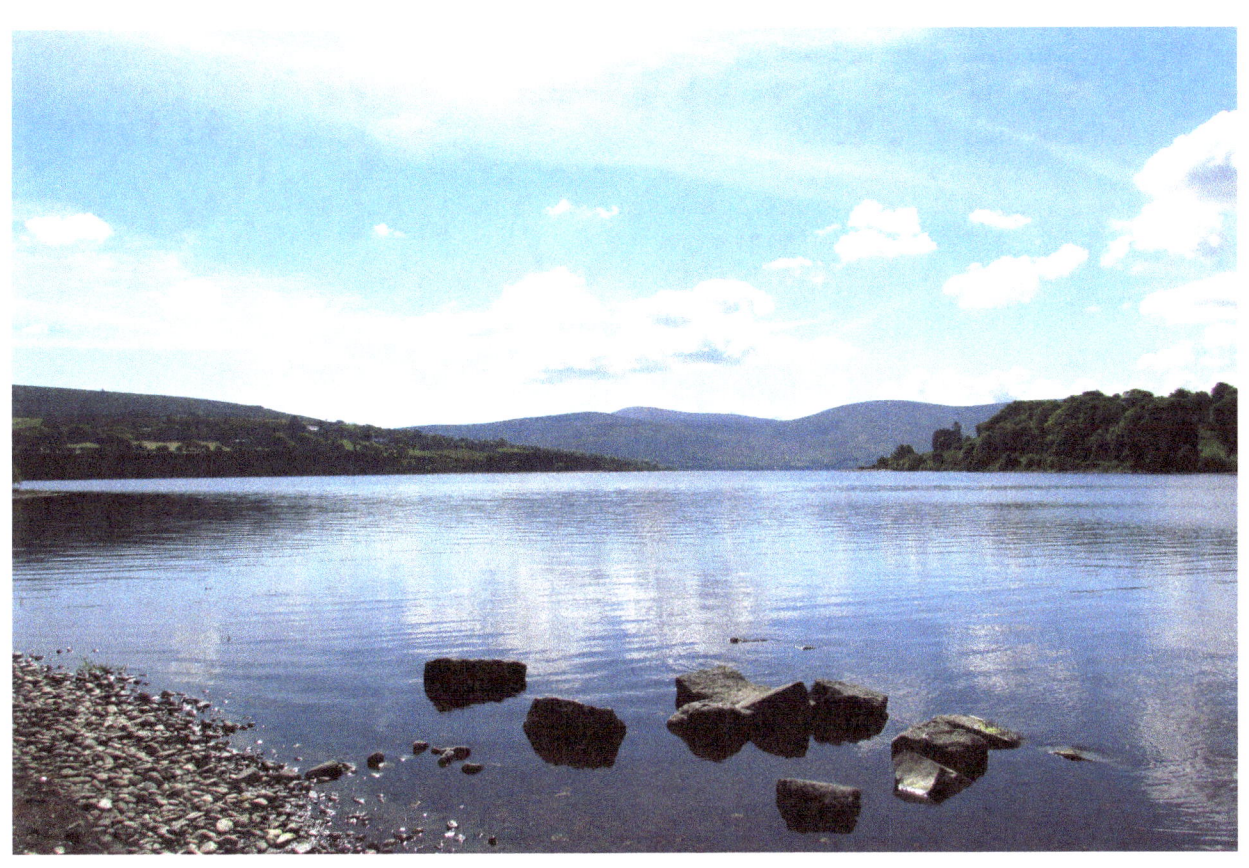
Burgage Shoreline looking towards Lackan and beyond

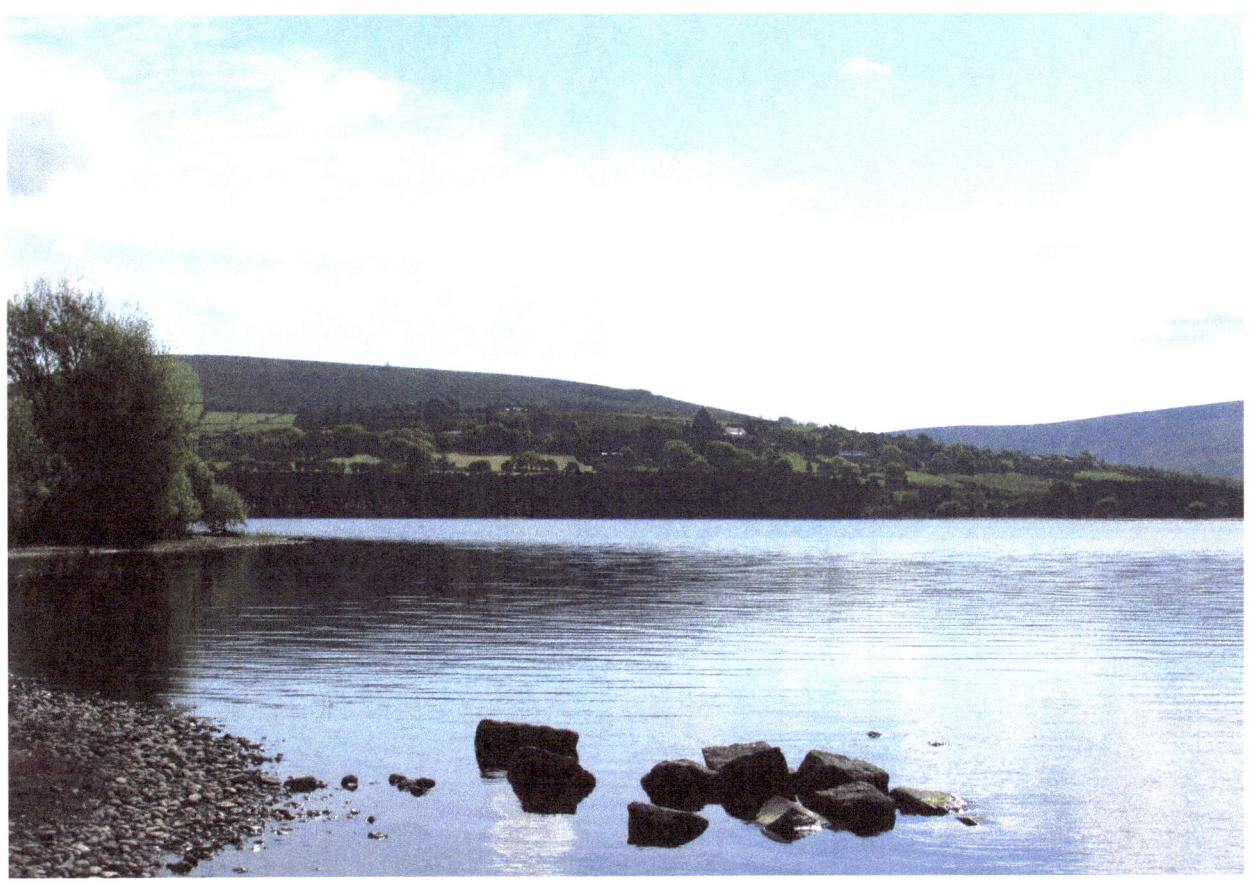

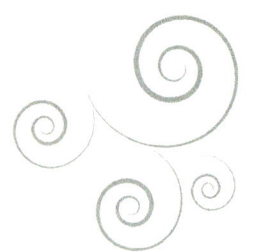

ST. MARK'S CROSS

St. Marks Cross is situated in Burgage Cemetery at Burgage More

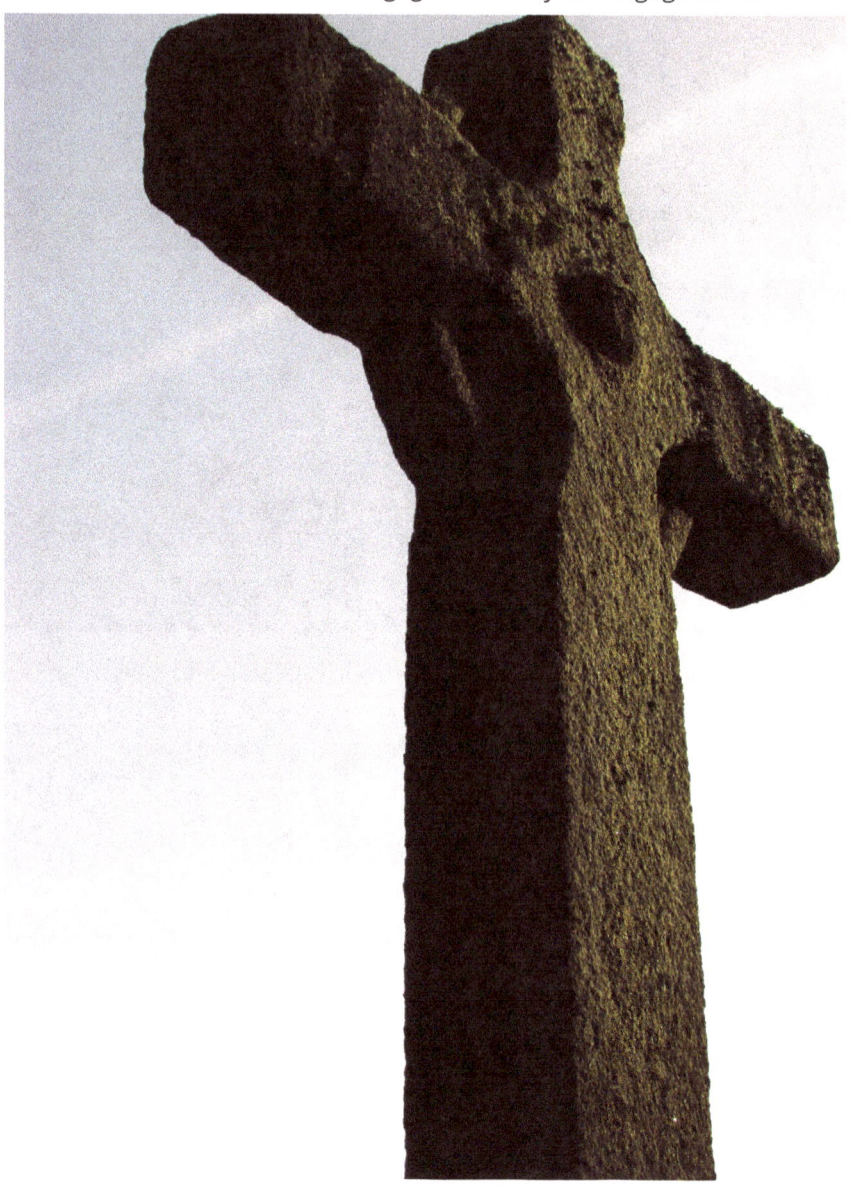

There's a 12th century cross in Burgage Cemetery that was moved from the Burgage shoreline before the flooding. It known as St. Marks Cross, but apparently its original name was St Boaithin's Cross and it was called this up to the 19th century. It was named after a saint from Kildare who was said to have founded a church at Burgage. The cross is approximately 14 ft high and is unusual as it doesn't have openings between the arms where crosses of a similar time period have on the ringed head. It is made of granite and not as ornate as other crosses. Two circular bosses are situated in the middle of the cross face on both sides, these are believed to depict the centre of the universe with the sun or Christ at its centre. There is some ancient Gaelic lettering at the base which is badly worn and not easy to read.

BURGAGE TOWER

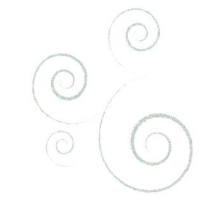

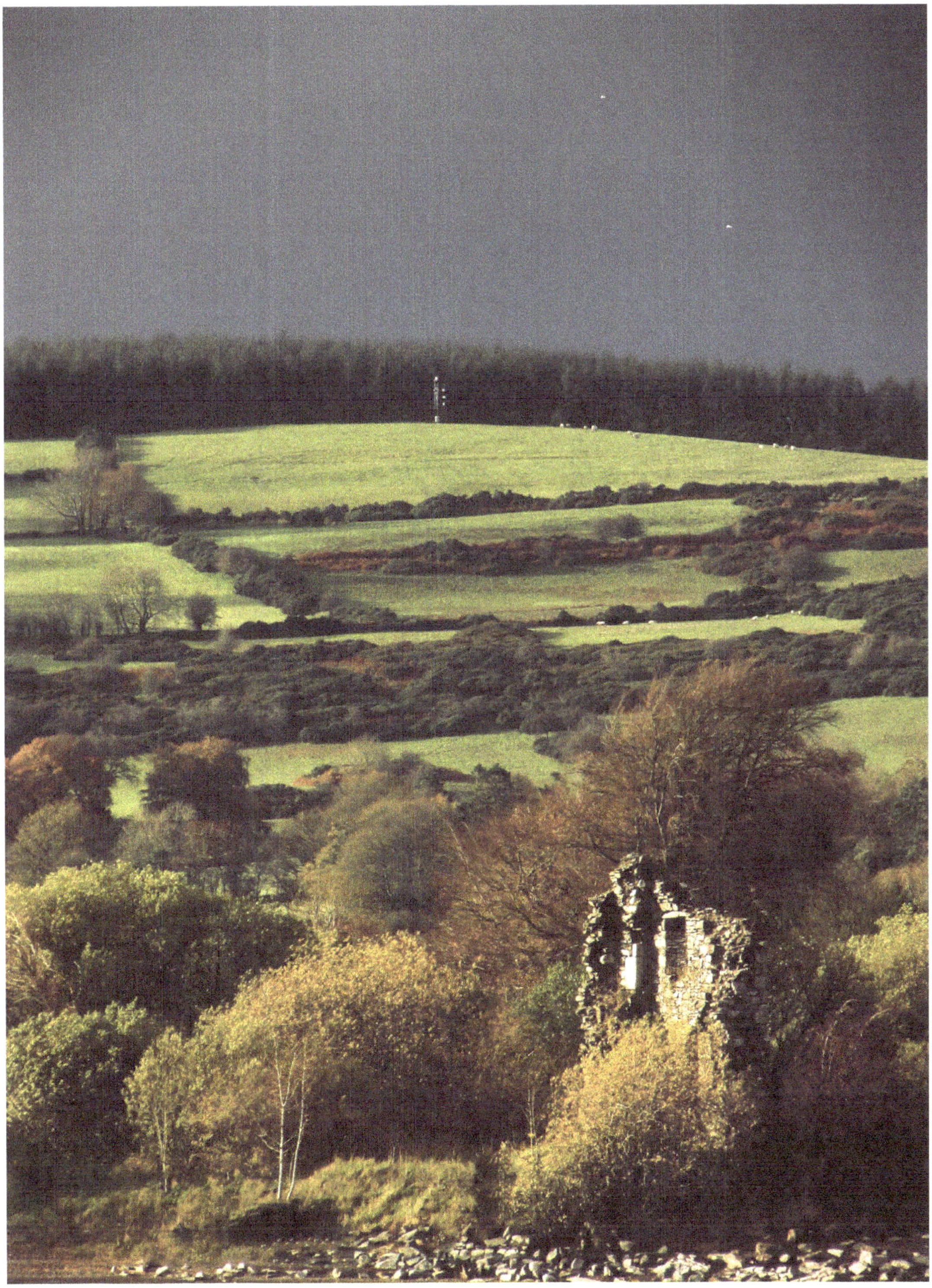

Burgage Castle Tower House taken from the opposite side of the Lakes - it's so easy to imagine what it might have looked like in the distant past.

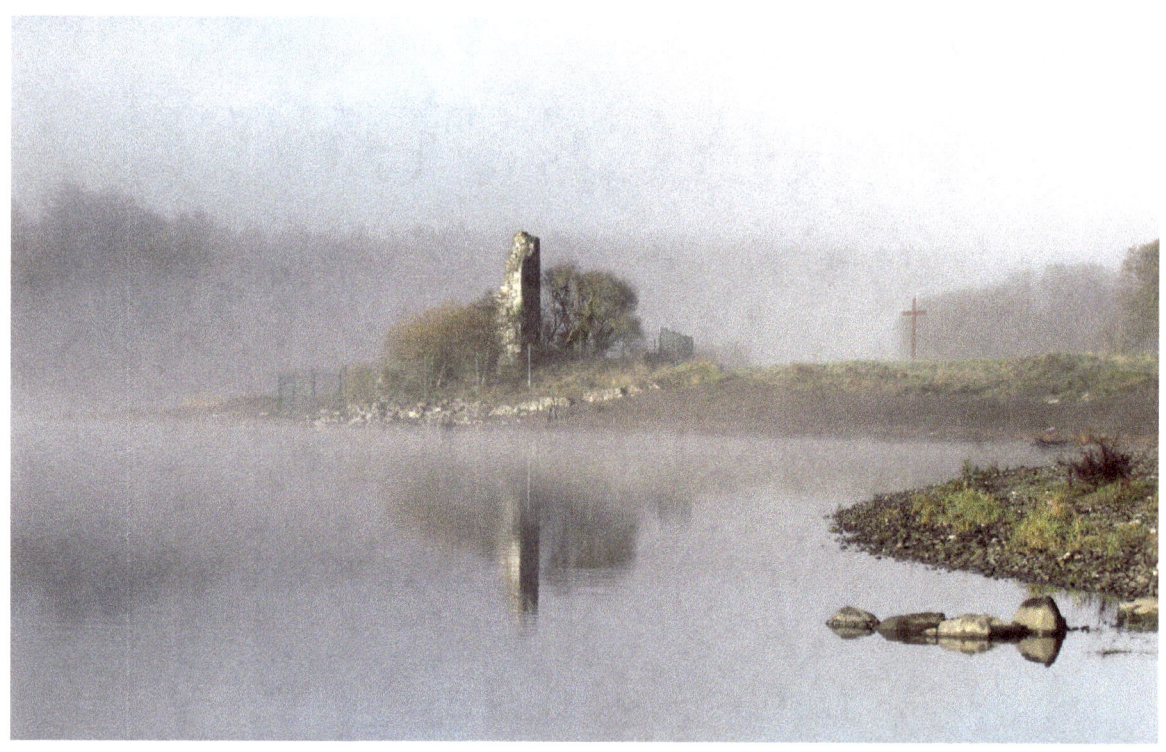

It wasn't long before I heard that there was an old castle ruins on the lakes near Burgage and so I went to check it out regularly. Each new day brought more and more interesting photos of this lovely ruin. The wooden cross is placed where the original granite cross St. Mark's Cross or St Boaithin's Cross once stood beside a church and holy well. While a lot of the remains from the graveyard were brought to the new cemetery, some are believed to be still here. Burgage Tower is now in the process of being restored and has a high board fence around it, so I'm really glad I got these photos while I could.

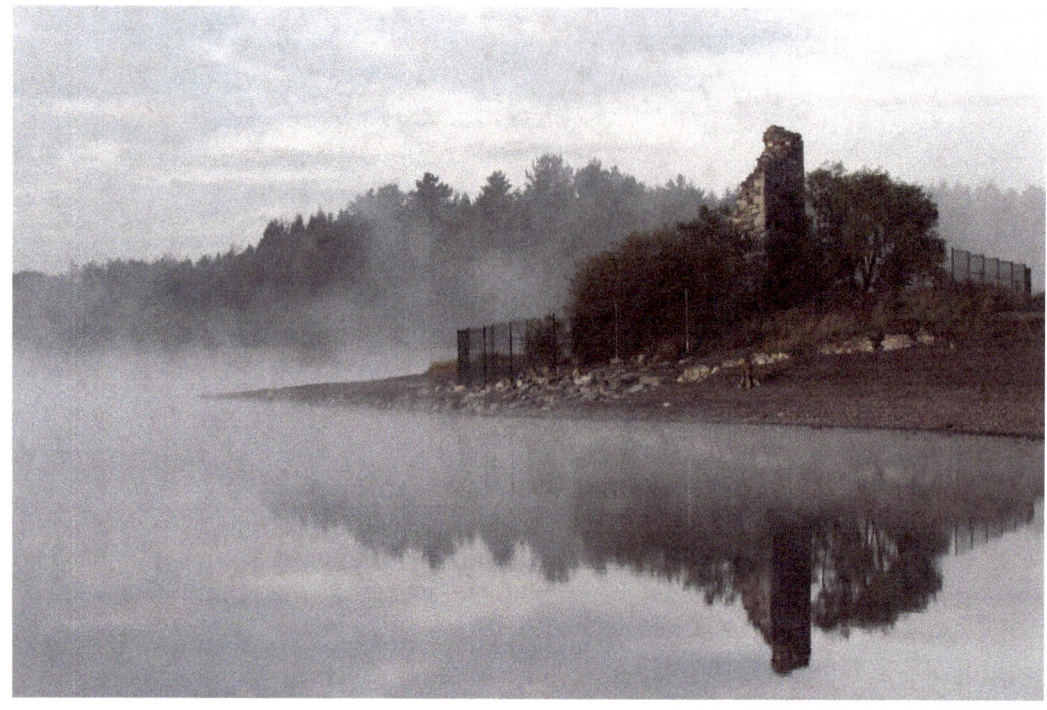

Burgage Castle Tower House on a misty morning is always amazing!

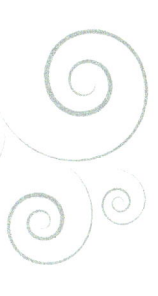

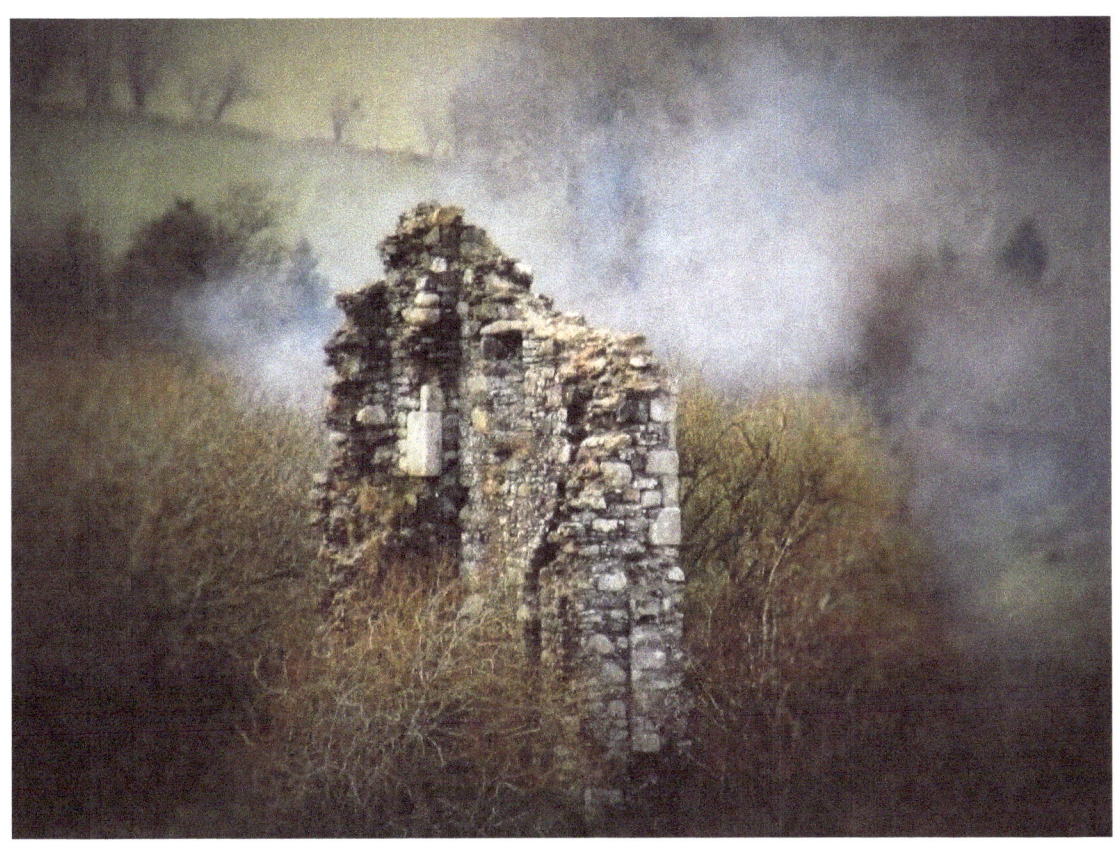

I was lucky to get this shot of Burgage Tower with the smoke of a bonfire behind it.

A sunset makes for a great photo but it looks great in the daytime too

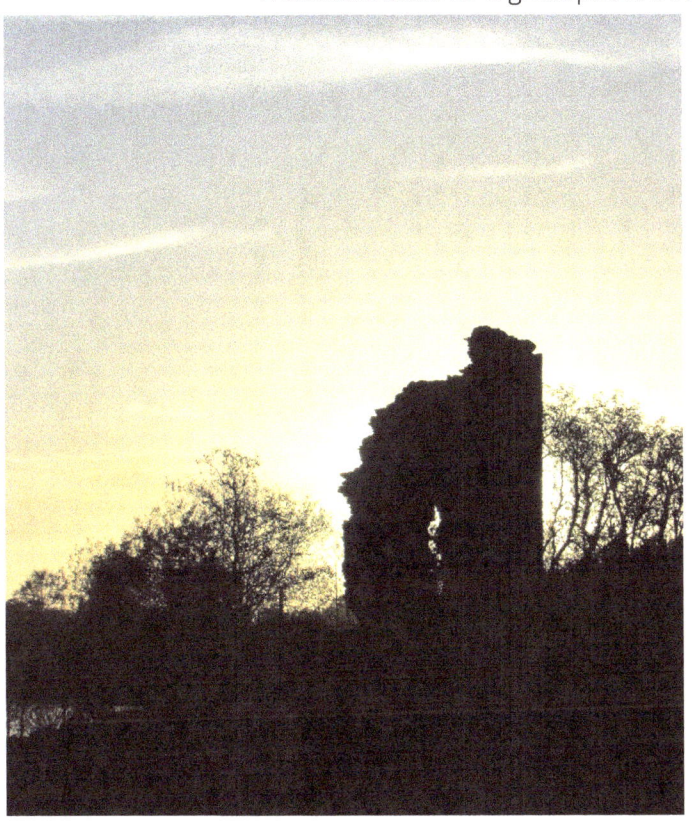

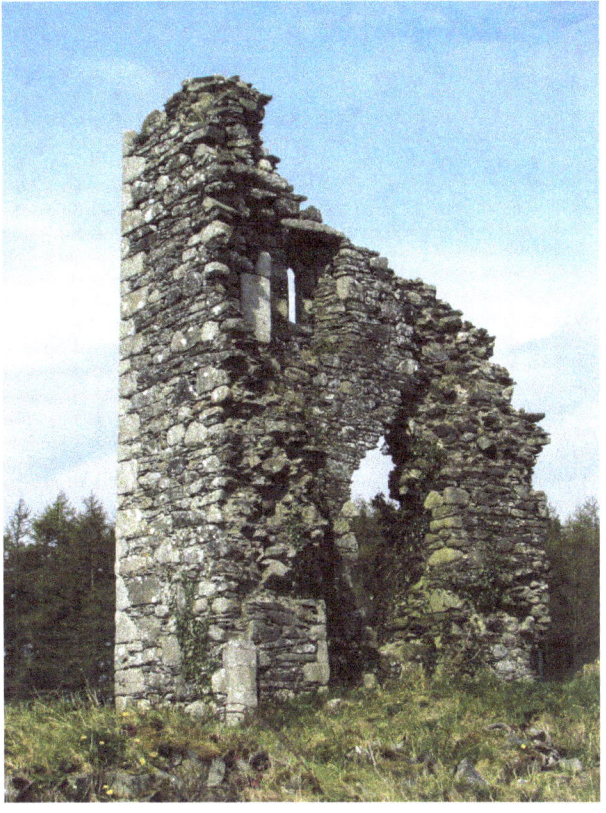

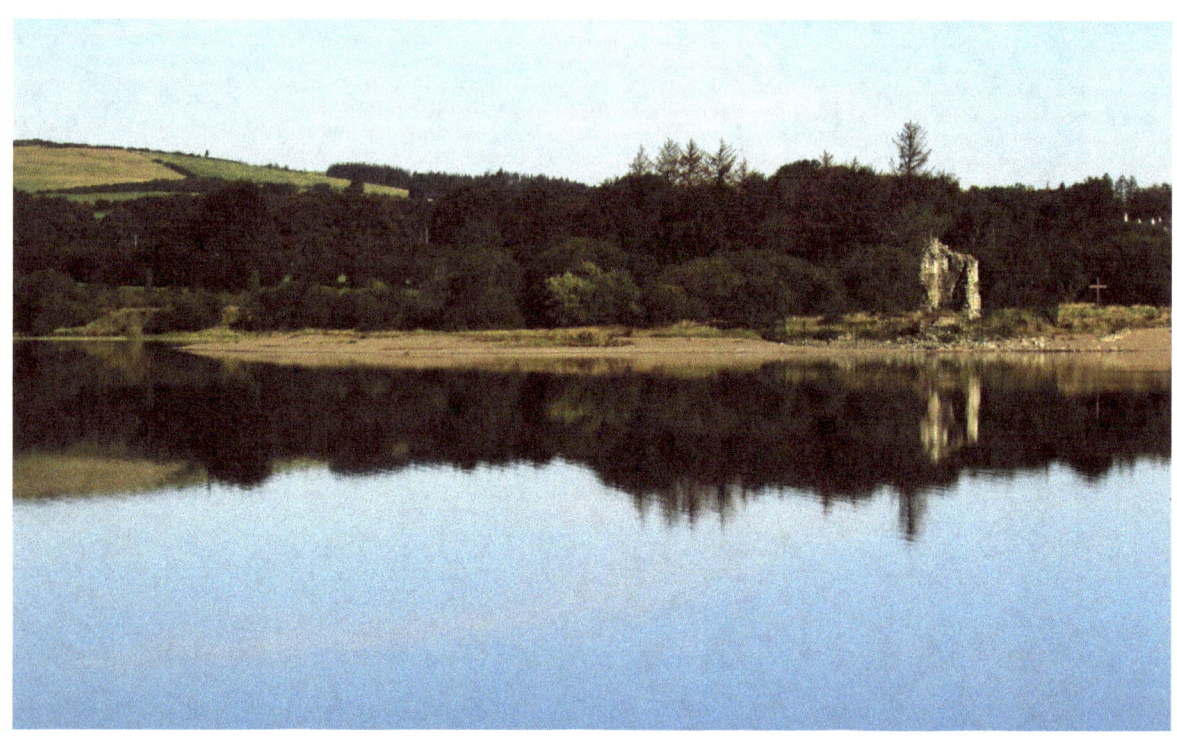

Burgage Castle, a Tower House is thought to have been built around the 12th Century during Norman times. It's believed to be beside an ancient ecclesiastical site called Burgage More which was inhabited until approximately the 1400's. As you can see by my photos there is only one wall remaining. I did however find a photo that was taken in the 1980's which shows the four walls with a huge crack in the structure, which later crumbled. I did a painting of it in vivid colours. I had set myself an Art vs Photography challenge, more about this later. The original photo, that I used for reference for my painting, which was taken by Patrick Healy can be seen at the end of the book, where I show original photos and the paintings I did based on them.

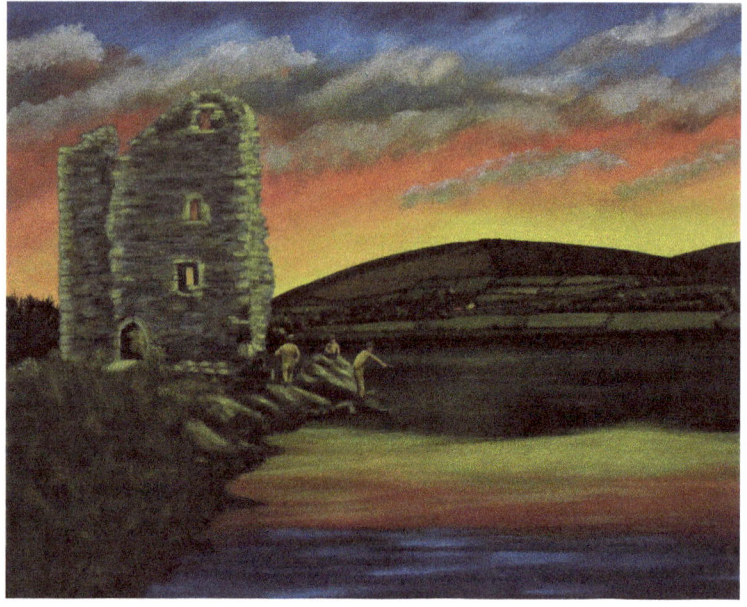

My painting of Burgage Castle Tower House in the 1980's, based on a Patrick Healy Photograph, more details further on in book.

In Medieval times as mentioned previously, Blessington was called Munfine and was part of the lordship of Threecastles. There is a structure which is very similar to Burgage Castle Tower House in Manor Kilbride, which is approximately 300 metres 0.3km from Burgage Castle, and it is documented that there was a possible underground tunnel between the two at one time, however that might just be a story. Maybe a Ground Penetrating Radar could confirm this. It was thought that the Threecastles included Burgage Tower, but I was speaking with Aidan Cruise, a local Historian, who told me he reckoned that Burgage Tower wasn't one of the Three Castles, and that they were located near Oldcourt, one of them being currently part of a house at present.

A similar structure is Threecastles in Manor Kilbride

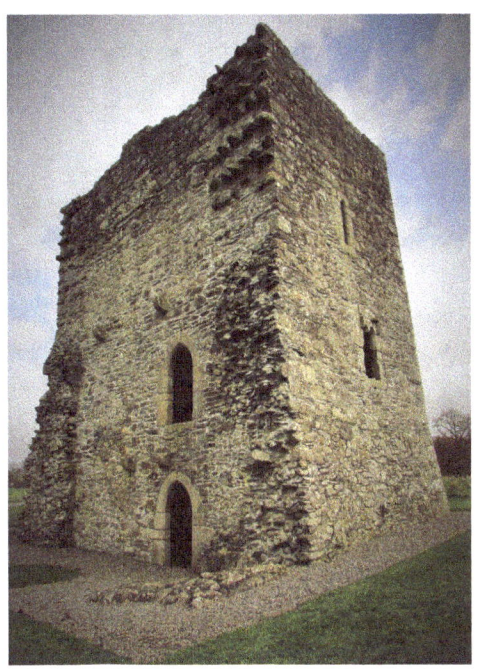

In 1546, after when the monasteries were dissolved due to the Act of Suppression in 1536, Burgage Castle came into the possession of The Earl of Kildare. It later came to be owned by the Cheevers Family of Monkstown Castle, Co. Dublin. It is believed that Cromwell was involved with the destruction of Burgage Castle and church in 1649. The Castle was later sold for £1000 to Archbishop Michael Doyle, who established Blessington.

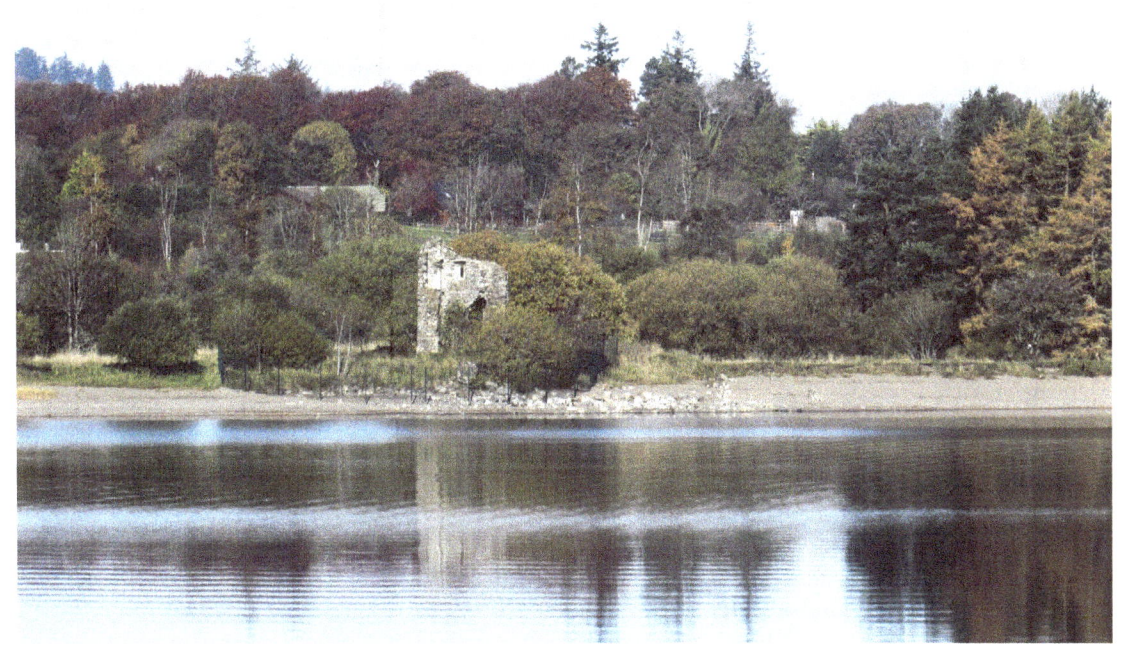

BLESSINGTON GREENWAY

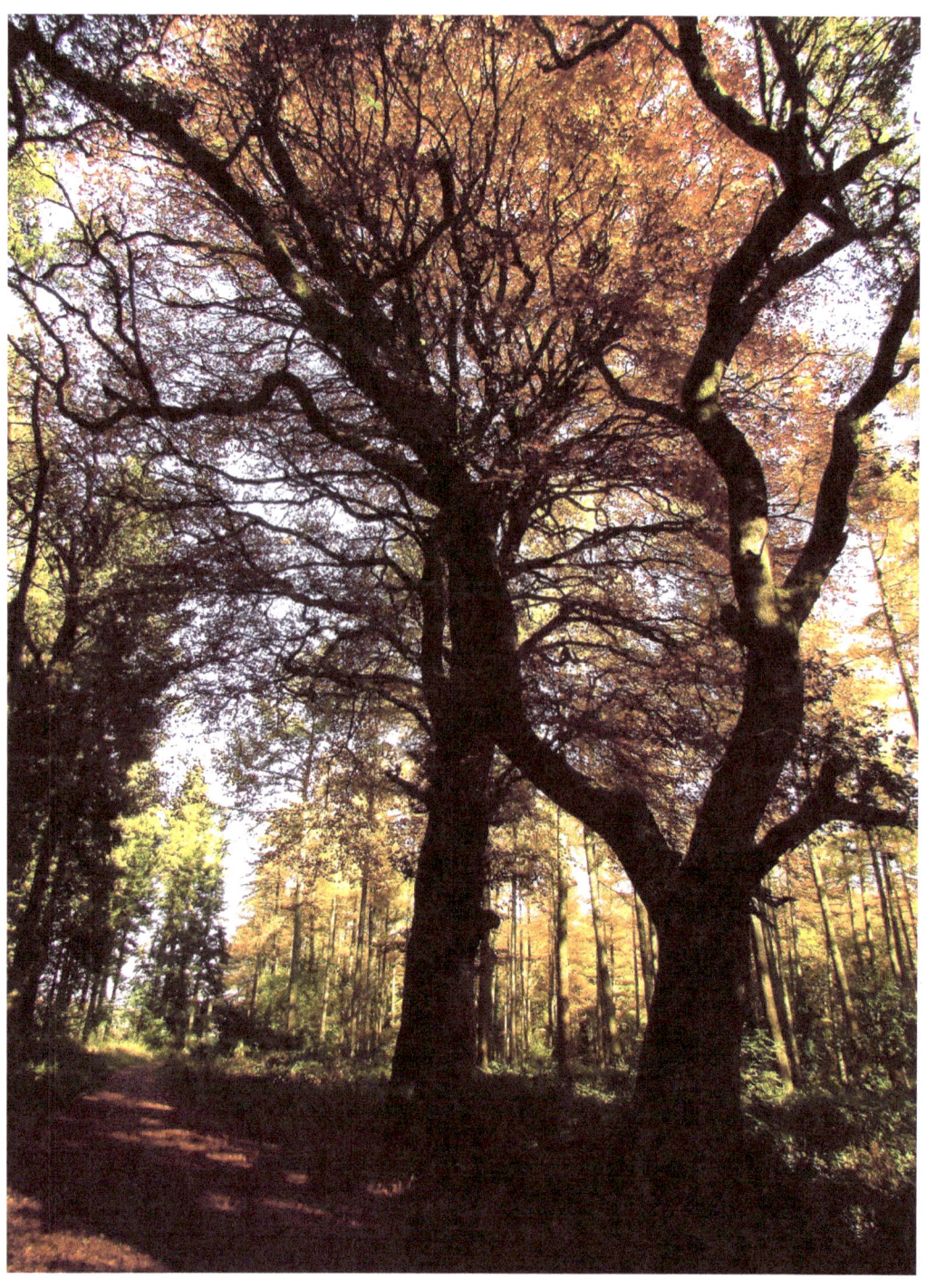

Beautiful Autumn colours - Blessington Greenway at Russellstown

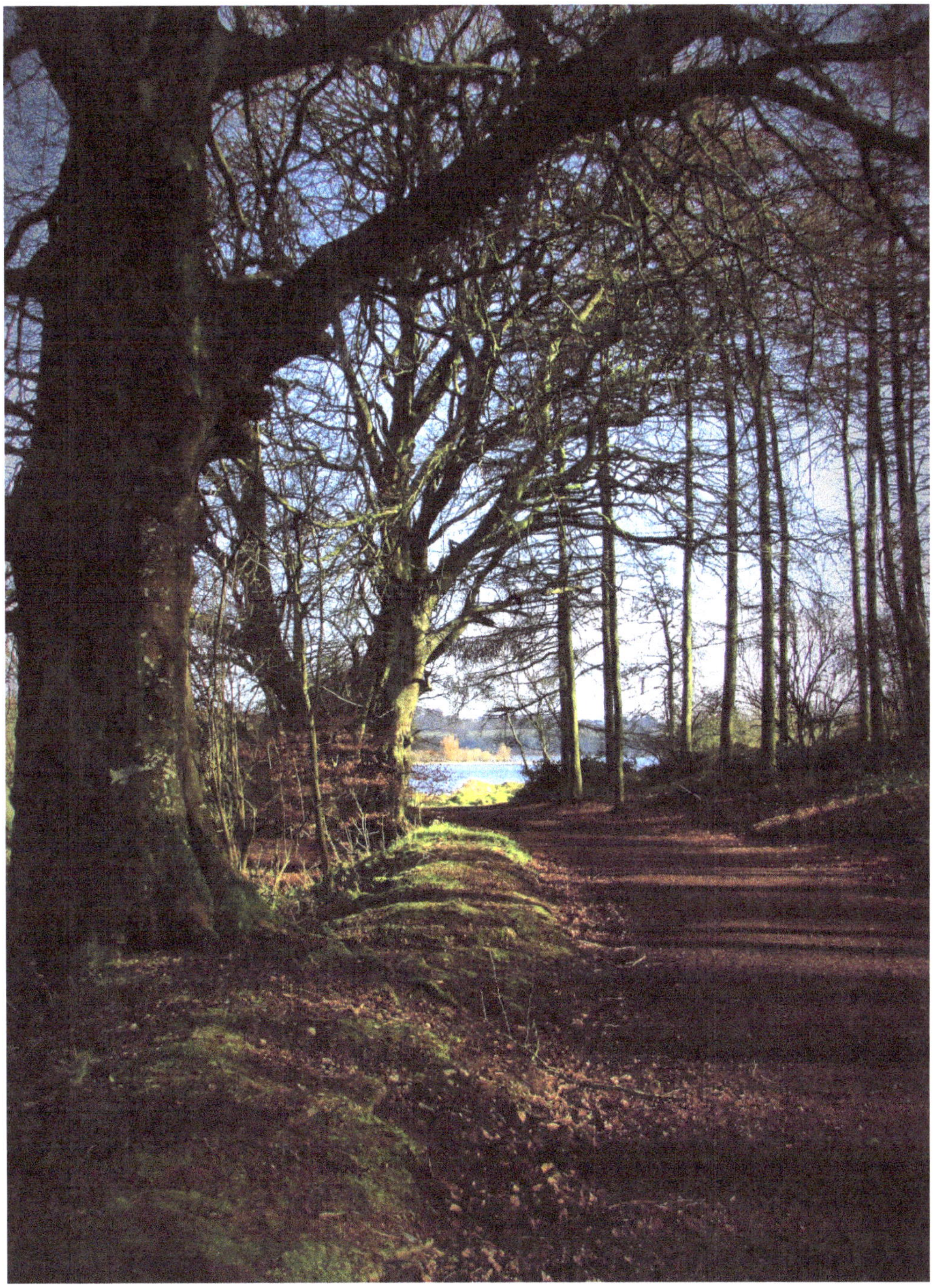

Blessington Greenway off the Valleymount Road

Blessington Greenway is an amazing series of pathways that begin at The Avon Lakeshore Resort and weaves its way around the Blessington Lakes, through forests, past an ancient Medieval Ringfort, then onto the N81, following then into Burgage Moyle Lane, crosses the Valleymount Road and then to Russellstown Bay, and finally across the N81 to the Palladian Mansion, Russborough House.

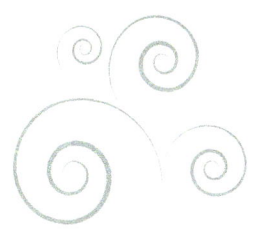

I was in communication with John Horan who has been closely involved with the planning of the Greenway from the beginning, back in 2009 when the County Council's Outdoor Recreation Strategy was launched. After a feasibility study, carried out in 2010 on 'Recreation Opportunities at Poulaphouca Reservoir', Blessington District Forum identified a potential project for walking and cycling trails around the Blessington Lakes. John after leading study groups to view other successful Greenway developments, worked on behalf of The Forum to develop the first phase which was to be 6.5kms from Blessington to Russborough. It was officially launched on the 1st February 2014. I'd like to say thanks to everyone who made it happen, its amazing!

Blessington Greenway Boardwalk - N81 to Burgage

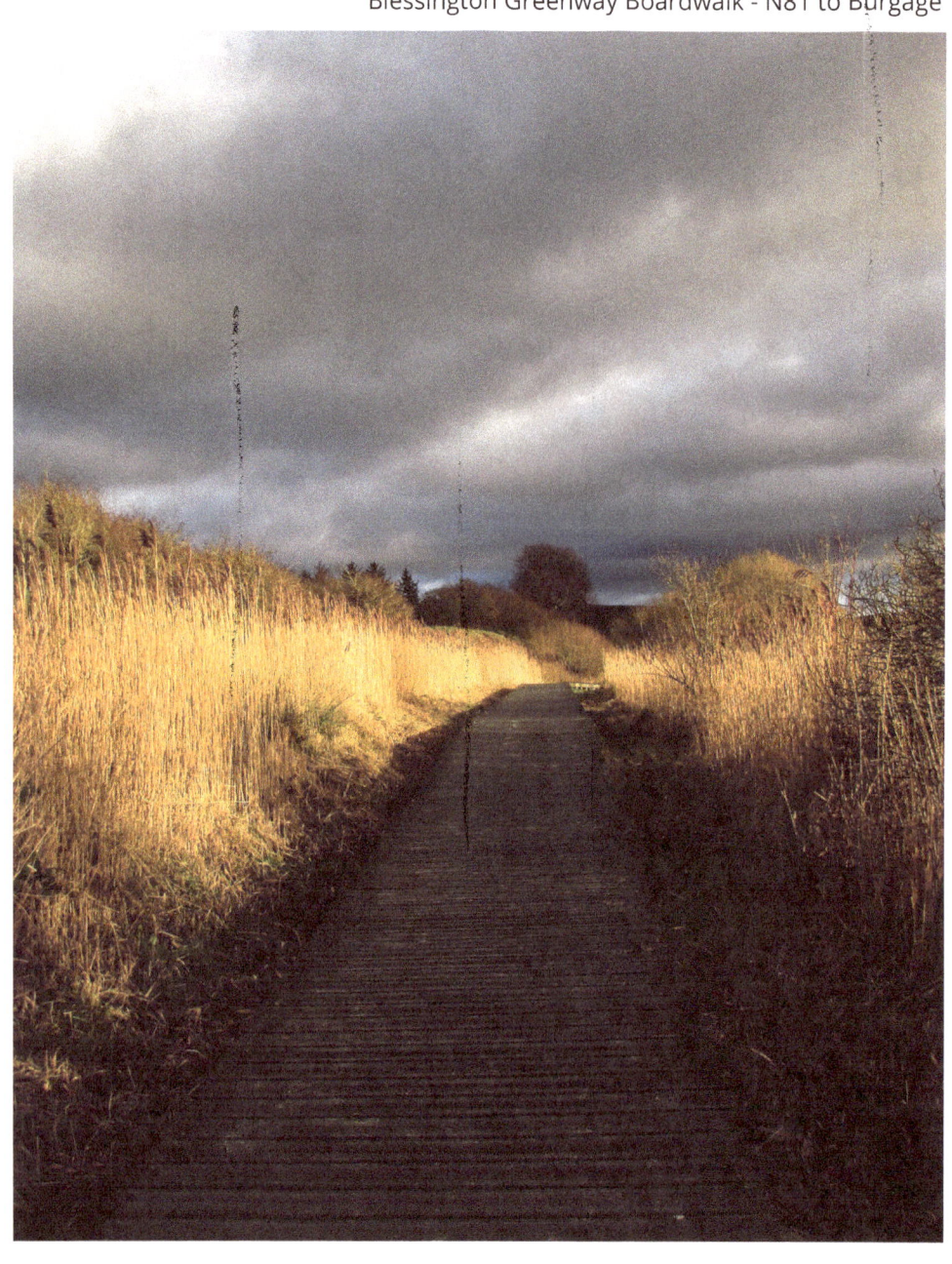

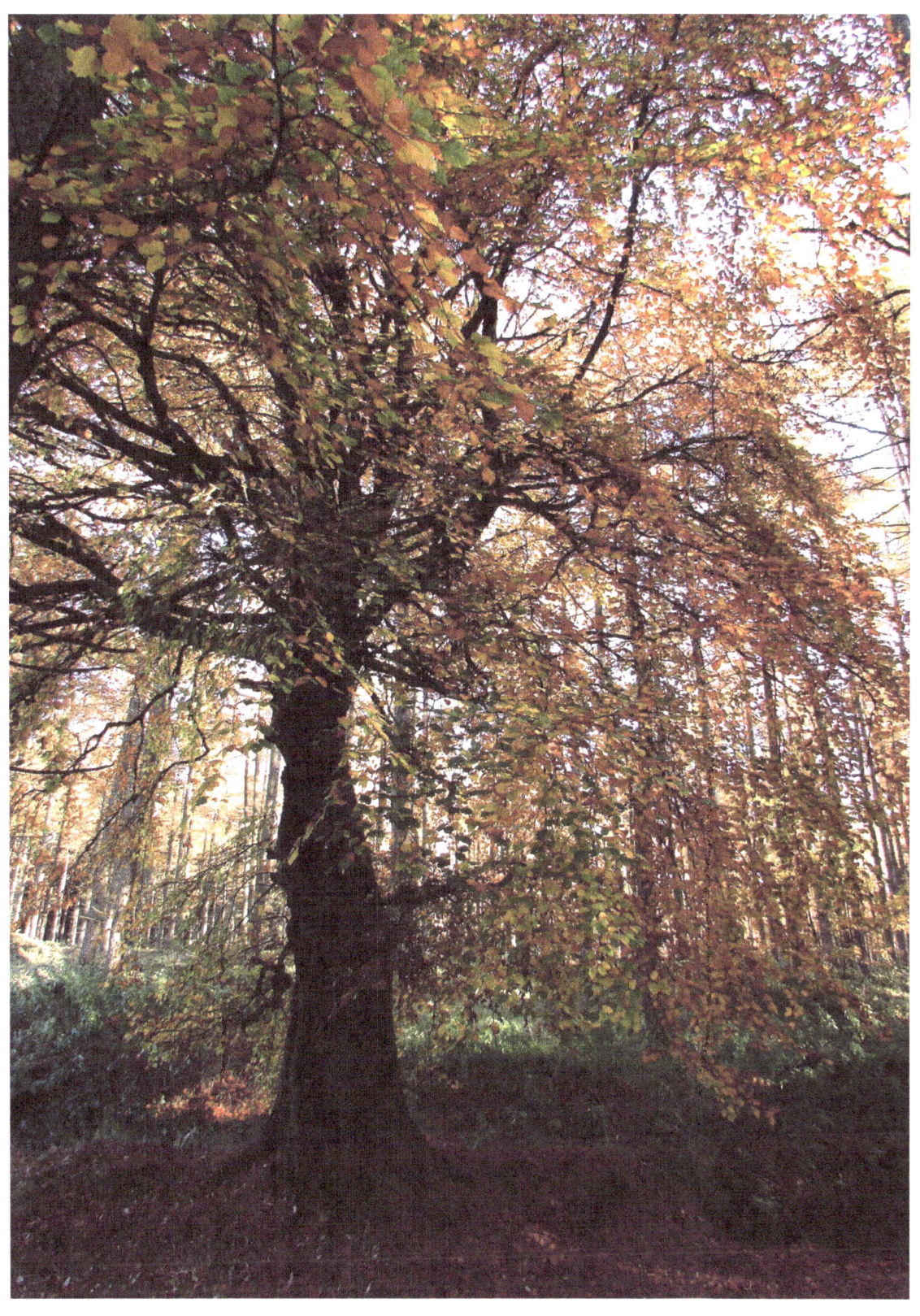

Blessington Greenway - Burgage Moyle

Plans are now underway, and funding has been secured to extend the Greenway. The new E-Greenway will have E Bikes with charging points along the route and solar powered charging points also for other electric vehicles. It will link in with a wider countywide project for E Cycling.

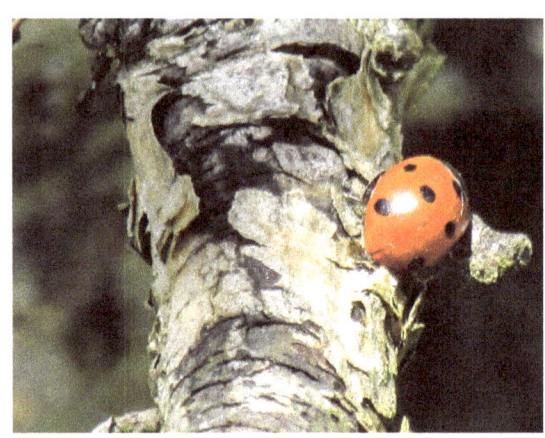
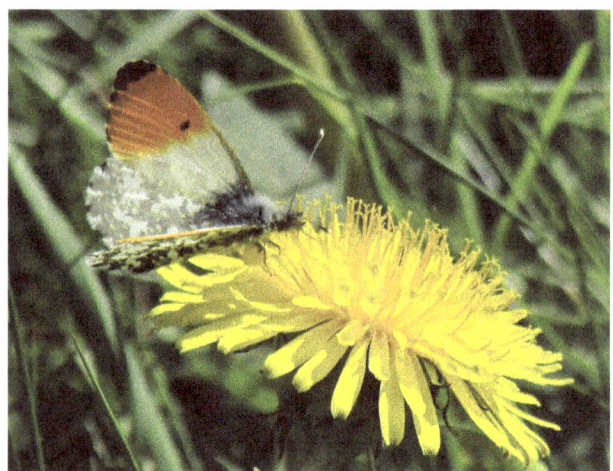

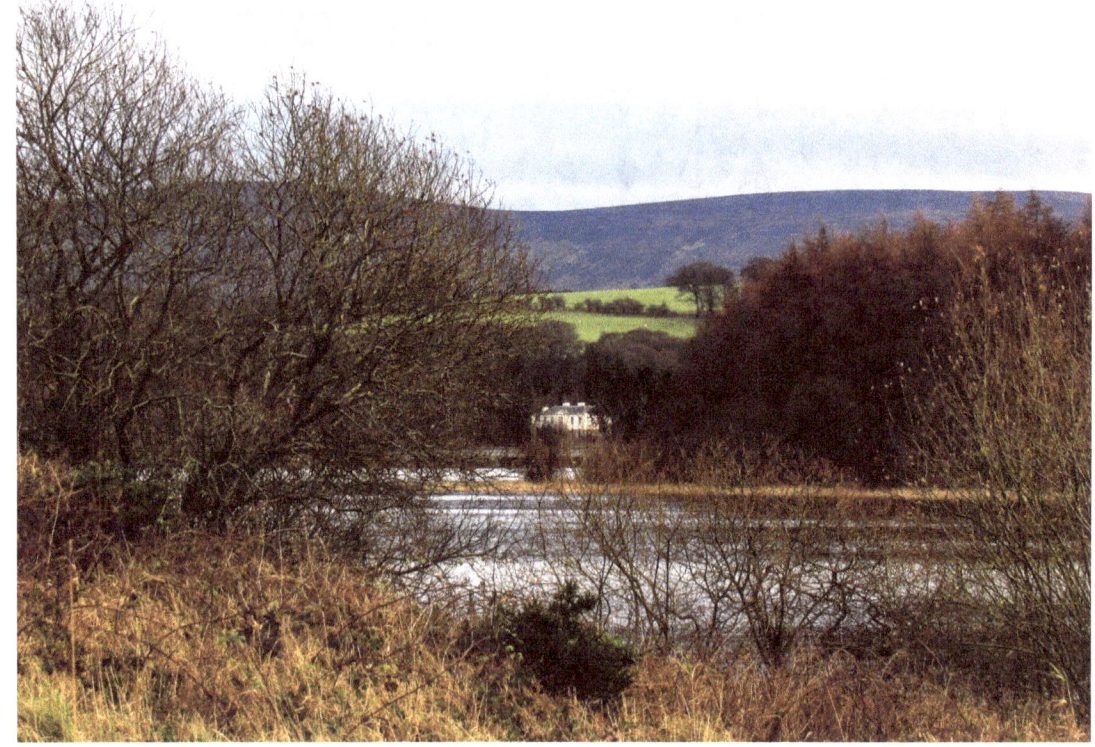
Blessington Greenway - N81 to Burgage - Baltyboys House in distance

The EGreenway will lead near to Russborough and Tulfarris and have loops to the villages of Valleymount, Ballyknockan and Lacken. It will cover a total of 42kms. There will be a new Blessington E-Greenway Interpretive Centre, situated on the Manor Kilbride Road near to the Greenway in Blessington.

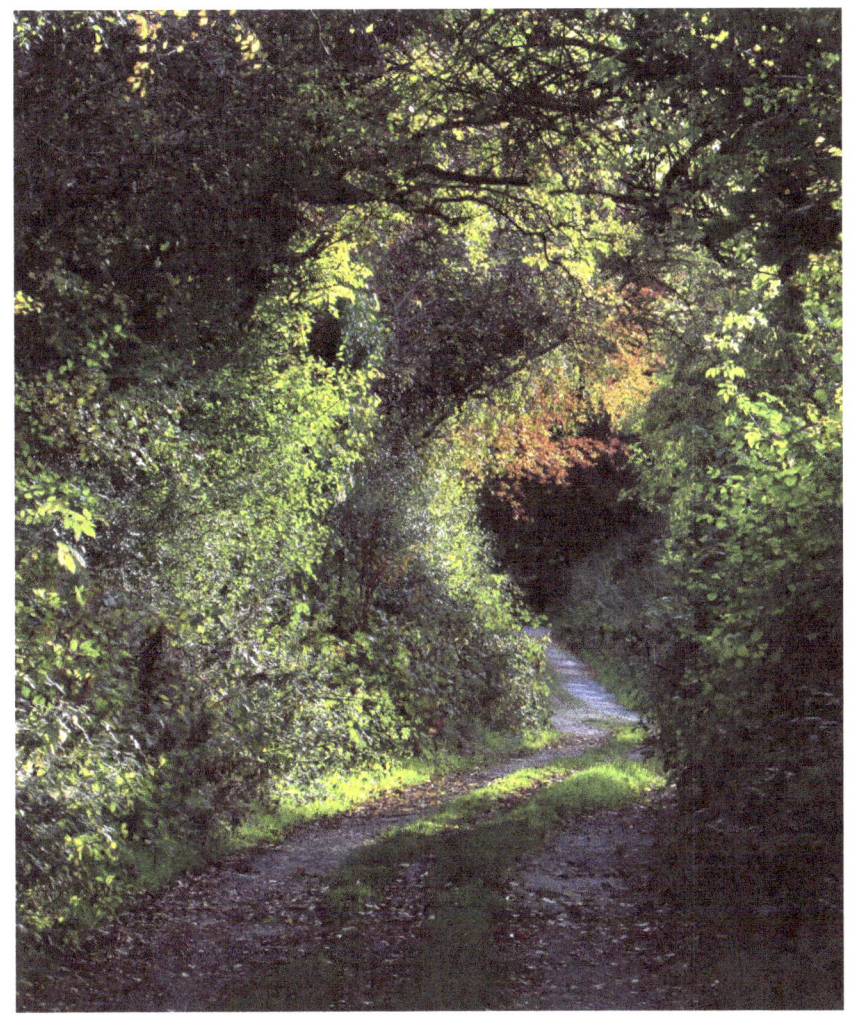

Blessington Greenway -Burgage Moyle

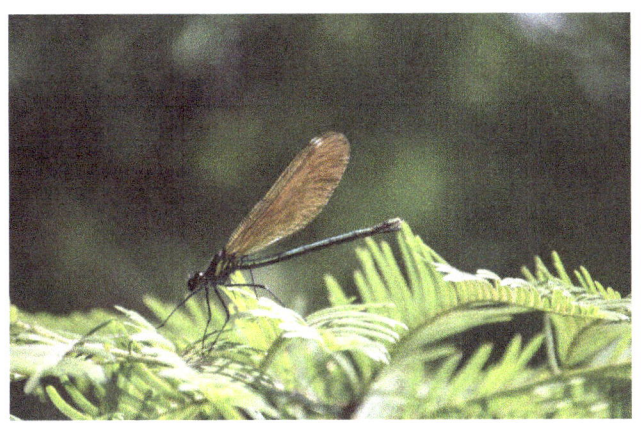 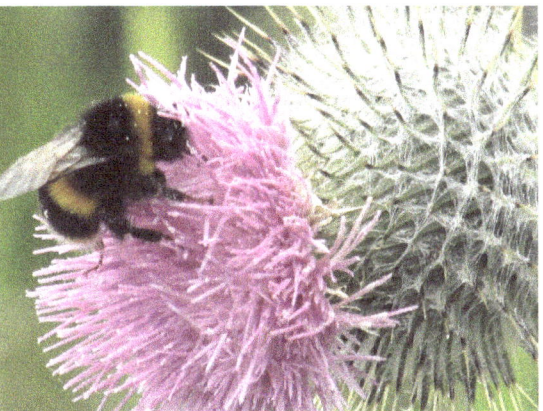

You never know what you'll see - from dragonflies to bees!

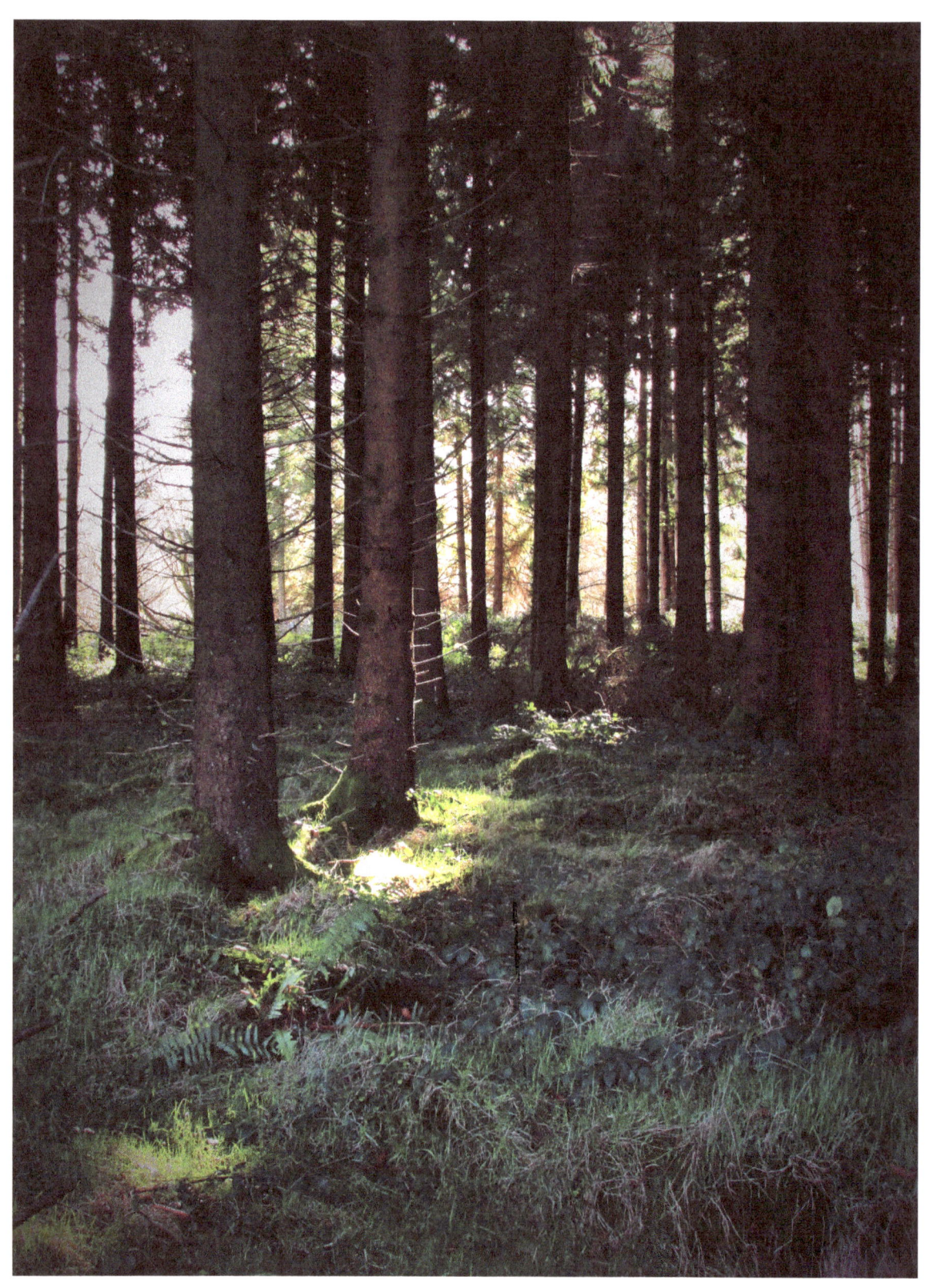

Into the woods I go to lose my mind and find my soul, or so they say!
Russellstown Woods on the Greenway to Russborough

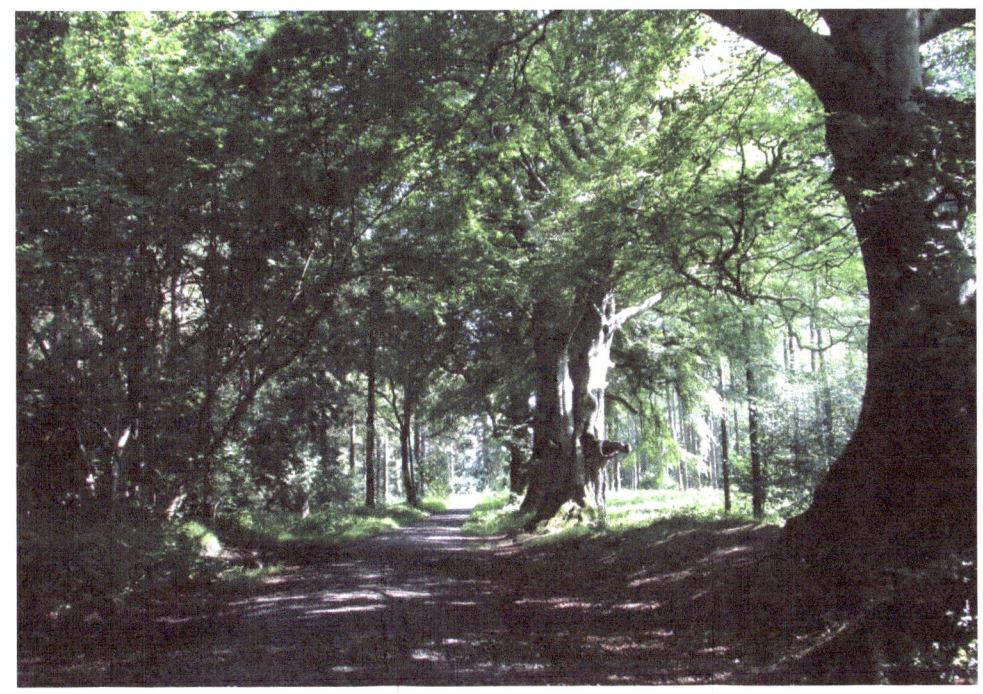

Russellstown Woods on the Greenway Path between Valleymount Road and Russborough

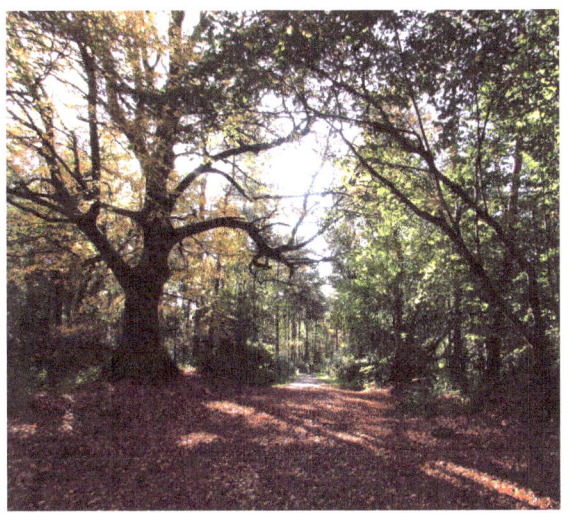 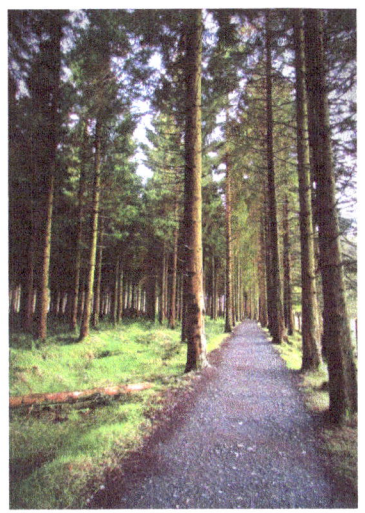 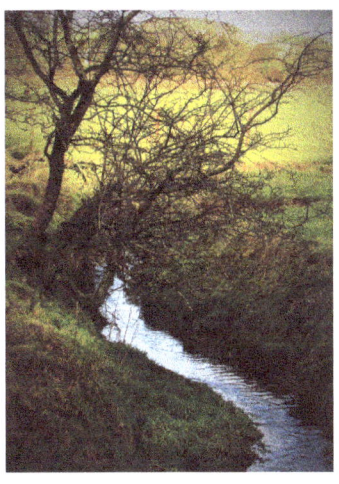

As I mentioned earlier, I used to drop my son to school and head off in search of new places to explore and photograph. Blessington Greenway has a path through Russellstown Woods, of course after taking many photos of that I wanted to explore more. A friend told me of a trail leading through the woods, off the pathway that was kind of a shortcut way to another part of the lake, and off I went. I went on and off over many different seasons. On one occasion the path had become overgrown and I ended up getting lost. At one stage I was so deep into the woods with no lake or path in sight and all I could see was large patches of briars around me. Fighting down a sense of panic, because I knew it was time to start heading back to get my son, I closed my eyes, calmed myself with my breathing, visualised myself walking back on the path and asked my Angels to point me in the right direction. I wished I'd remembered to do that at the time I got lost on Lackan shoreline! I got back out with great relief!

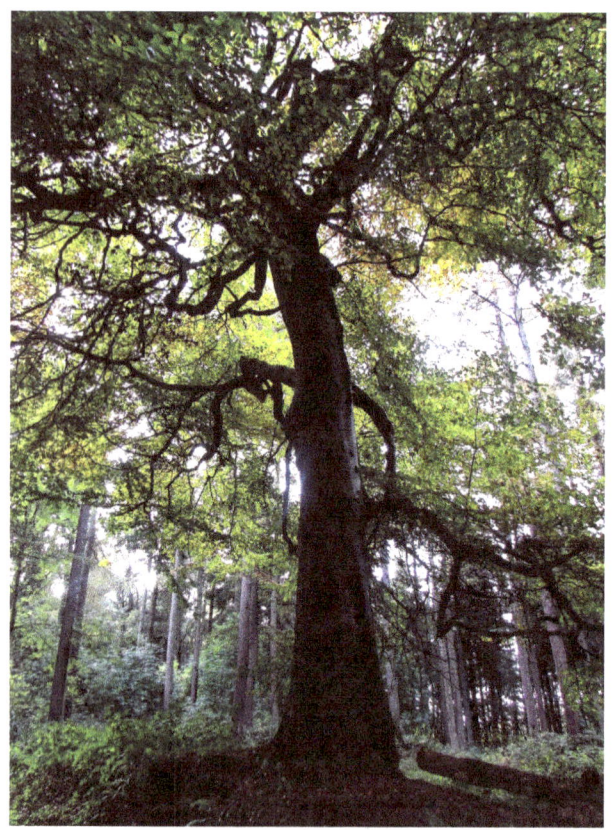

Beautiful tree at Burgage Moyle

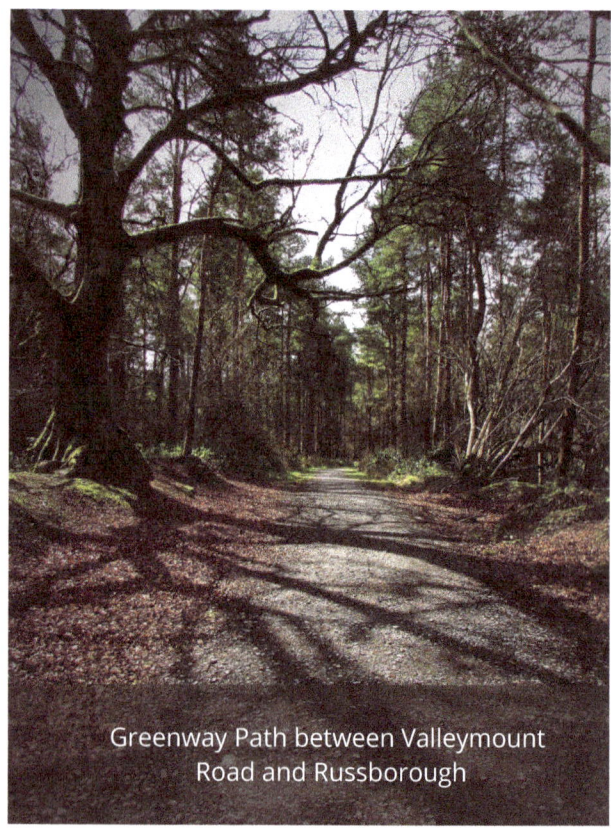

Greenway Path between Valleymount Road and Russborough

Wooden Cross on site of original St. Mark's Cross Burgage Greenway

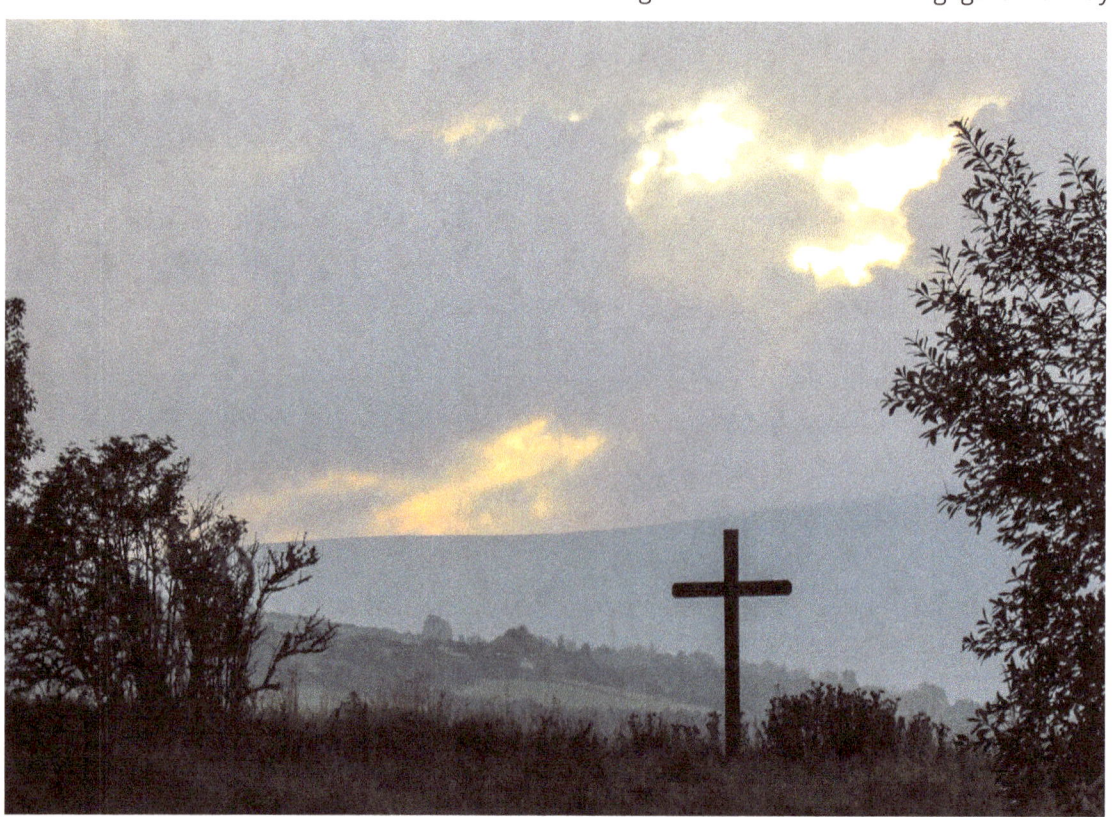

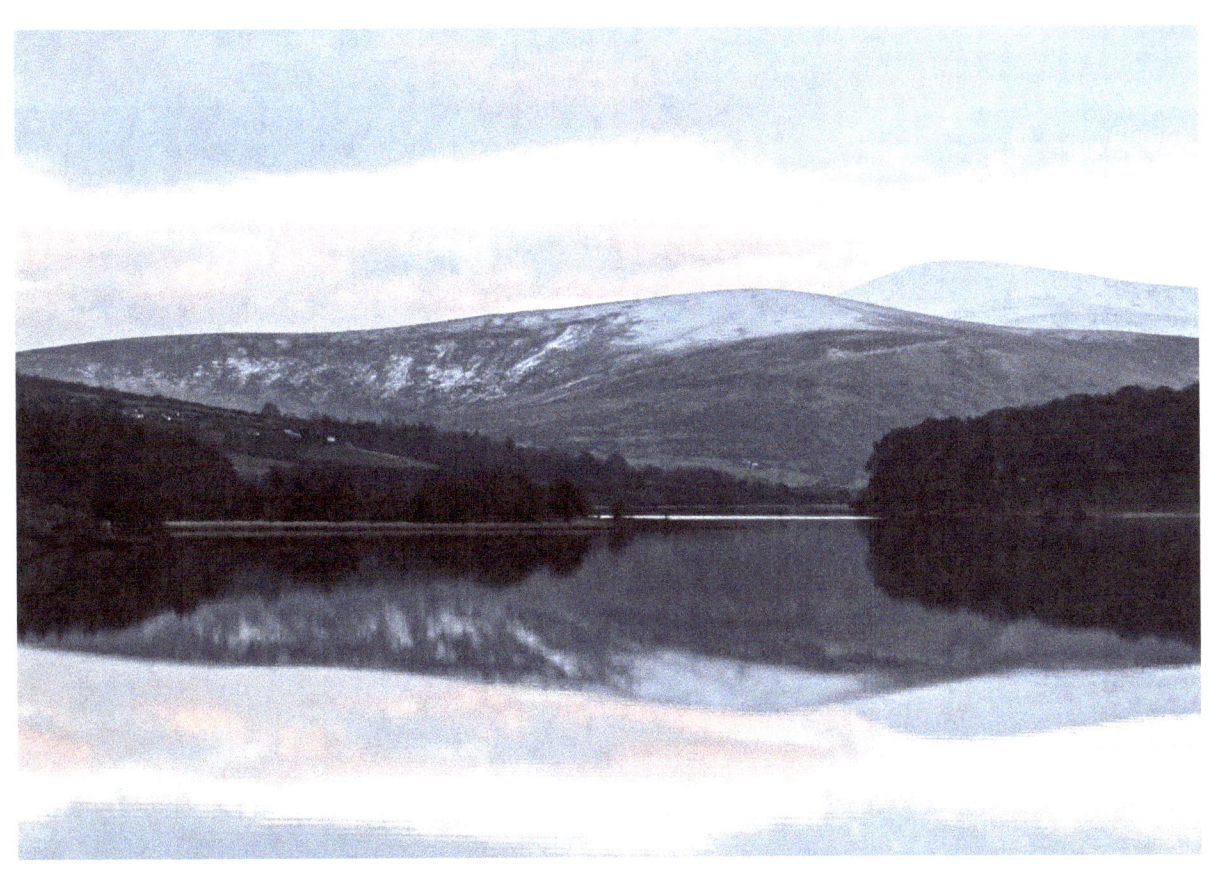
View from the Greenway path on N81 of Blessington Lakes

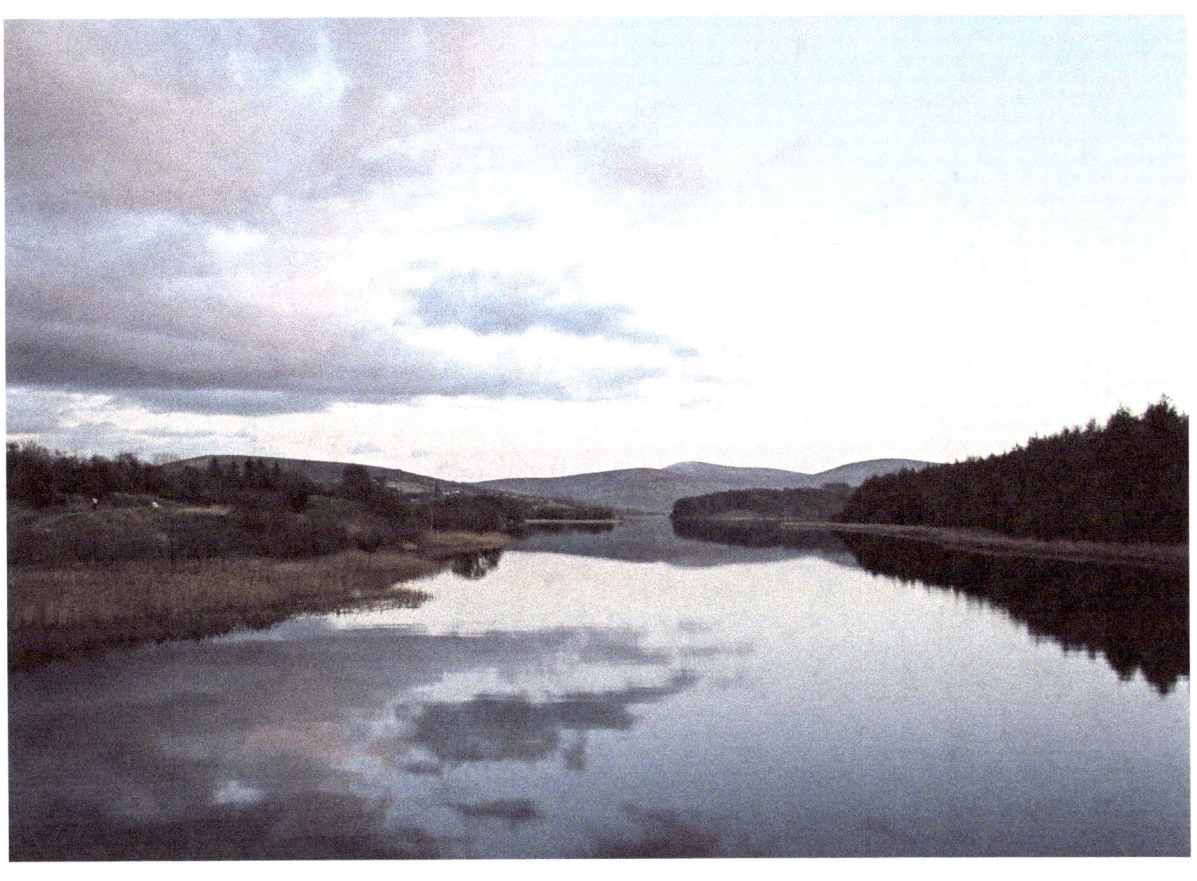

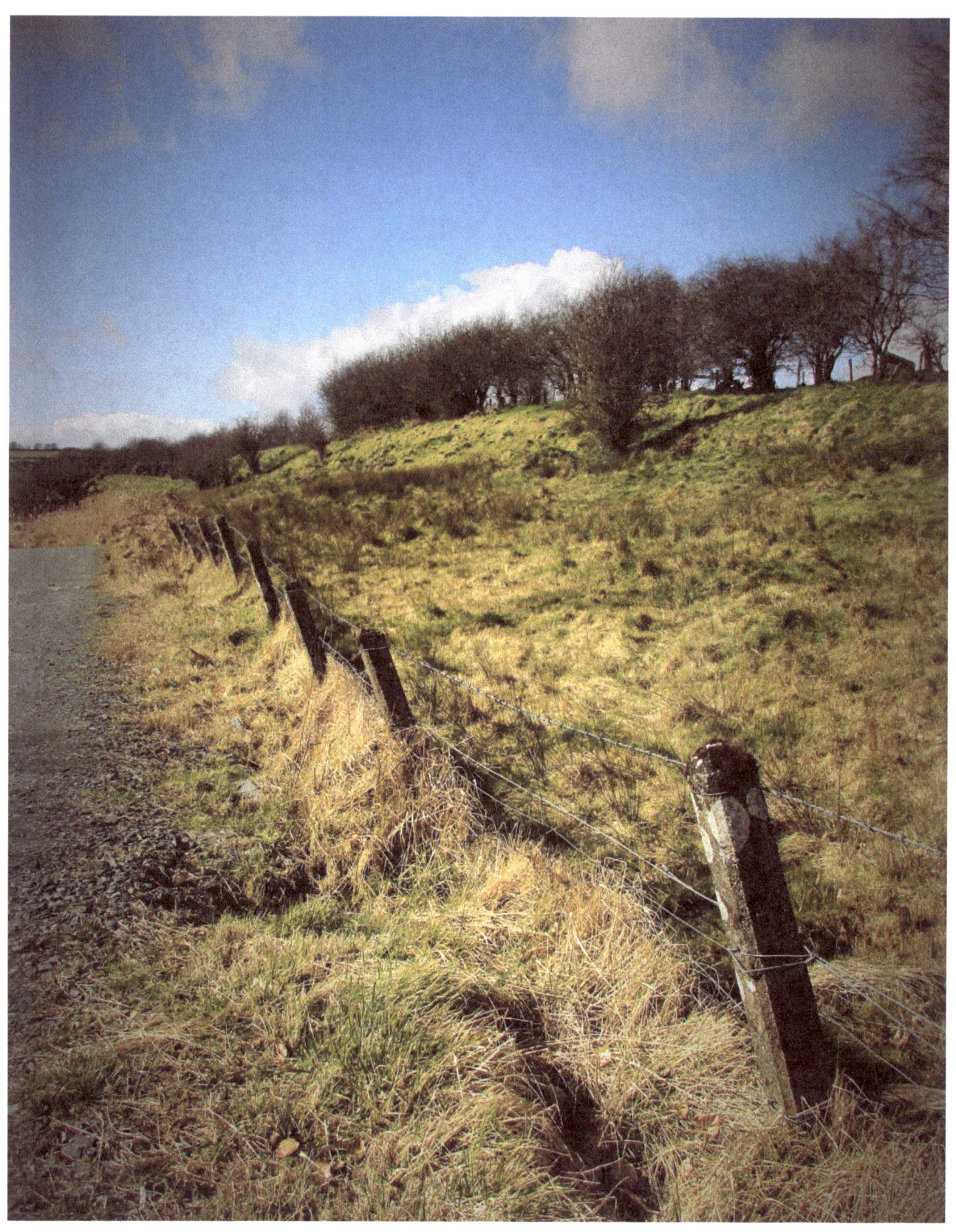

Greenway path, Burgage to N81

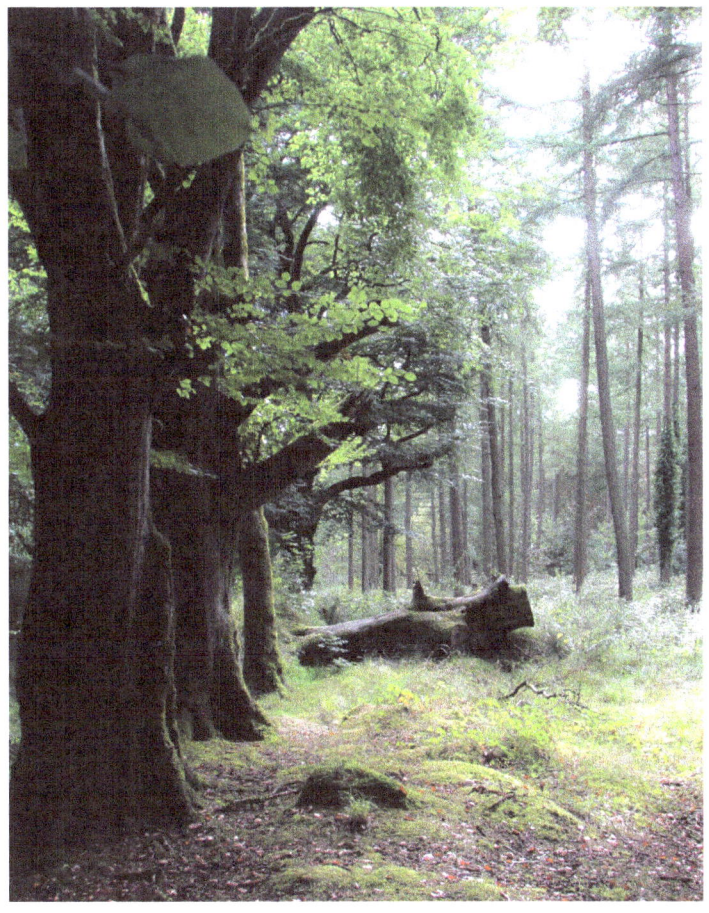

A fallen tree - in woods on the Greenway from Valleymount Road to Russborough

A heart shaped stone

A common blue butterfly

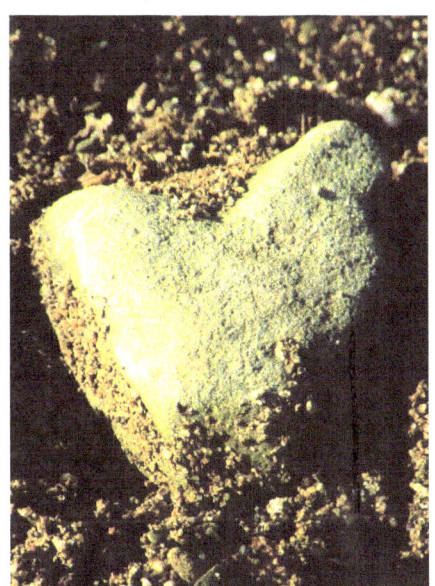

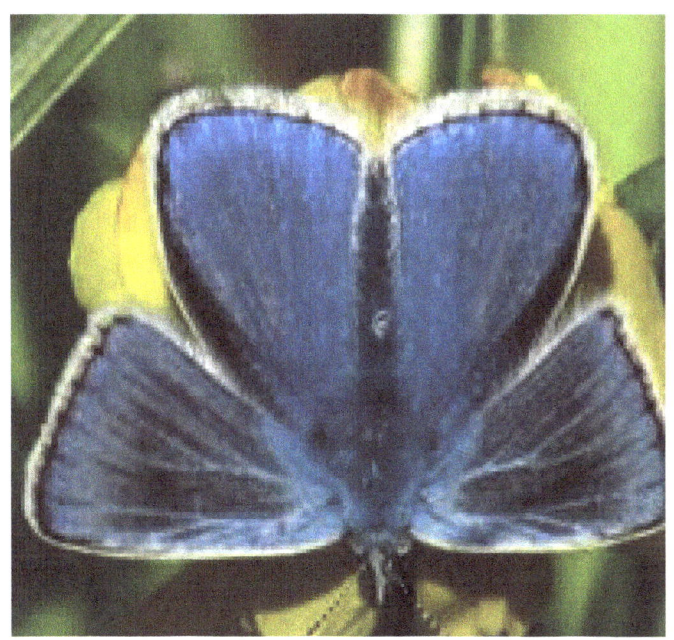

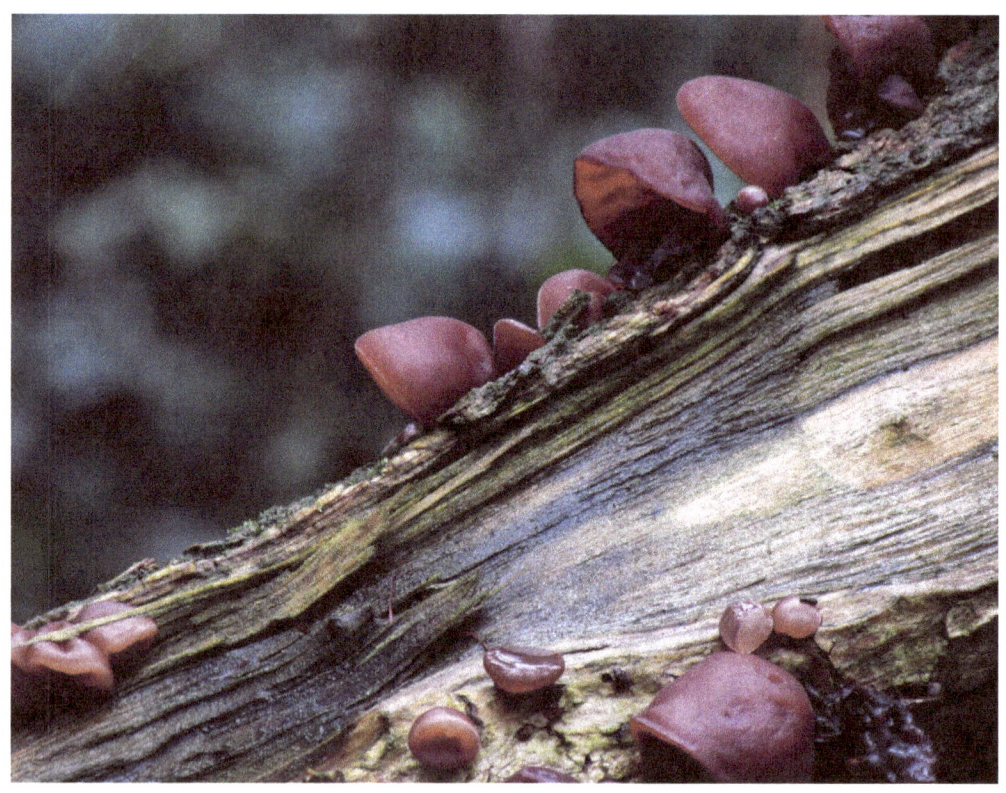

Scarlet Elf Cut Fungi - on a tree in woods near Burgage

Pussy Willow - Salix Caprea

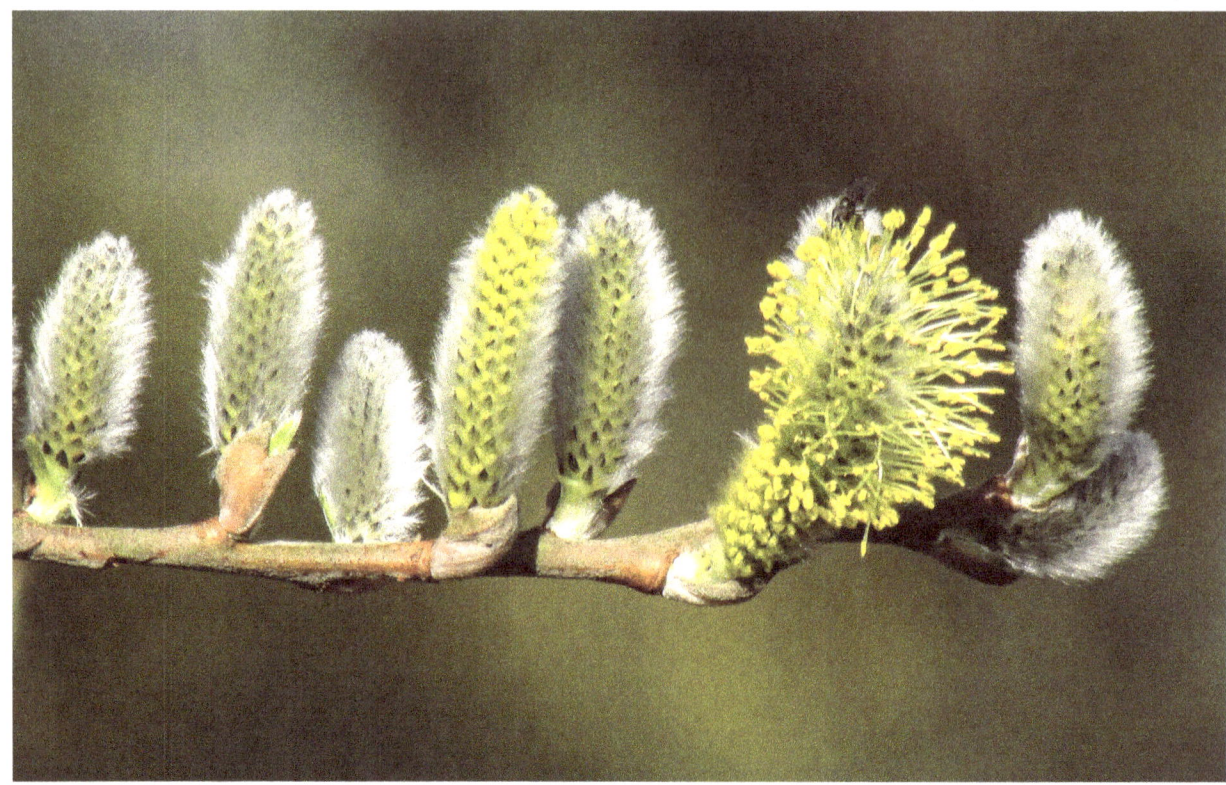

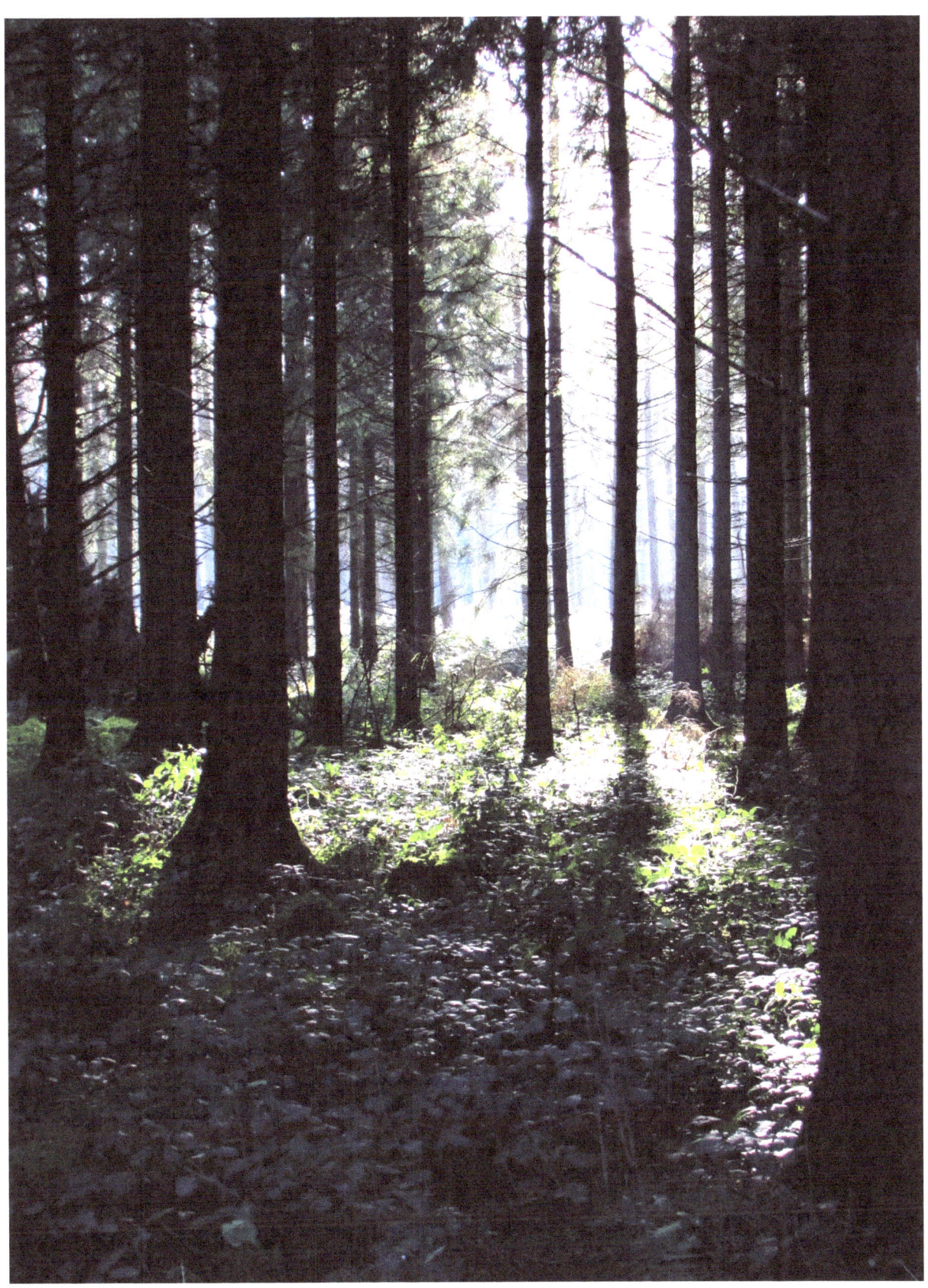

Morning sun in Russellstown Woods - wish you could hear the birdsong - heavenly!

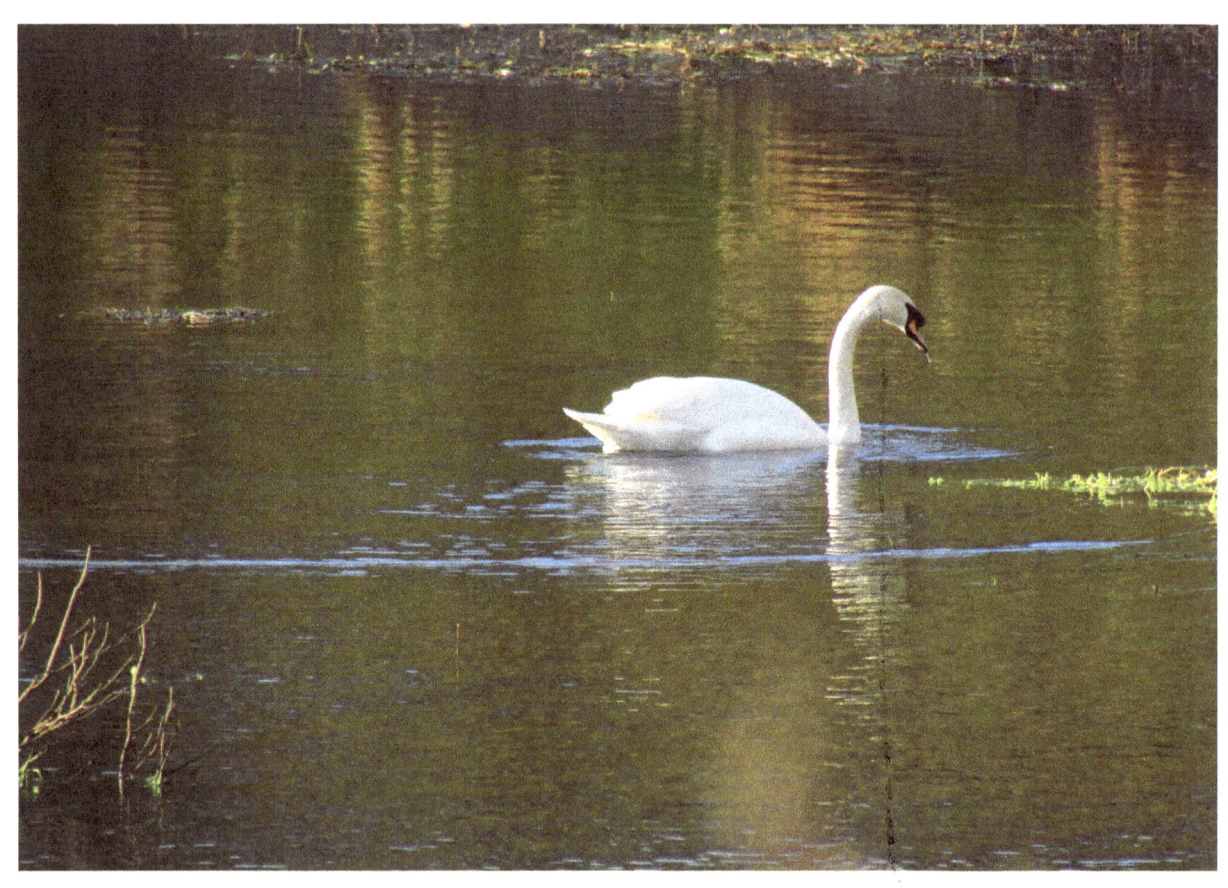

Swans enjoying the lakes near the N81 Greenway path

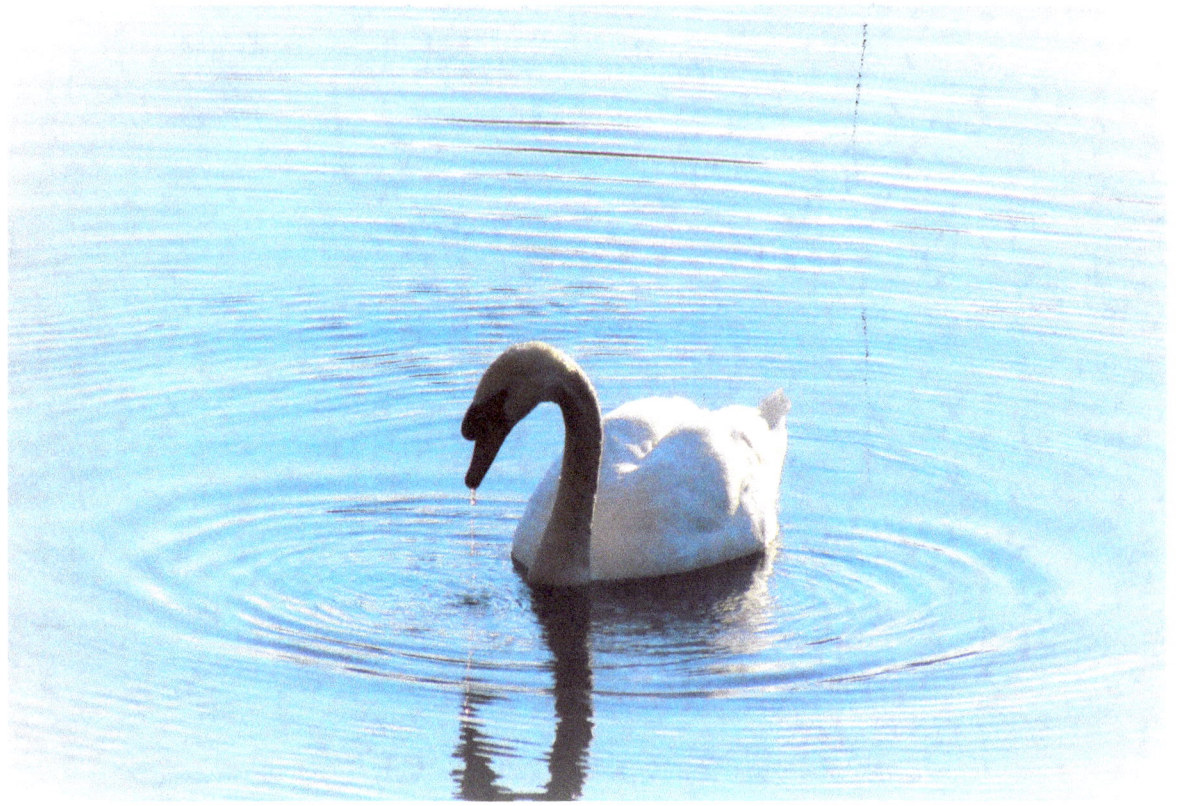

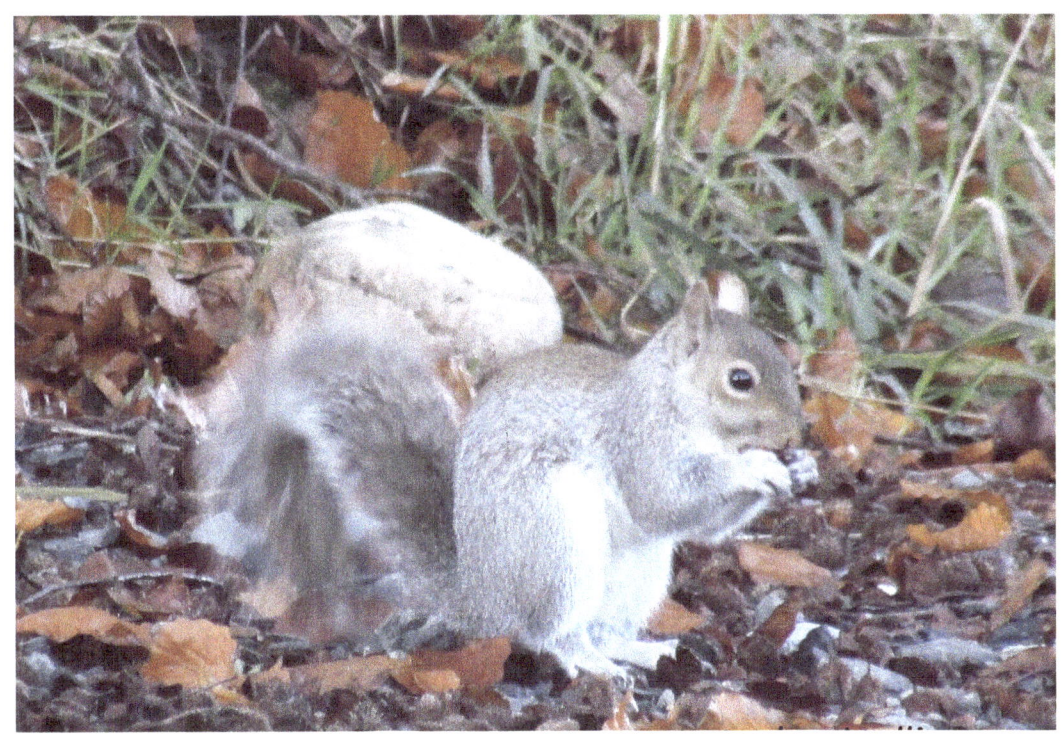

A cute grey Squirrel, a male Bullfinch and a Little Egret all spotted on my ramblings

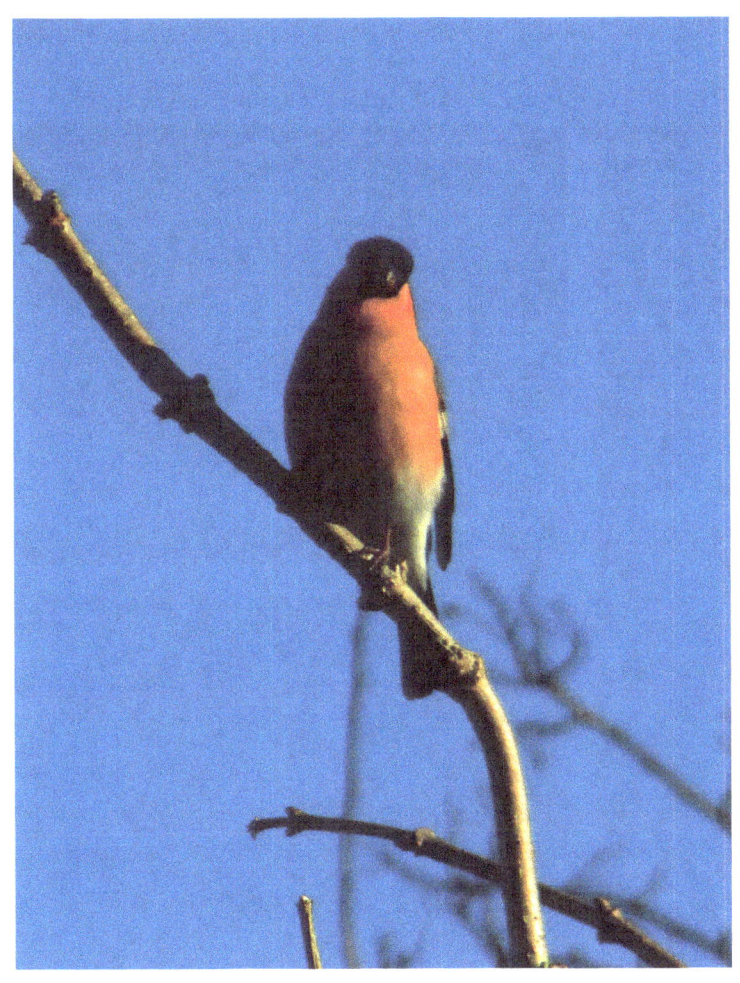
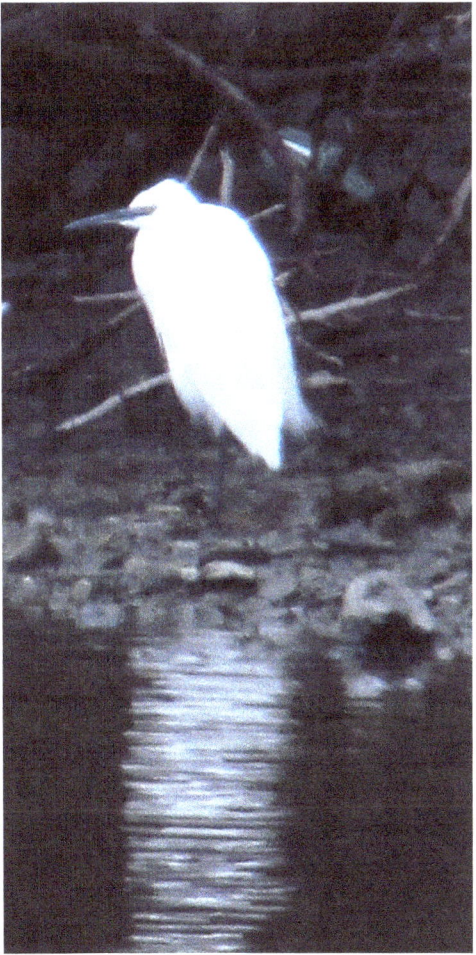

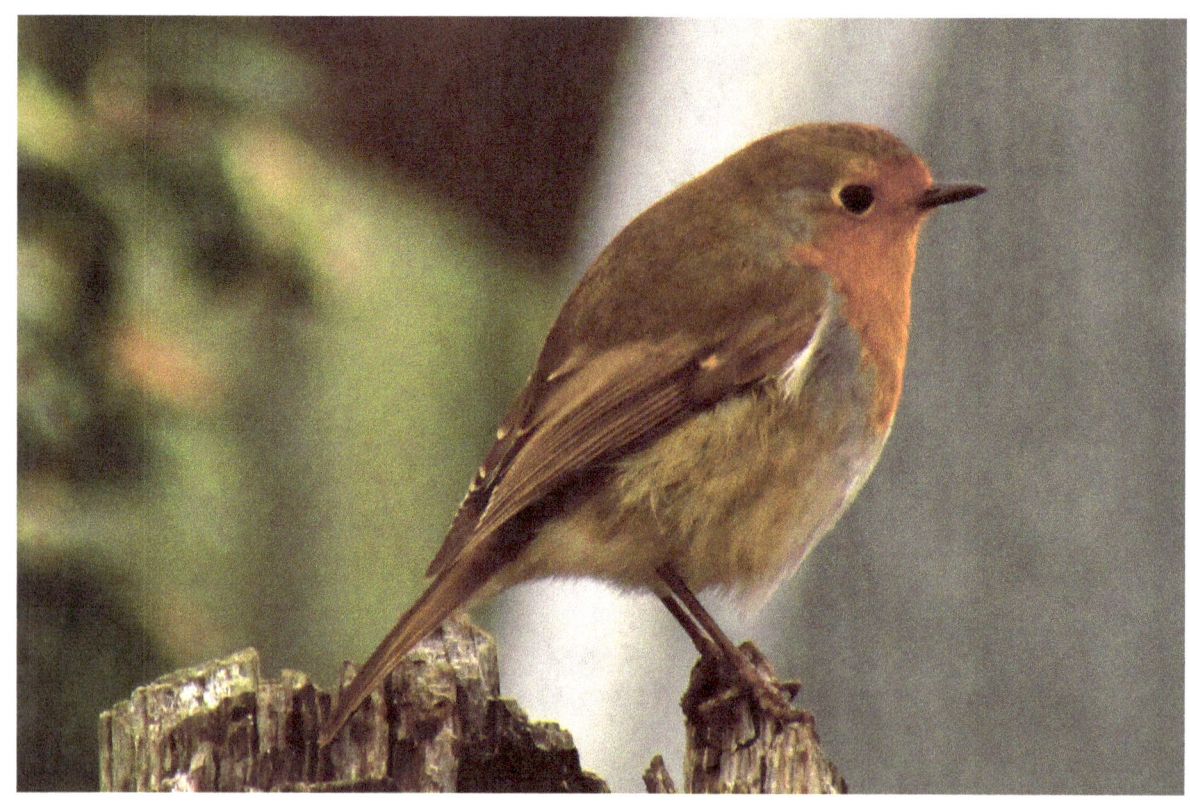

Beautiful Robin spotted in the grounds of The Avon

A happy cat shape in a puddle with a fish in its mouth, and close ups of various lichen - marvellous!

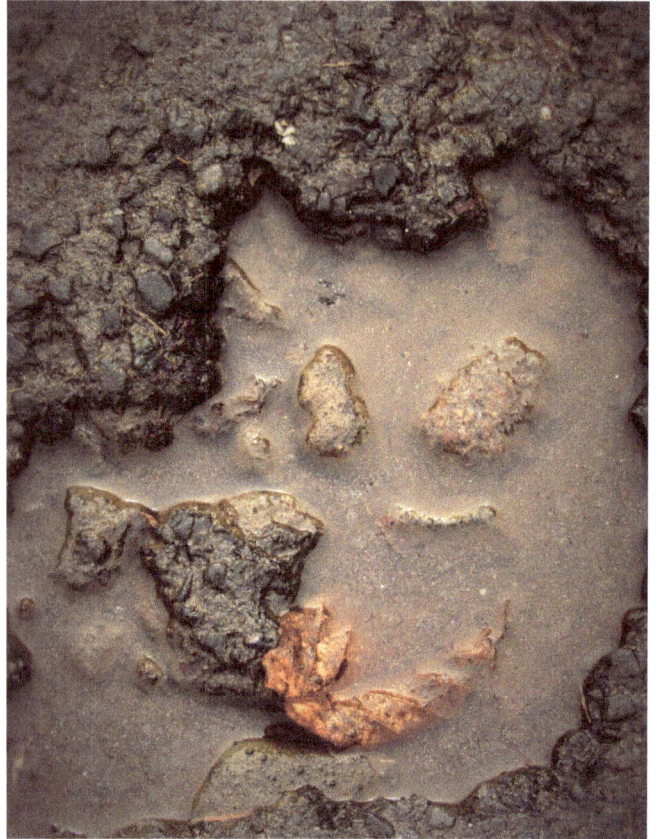

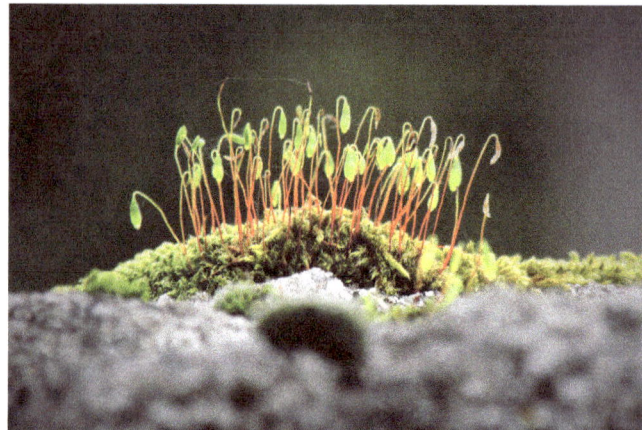

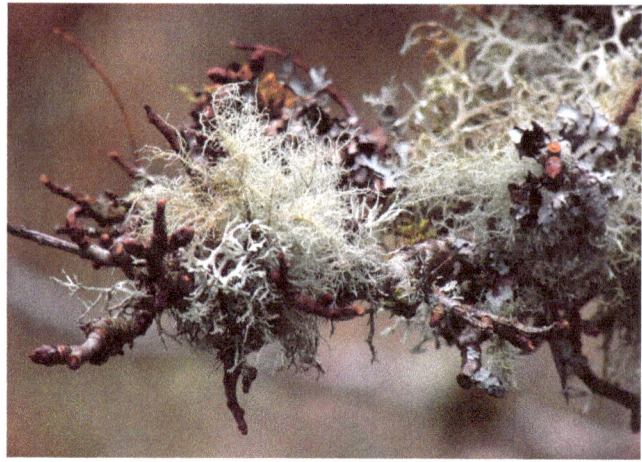

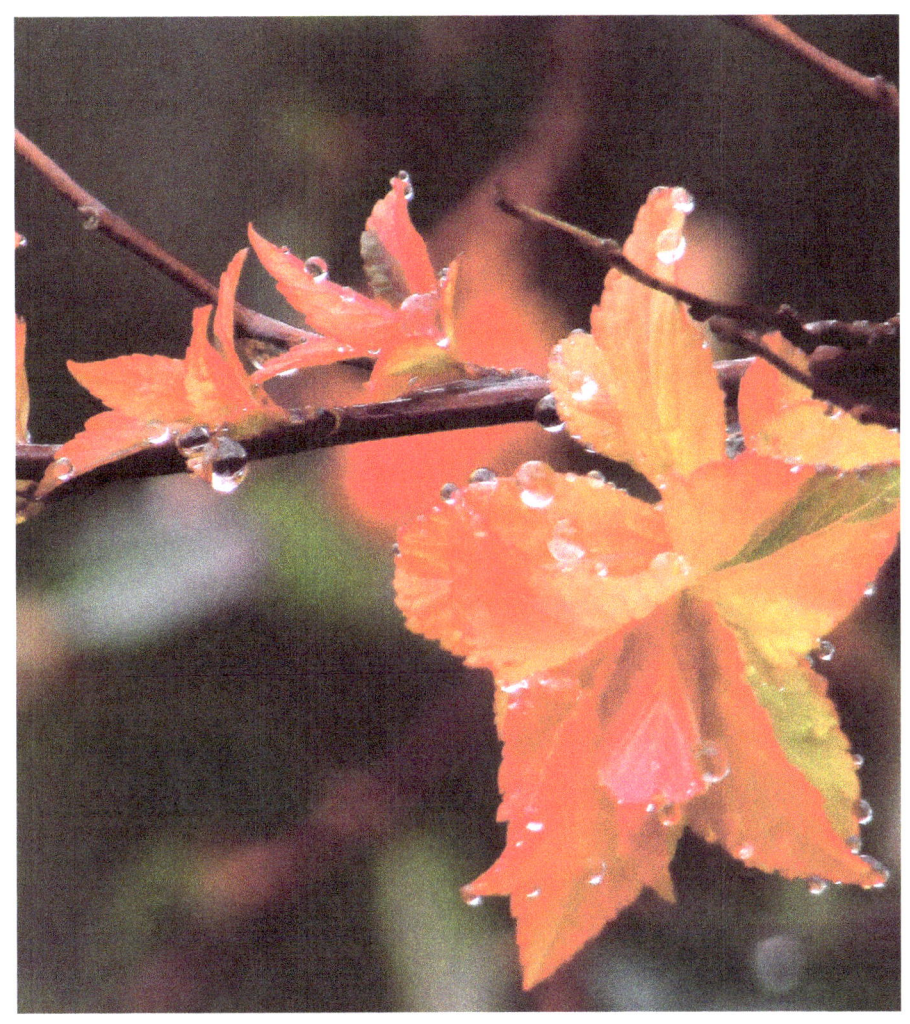

Beautiful raindrops on leaves

A whole little world growing on a cemetery wall & fungi in a tree

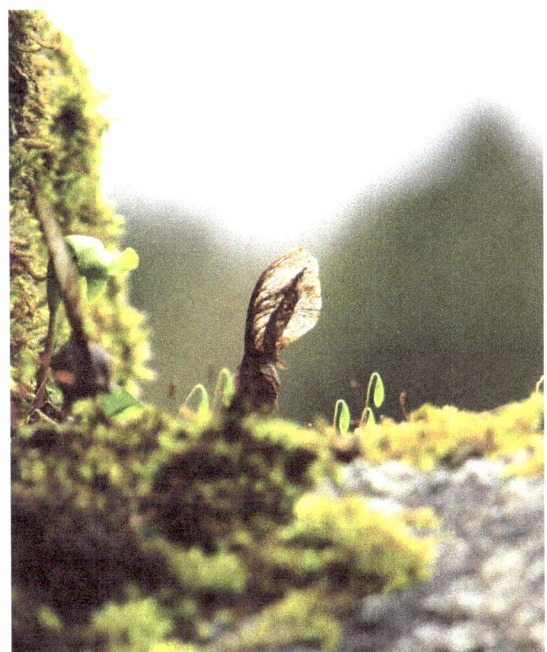
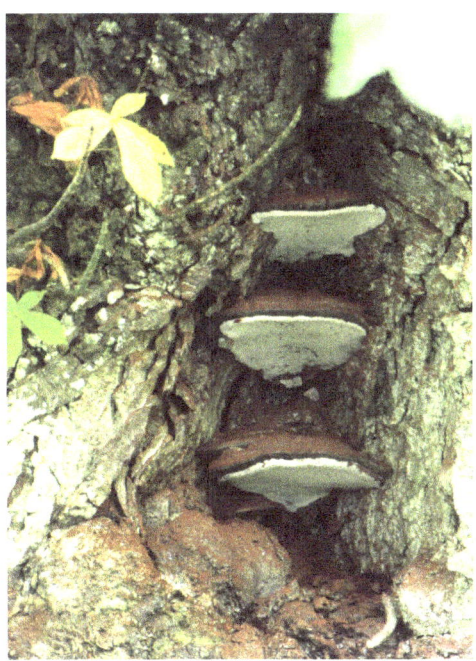

VIKINGS!

I was always on the lookout for anything that might make a great shot. In 2015 there were rumours and the occasional snap of the Film set of The Vikings appearing on the Facebook pages, they were elusive though and people were reluctant to say exactly where they were. But they were definitely filming on Blessington Lakes! So I set out with my eldest son, to find them. It took about an hour of searching, but we were so thrilled when we saw the Viking Ships moored and no one on guard! We were very respectful to leave everything as it was, but we did get some great photos.

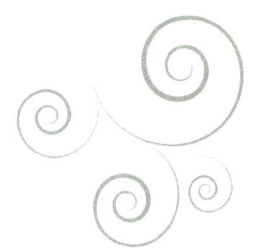

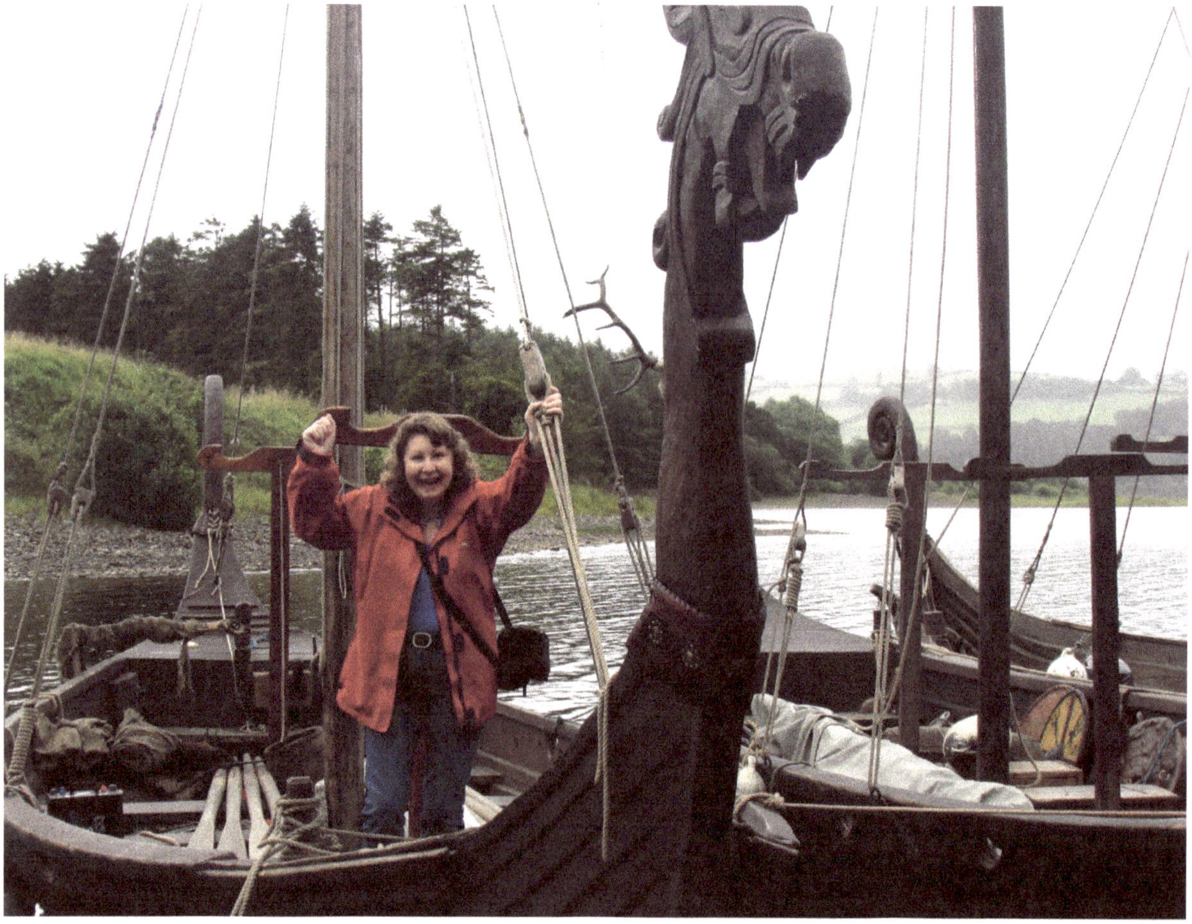

Me on one of The Vikings Boats 2015 -Blessington Lakes - photo taken by my son Josh

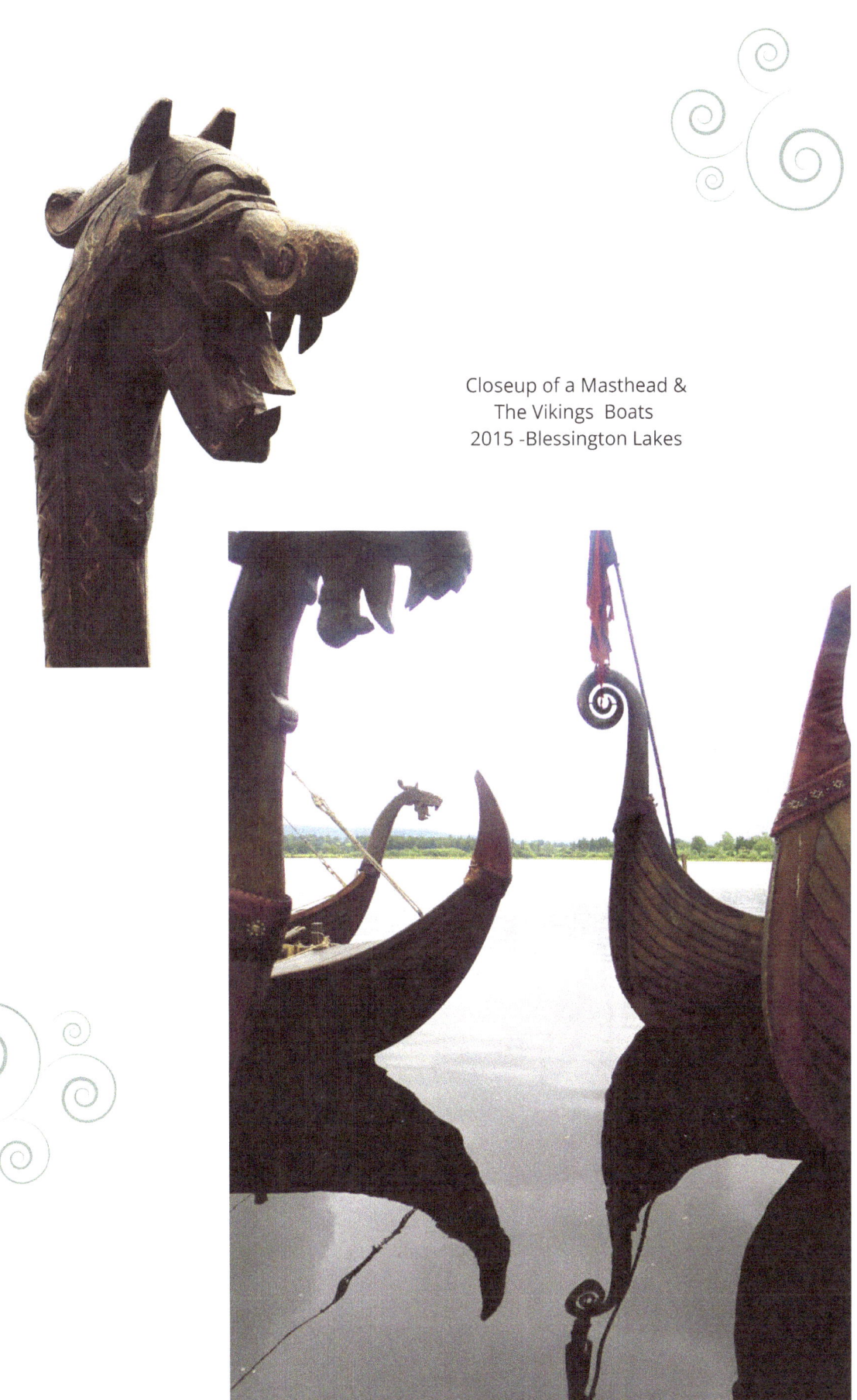

Closeup of a Masthead &
The Vikings Boats
2015 -Blessington Lakes

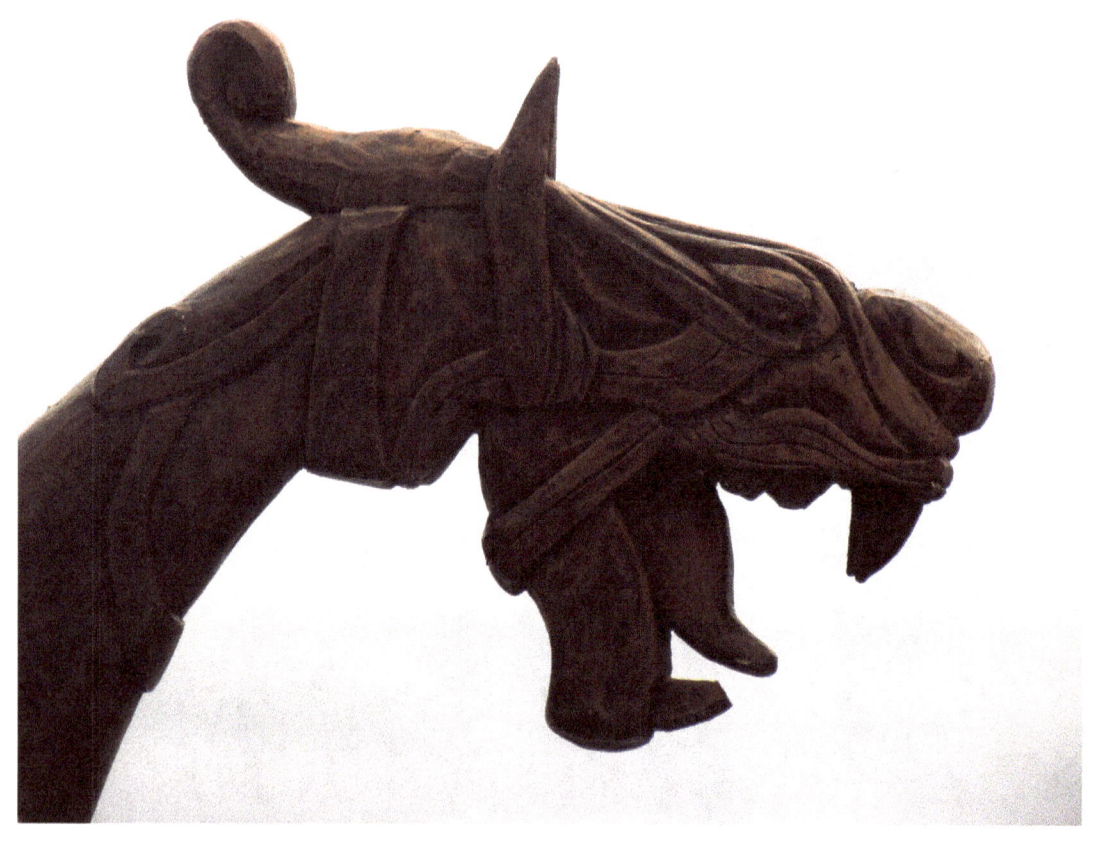

Amazingly beautiful detail and designs on the Viking Ships

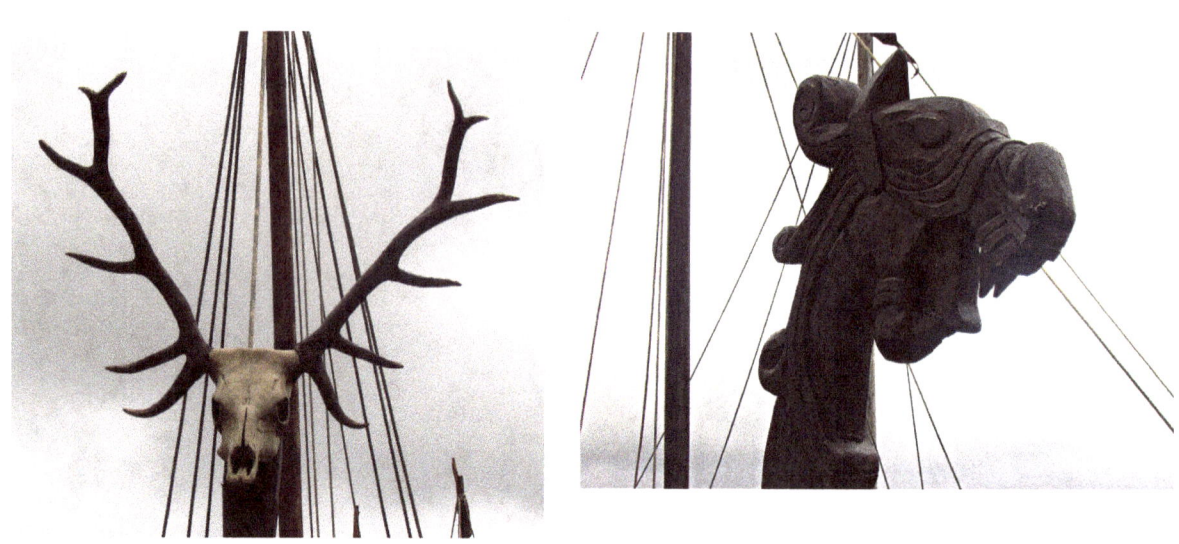

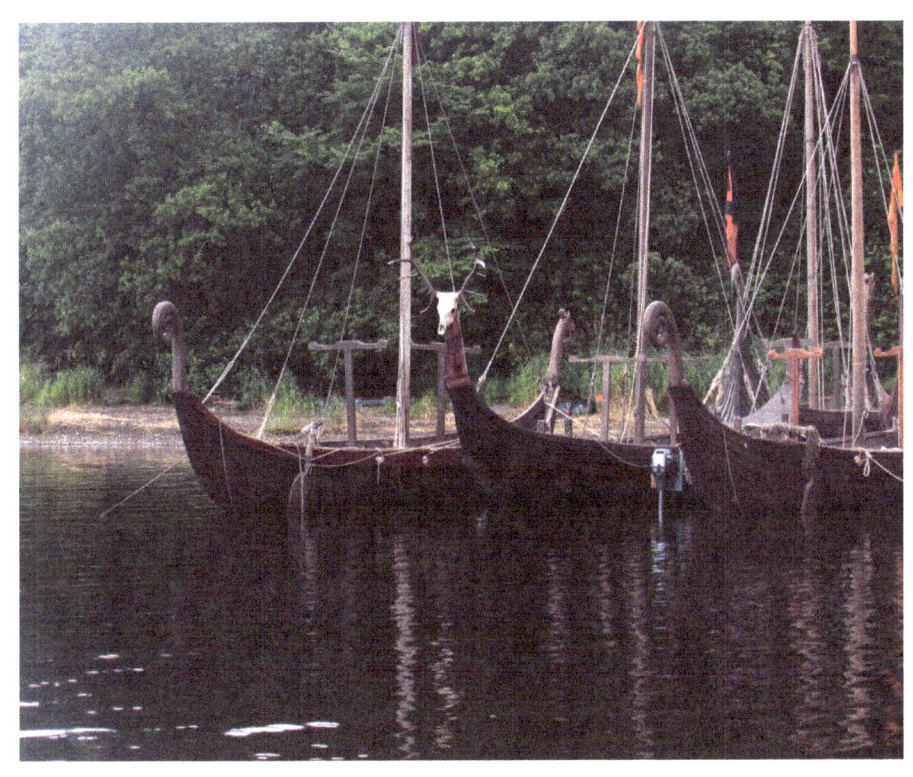
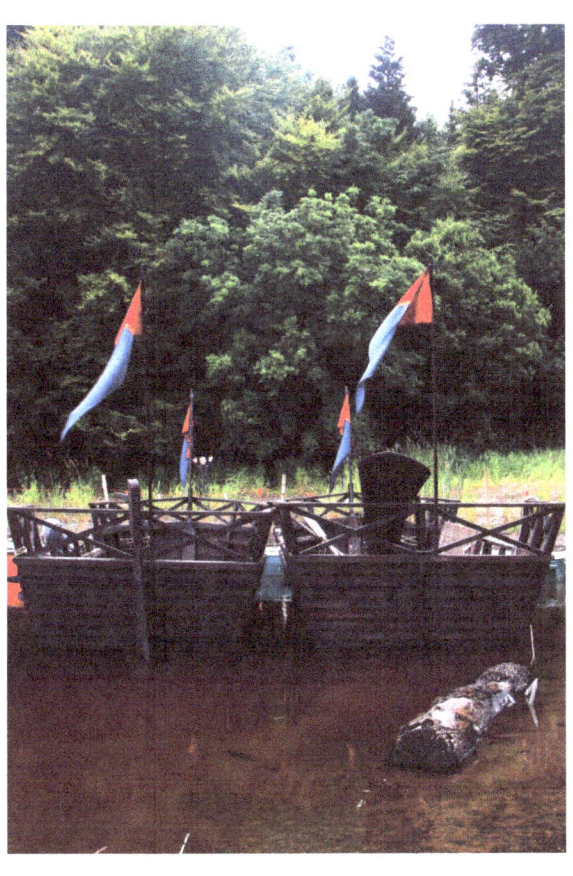
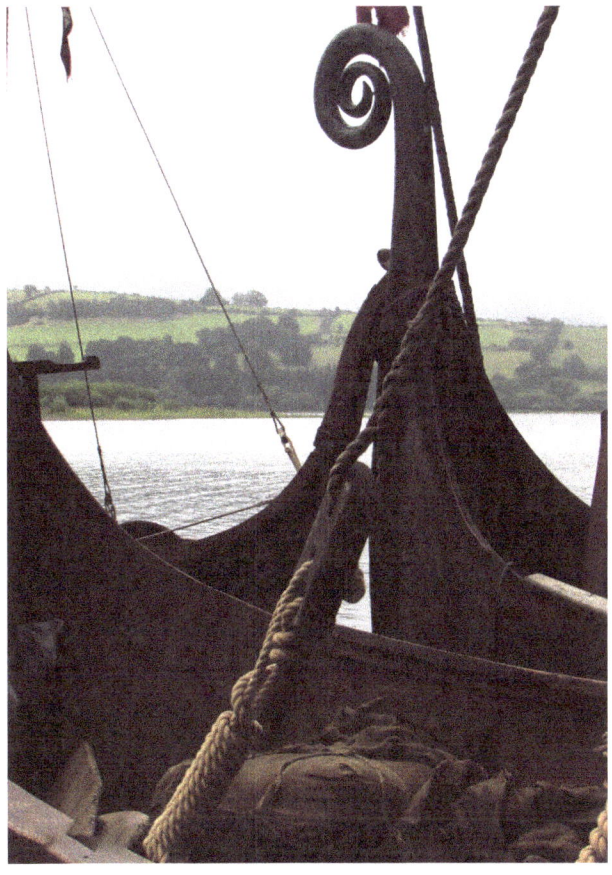

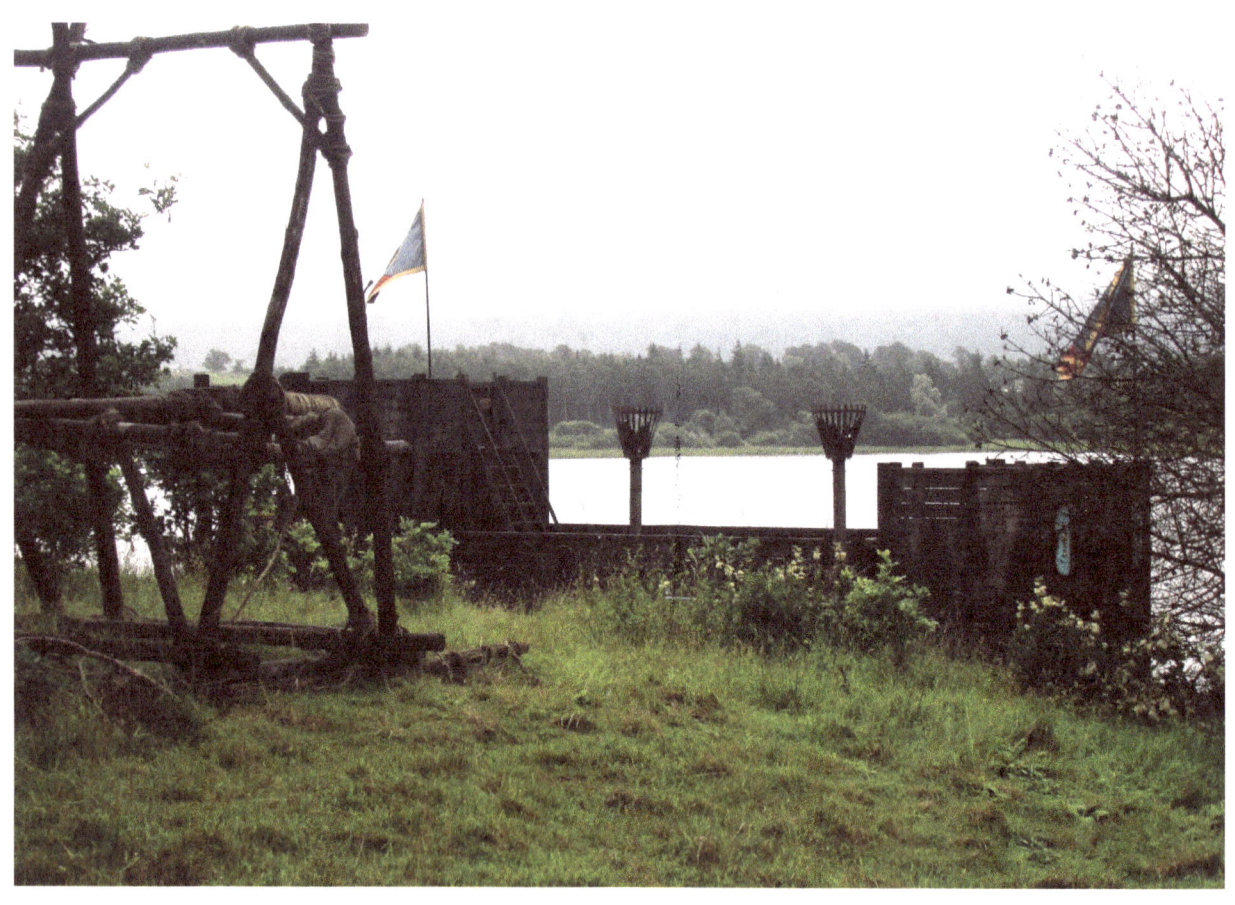

Film Set of The Vikings 2015 -Blessington Lakes

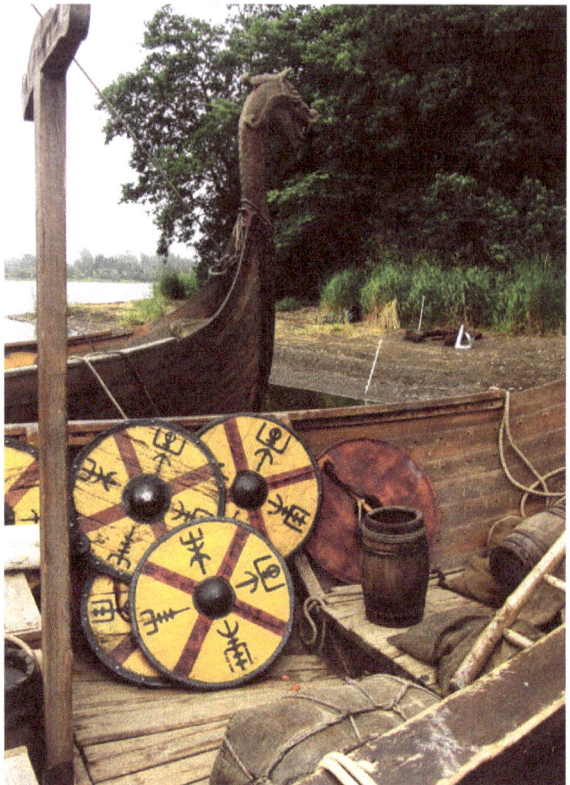
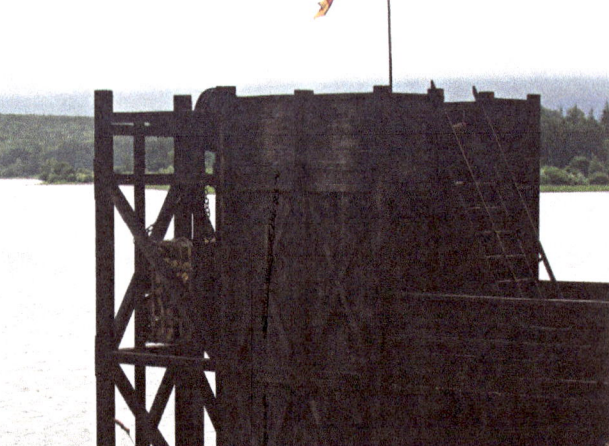

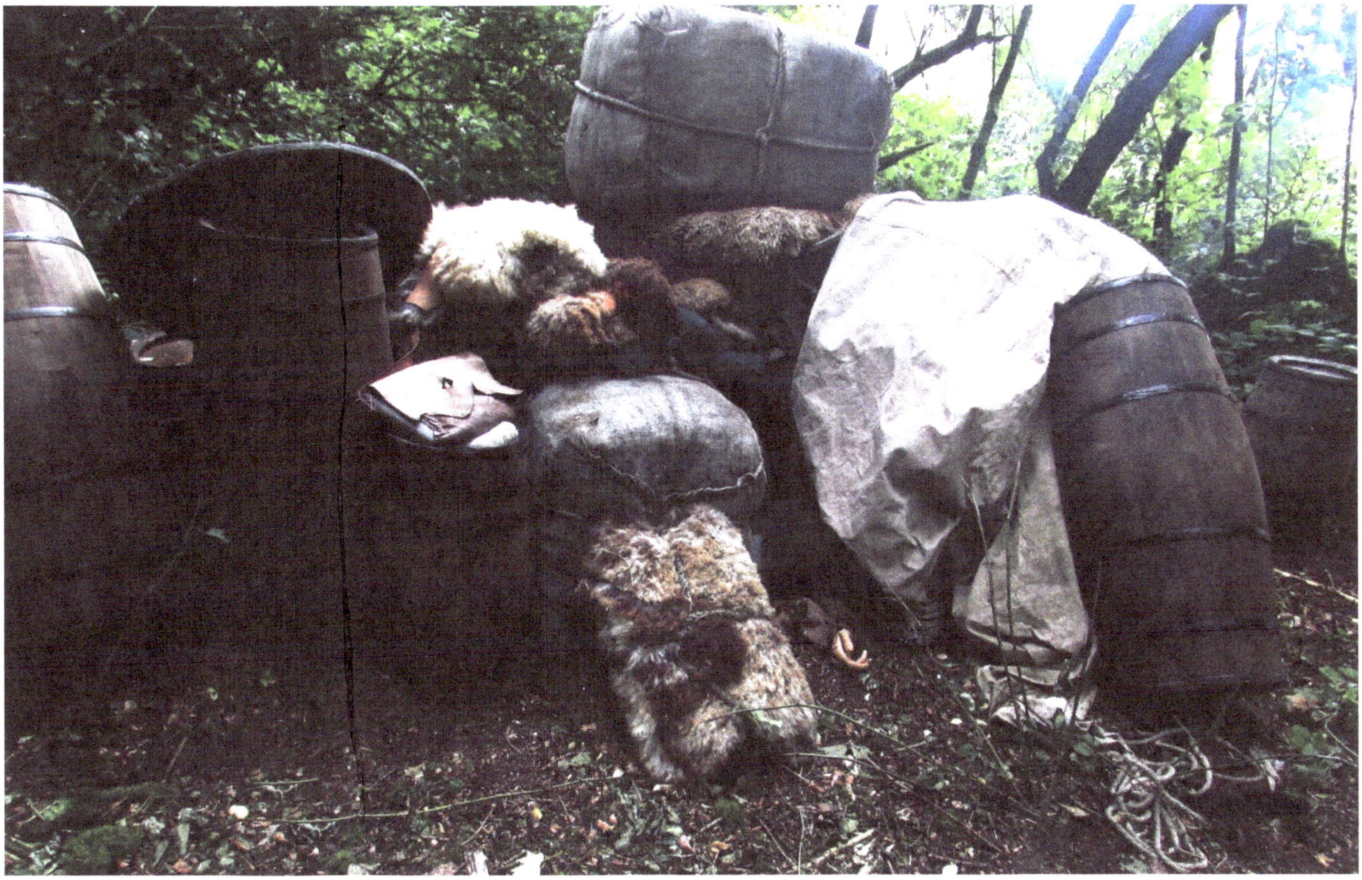

Some gorey additions to the props

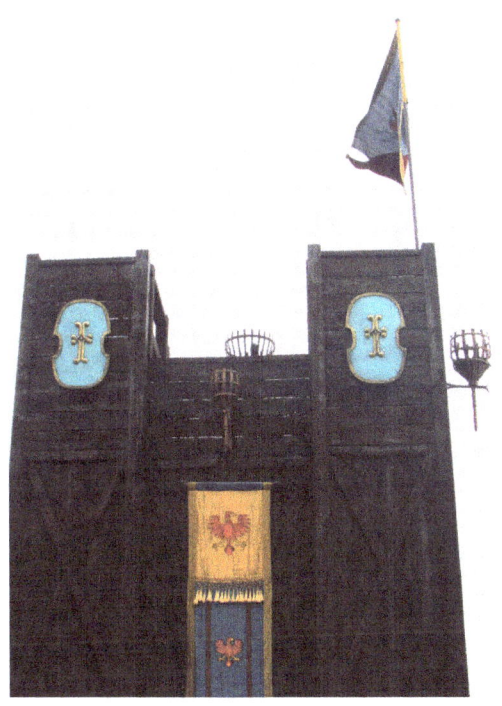

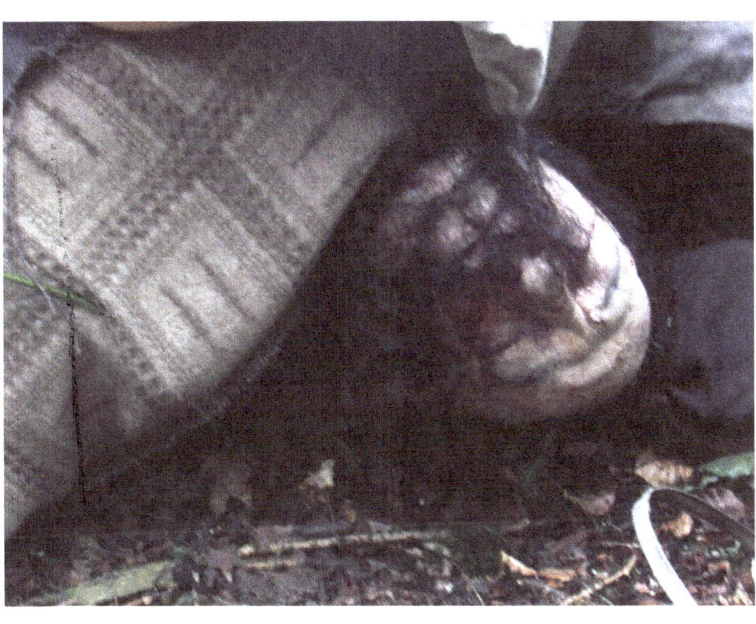

Burgage Castle Tower House surrounded by flood water in 2016

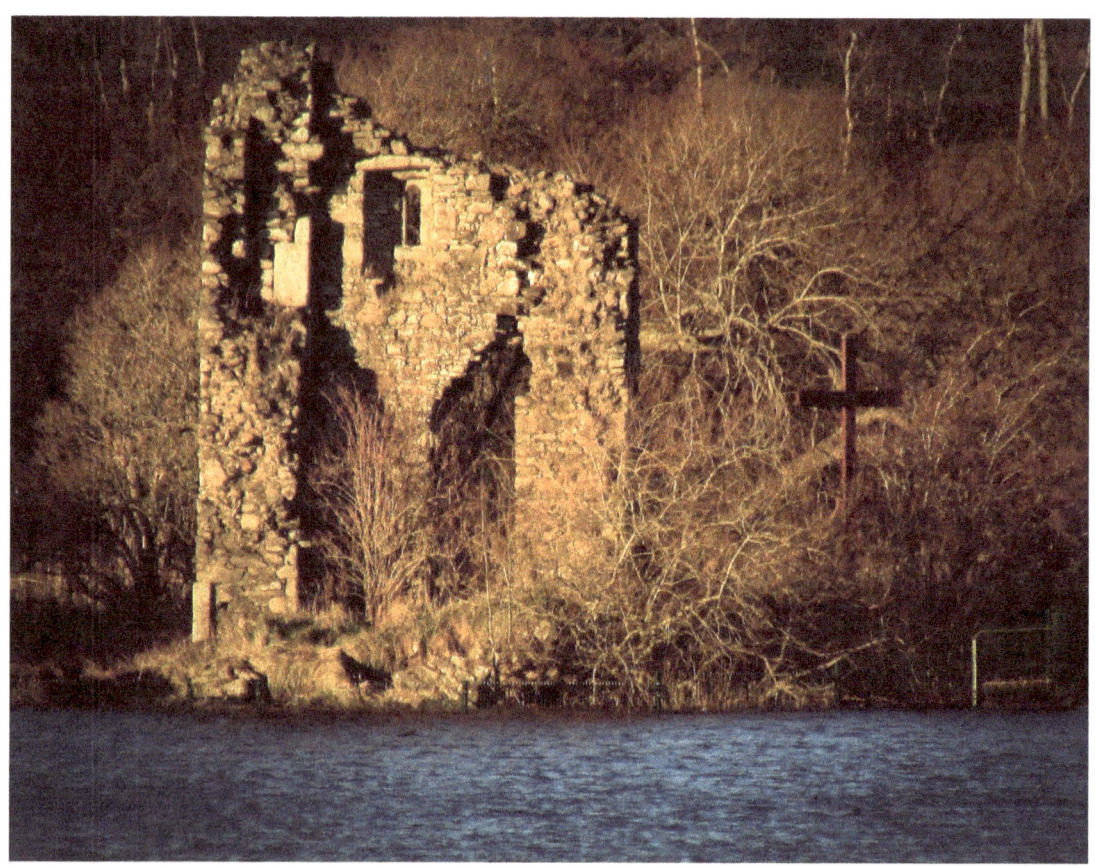

FLOODS!

In 2016 the waters rose significantly by about 6 foot in places, which some people believe was caused by heavy rains. Of course I was out with my camera trying to capture all the photos I could. The waters caused a lot of damage and covered many of the greenway paths, making it difficult to access. It gave me something to do for a bit until the waters got low, then there was another photo expedition for me!

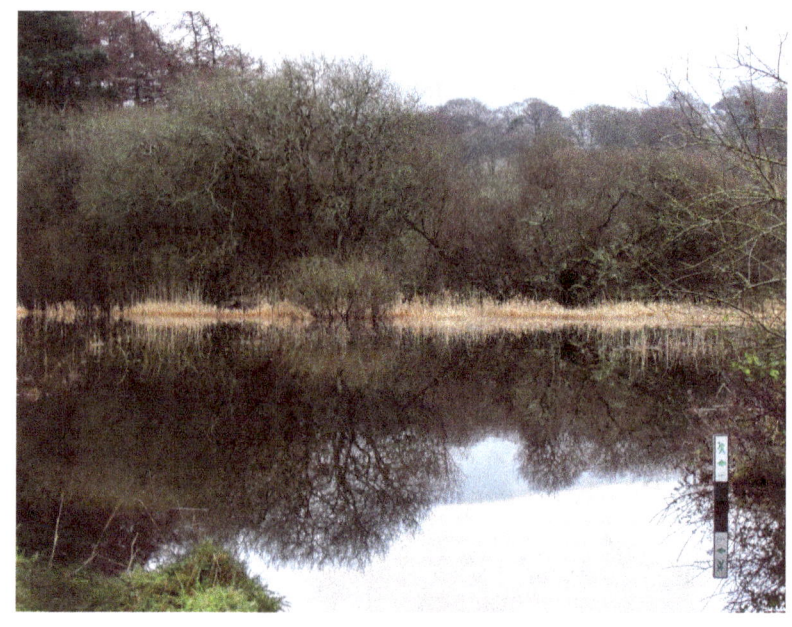

Blessington Greenway paths flooded in 2016

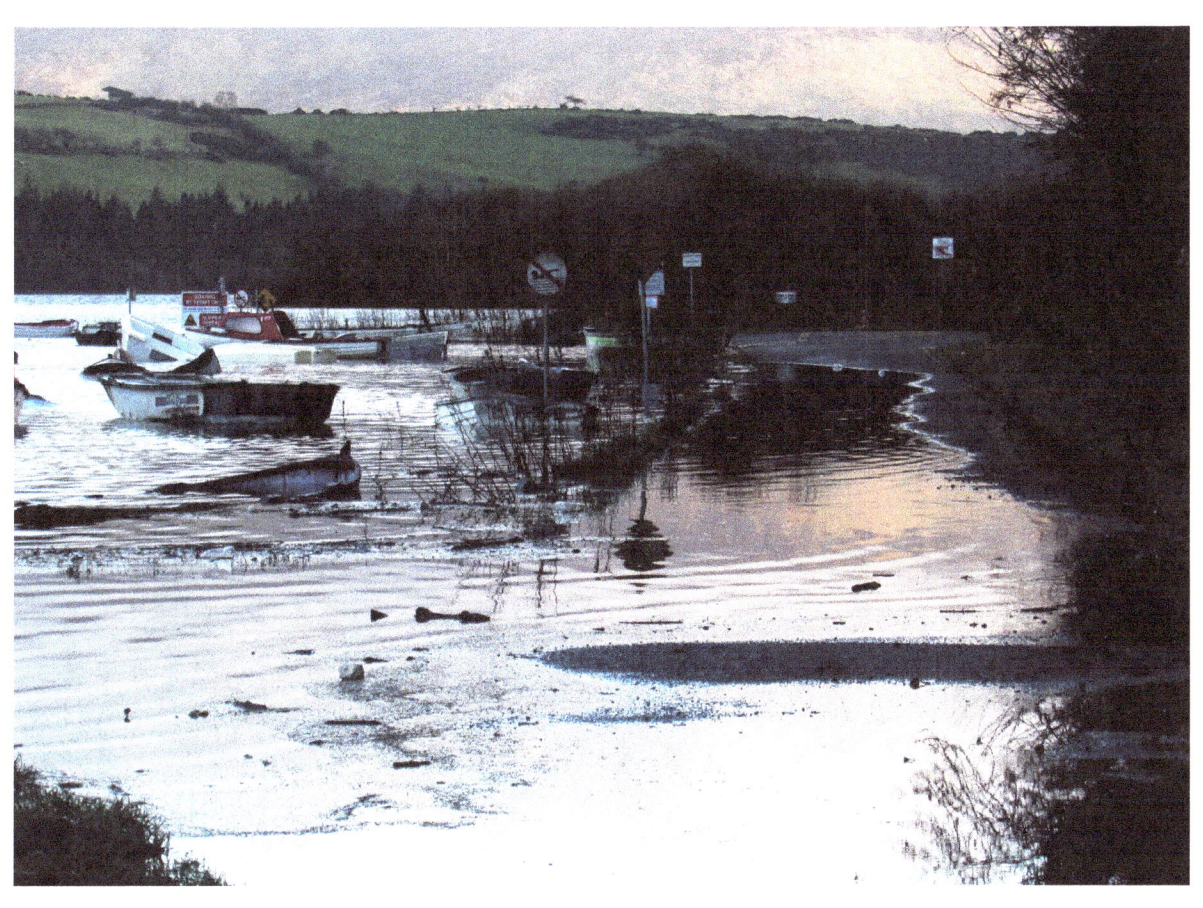

Harbour at Russellstown and Greenway paths were badly flooded in 2016

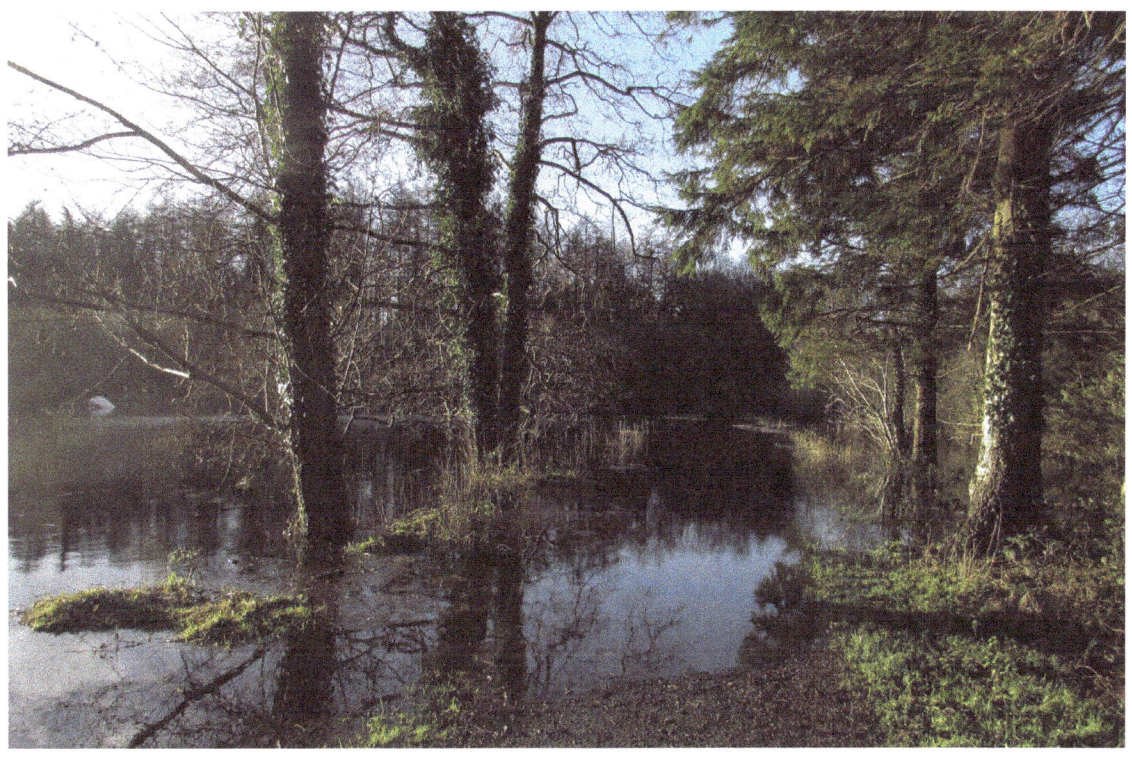

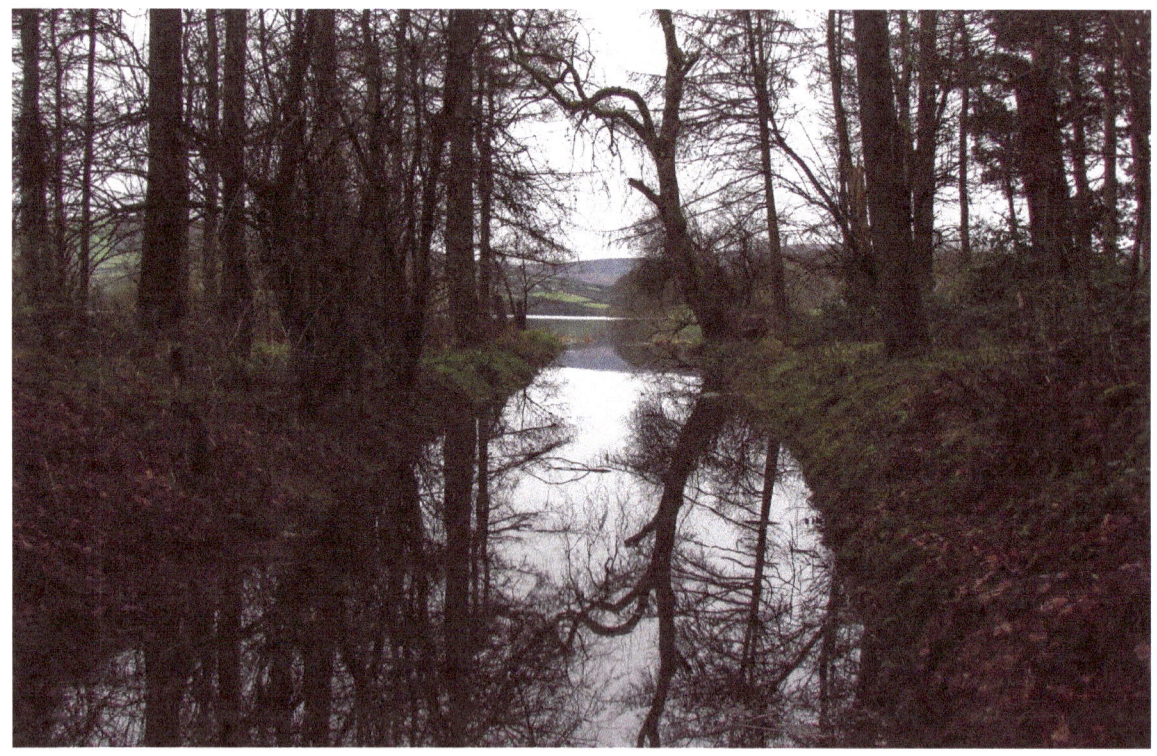

More flooding this time at Burgage Moyle Greenway path

One of the things I discovered while exploring around the lake sides, climbing under bridges, getting lost on shorelines and even in the woods one time, was that one of my boots was leaking, and I often got home with a wet, soggy left foot. That stopped in 2016! I actually bought myself a proper pair of waterproof boots! Whatever chance I had of keeping my feet dry under normal circumstances, it definitely wasn't going to happen with the floods. But with the waterproofs, no more wet feet, Yay!

Floods on the path near Burgage Bridge

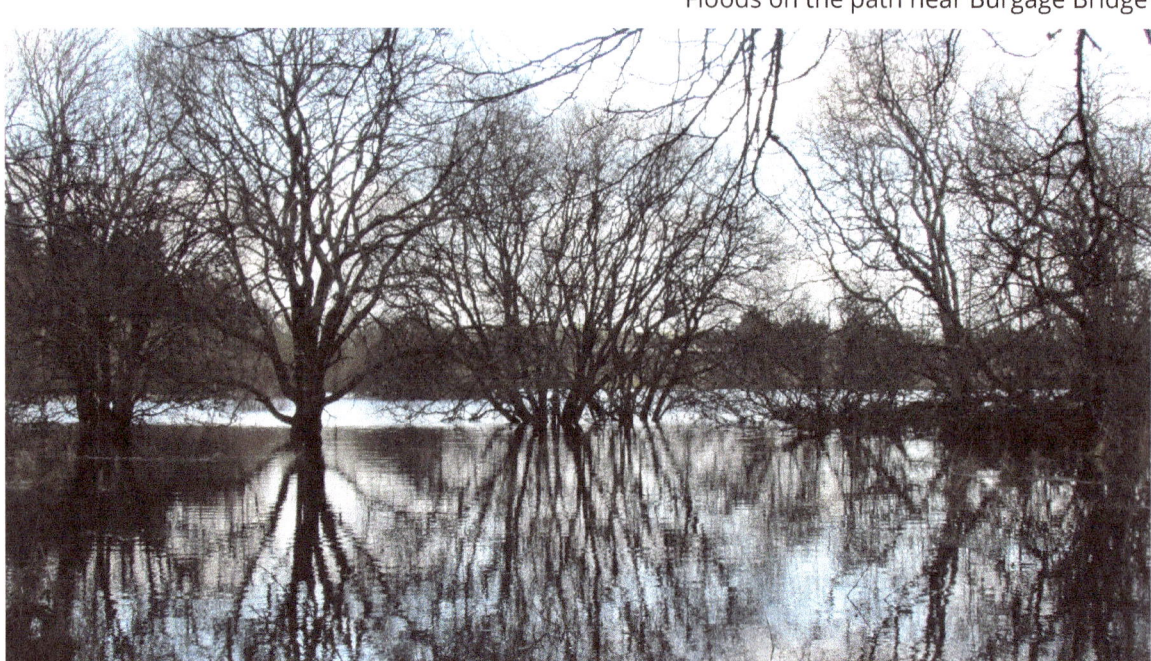

RUSSELLSTOWN

I first visited Russellstown Bay, I think in about 2008 not long after I had moved in to the area. The Greenway wasn't in existence at that time, but I was fascinated with the moored boats. The next time I visited it was around 2015. I was surprised how low the lake was and how many seemingly abandoned boats there were, alongside boats that were in use.

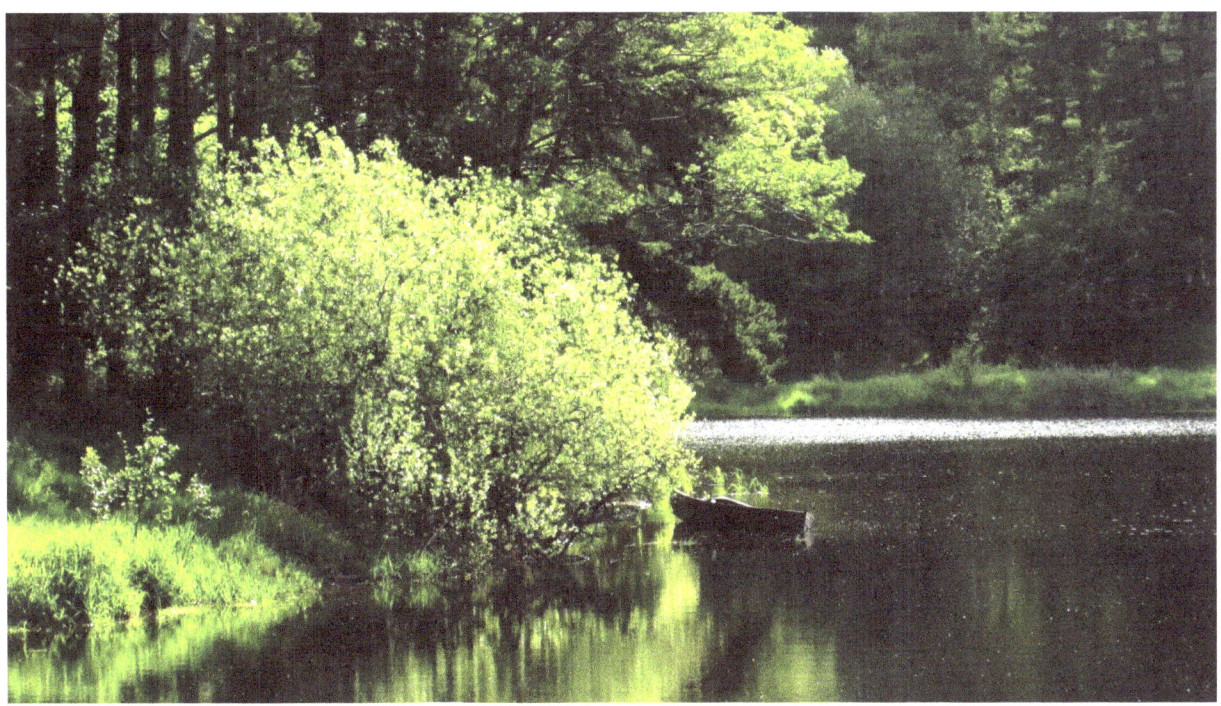

Its a fabulous place for a walk with two options for woodland trails, and if you're lucky and the lake is low, you can also ramble around the shoreline! I've taken many photos in all seasons there.

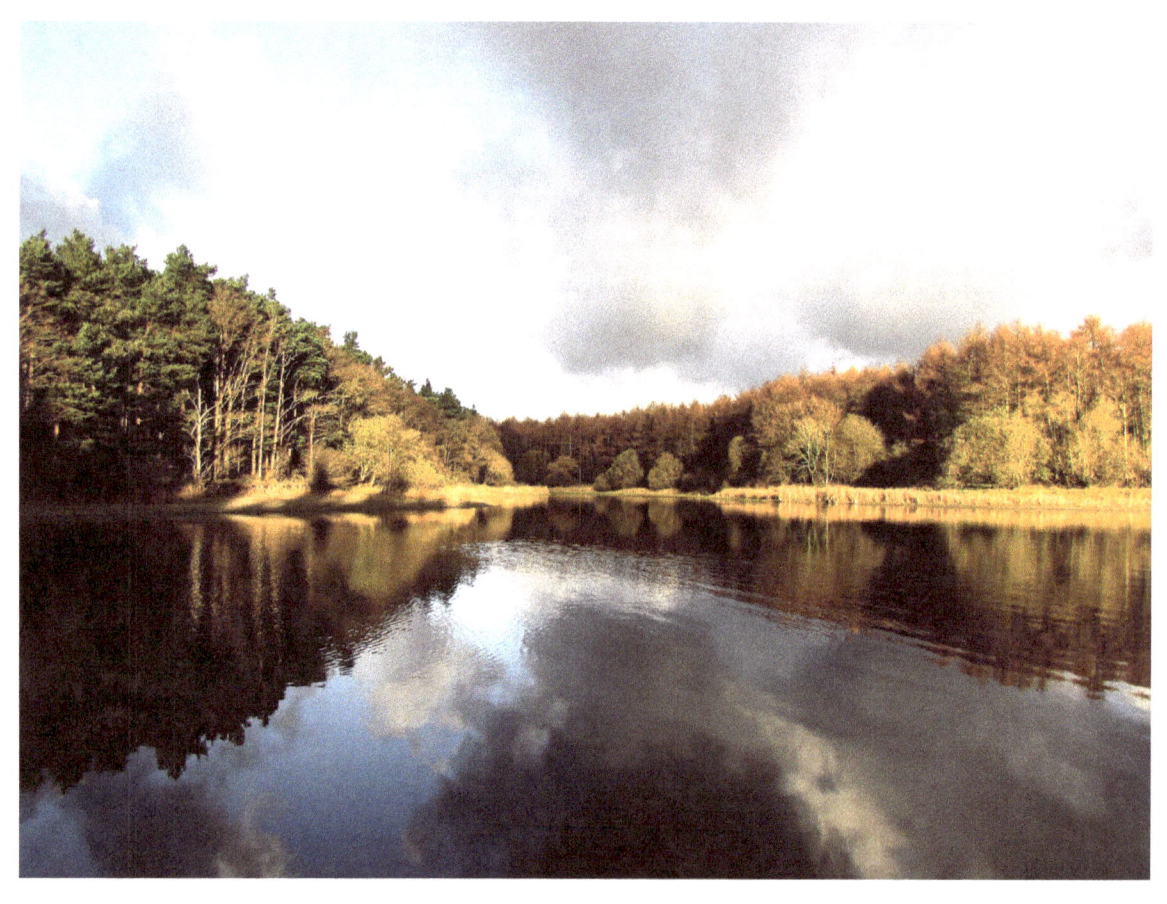
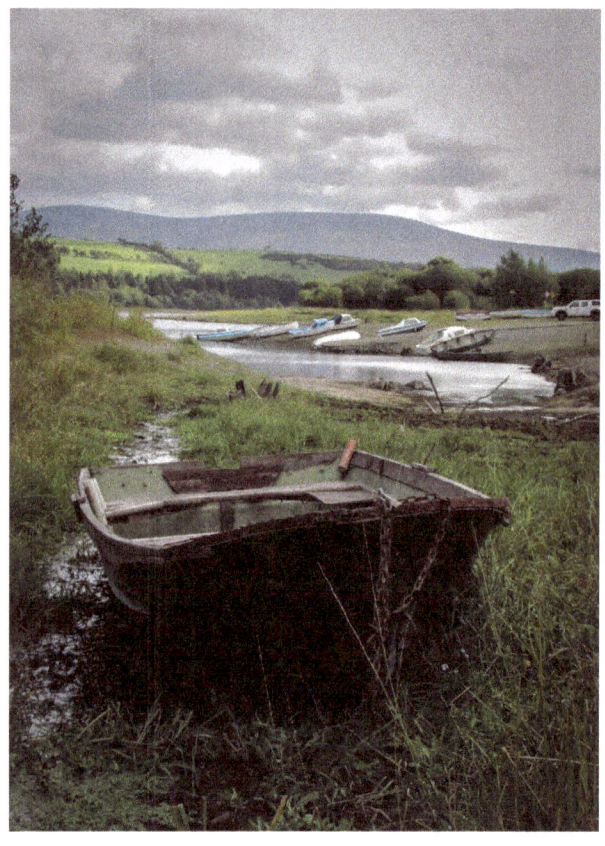
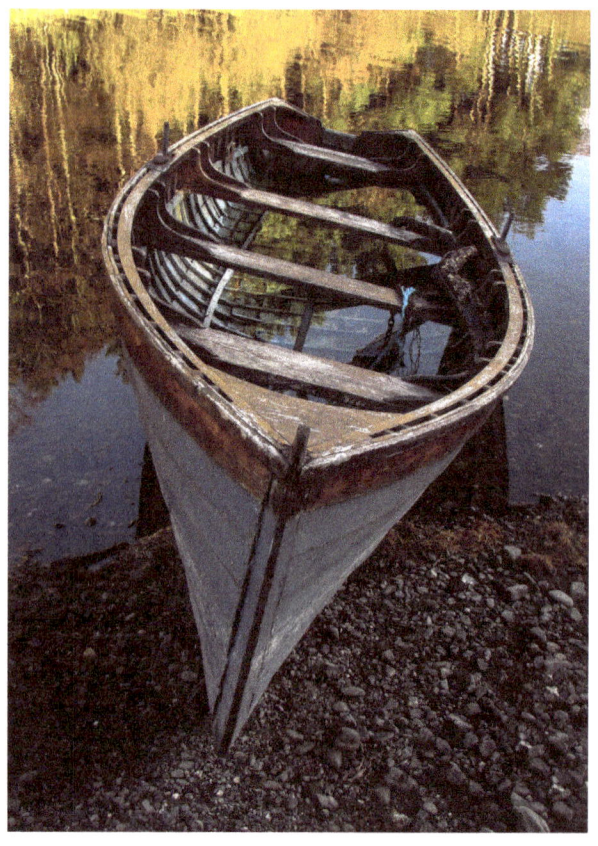

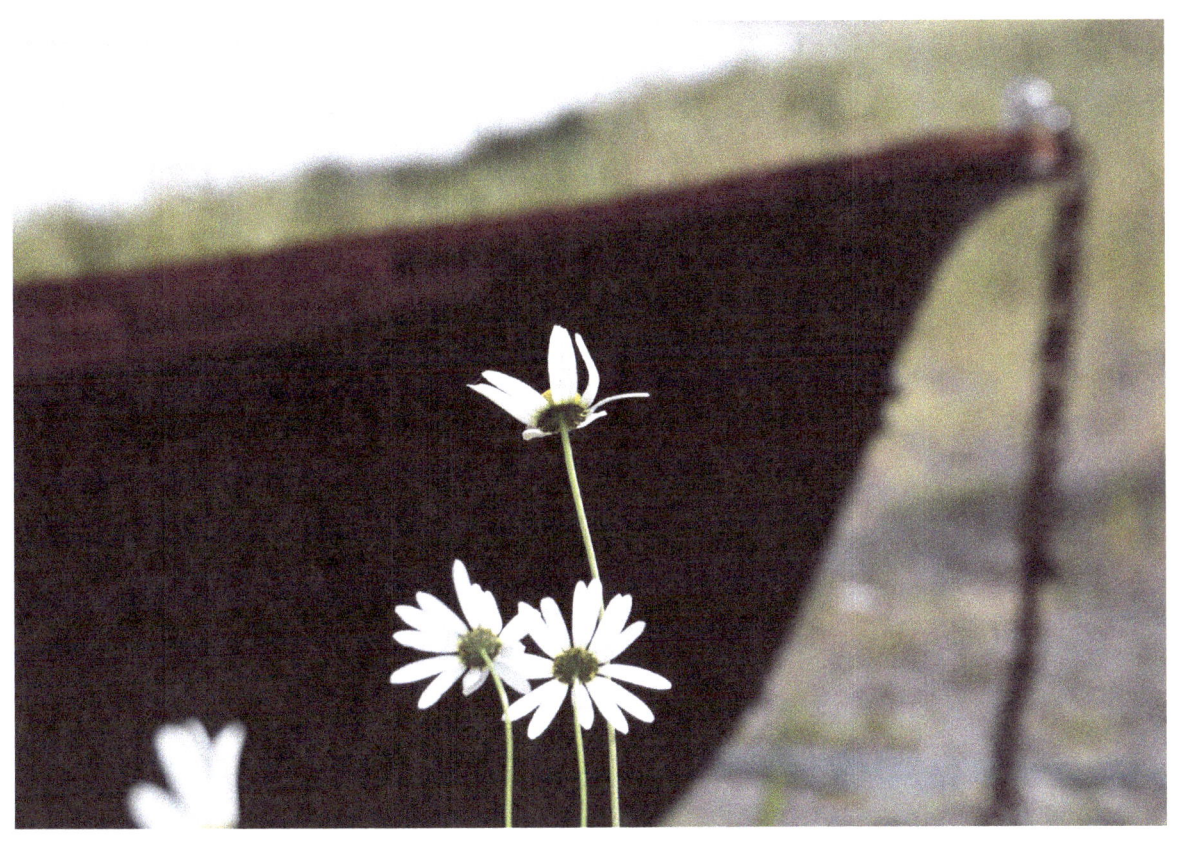
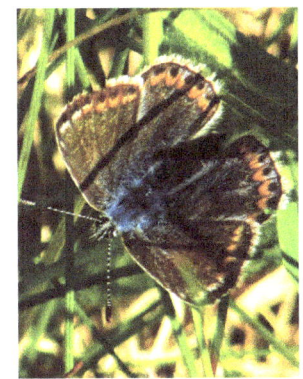
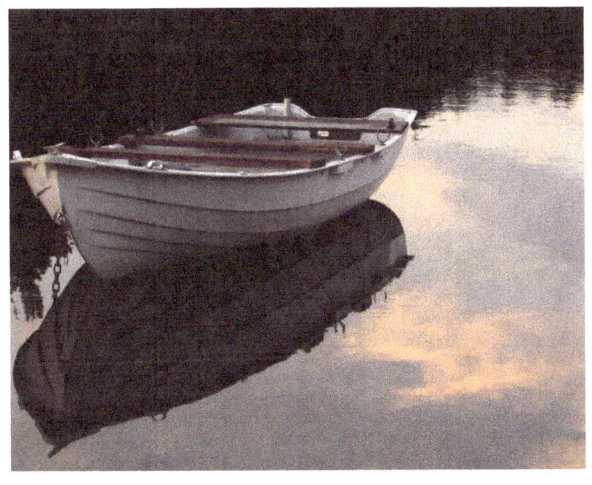
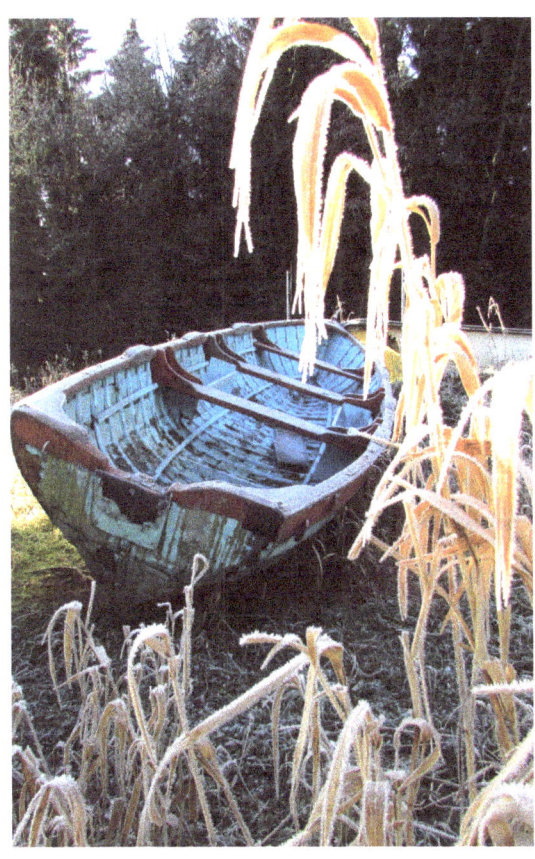

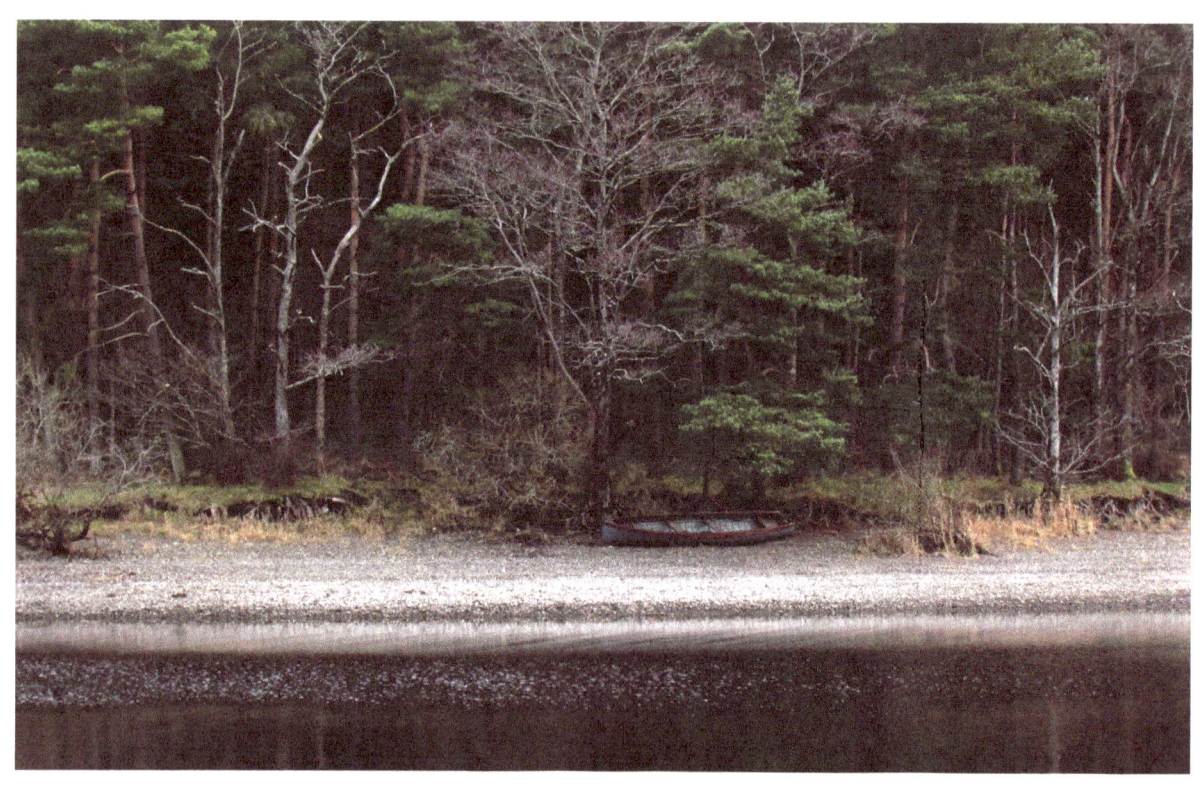
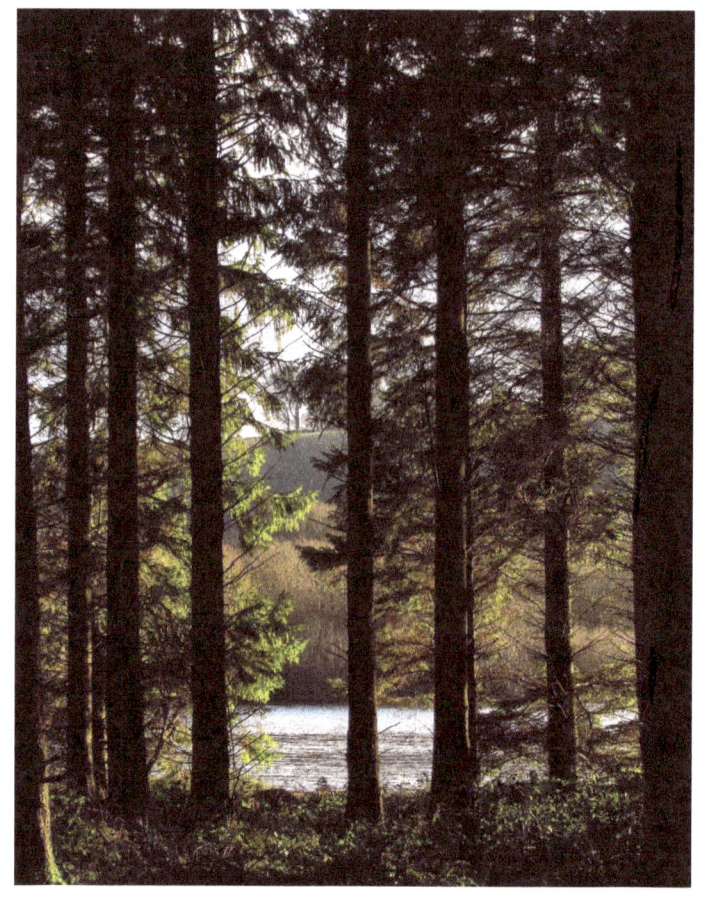

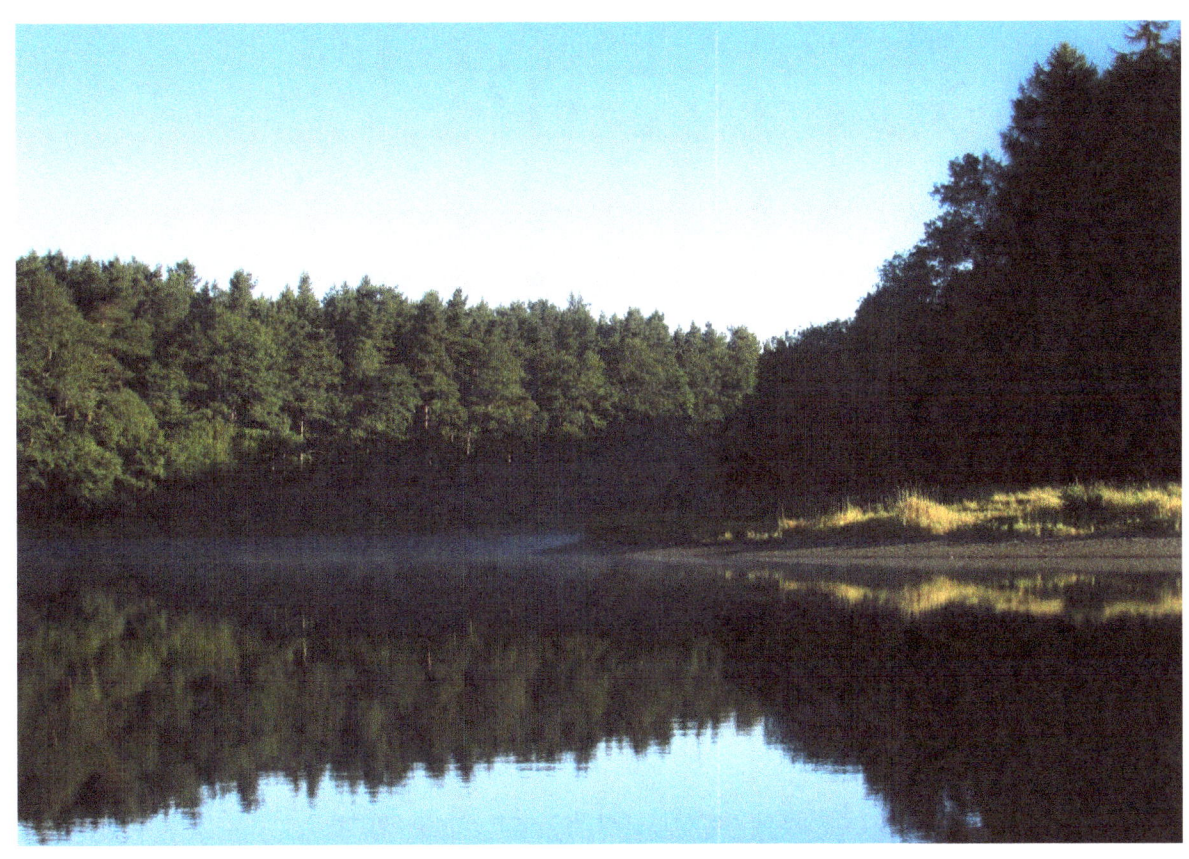
Shoreline at Russellstown

Baltyboys House from Russellstown shoreline
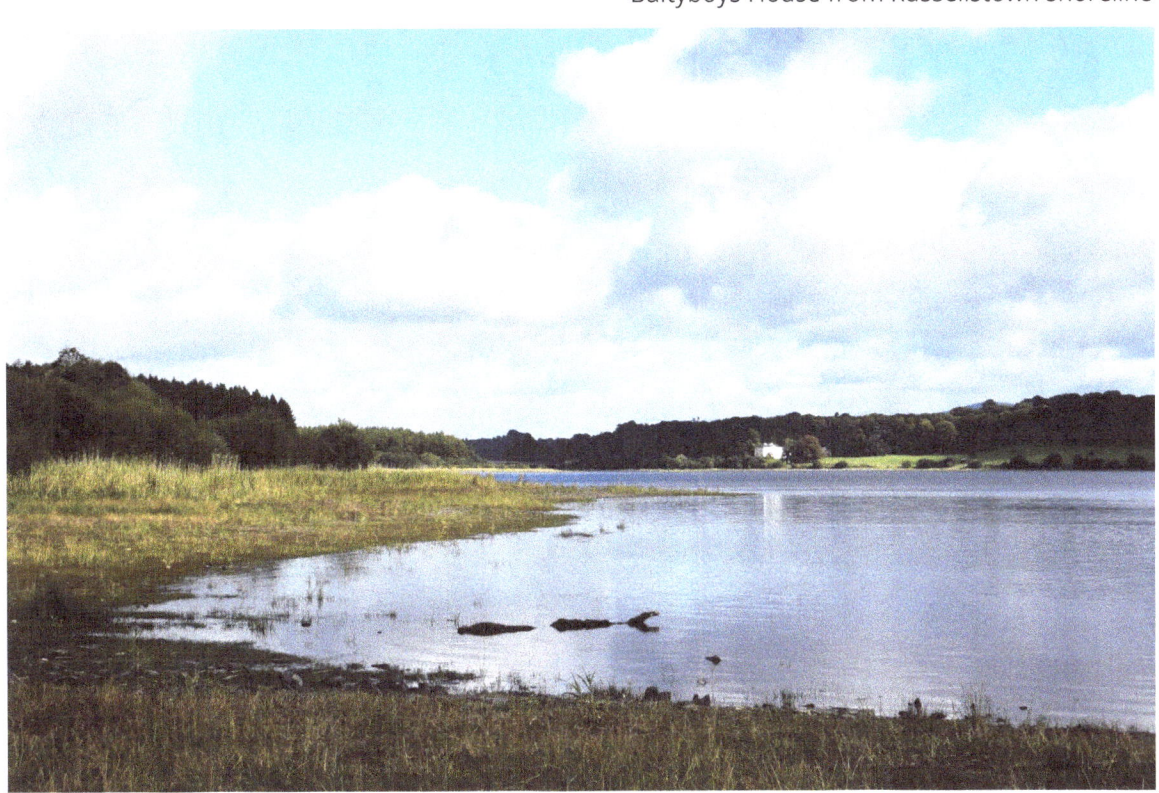

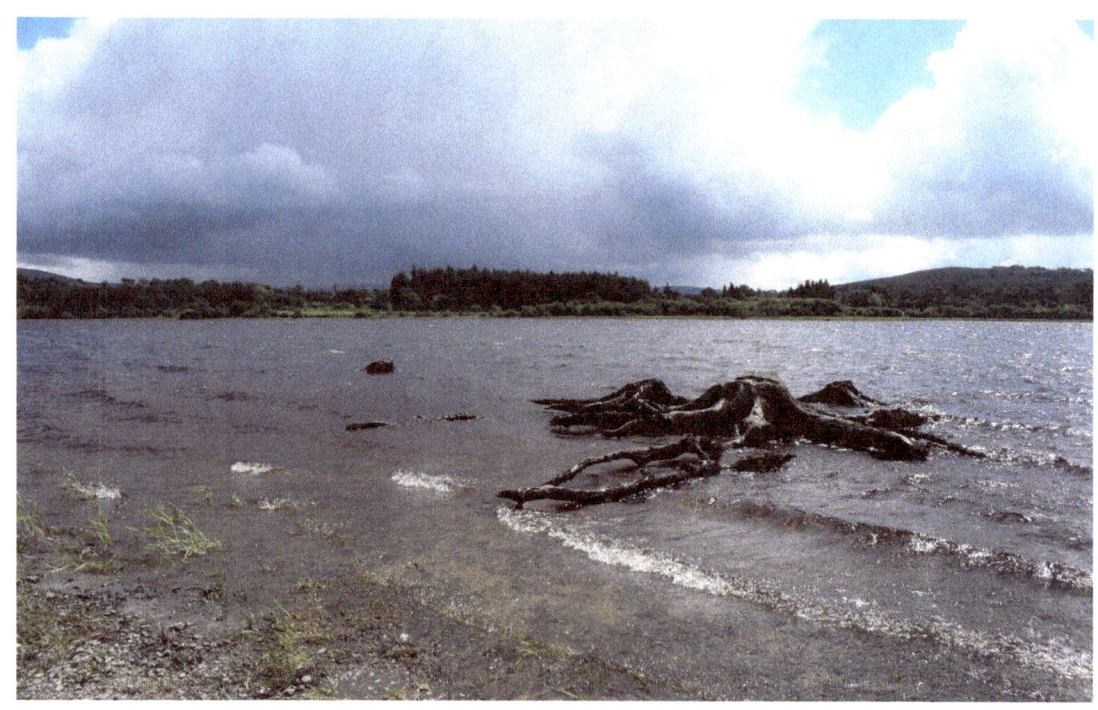
Old tree roots become visible at Russellstown not far from Poulaphouca

Lovely reflections
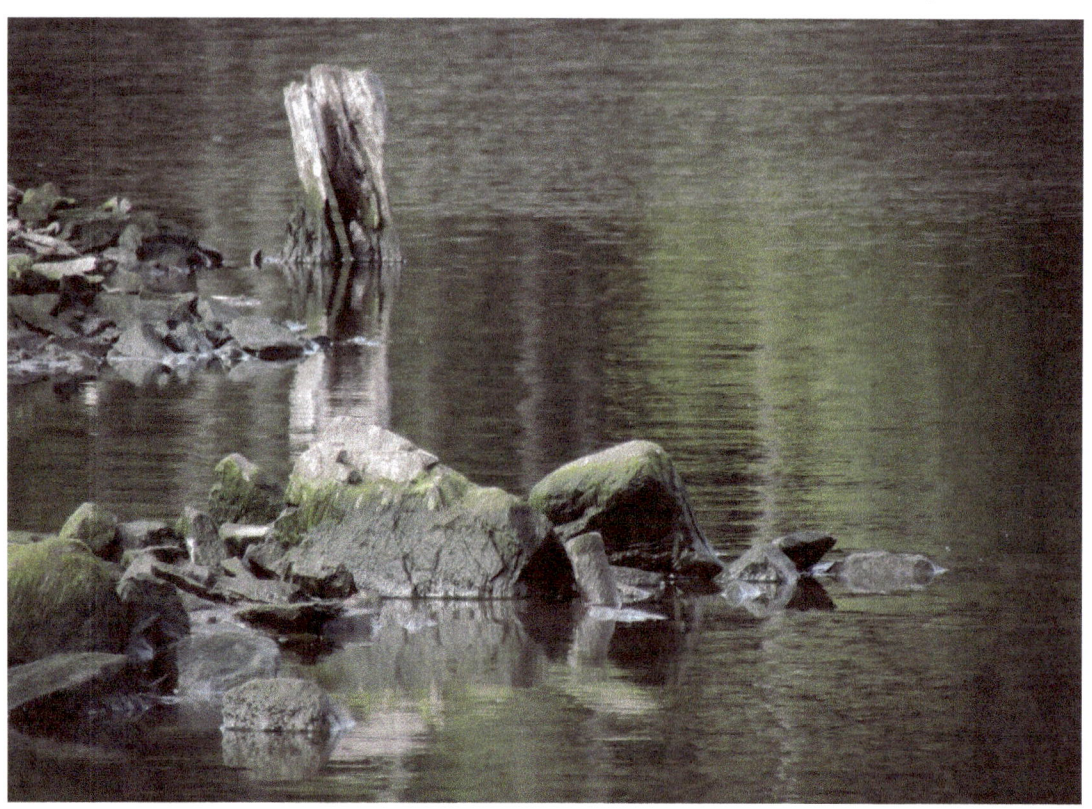

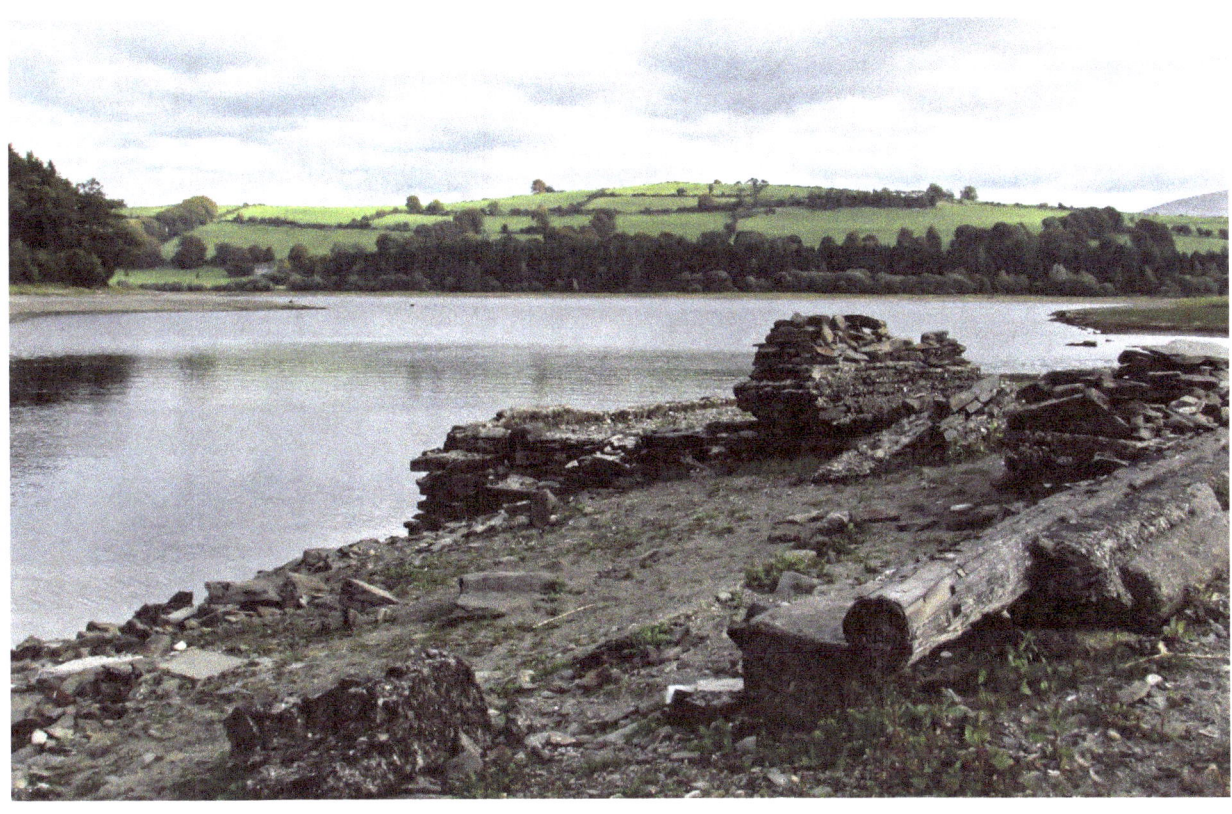

In 2018 when the waters were low on the lakes these remains of what I think was once known as Russellstown House became visible.

The exciting thing about wandering around the lakes, is that you just don't know what you might see! I get real excited when I spot a heron or the various butterflies!

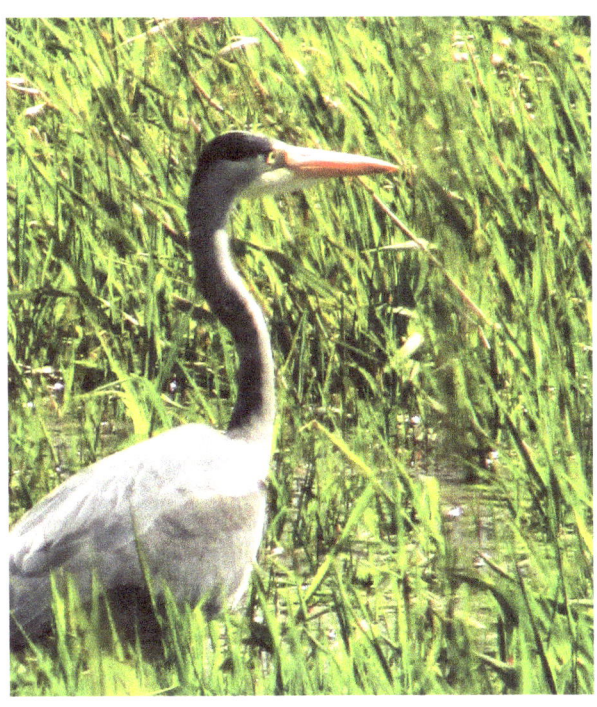
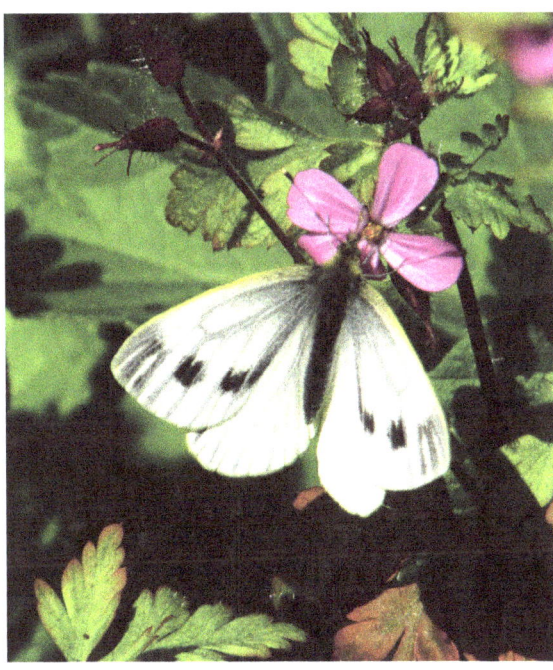

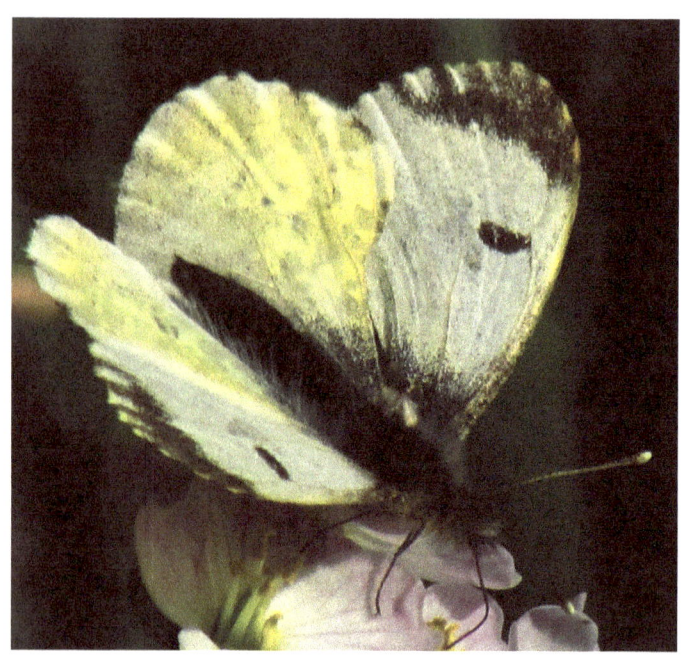
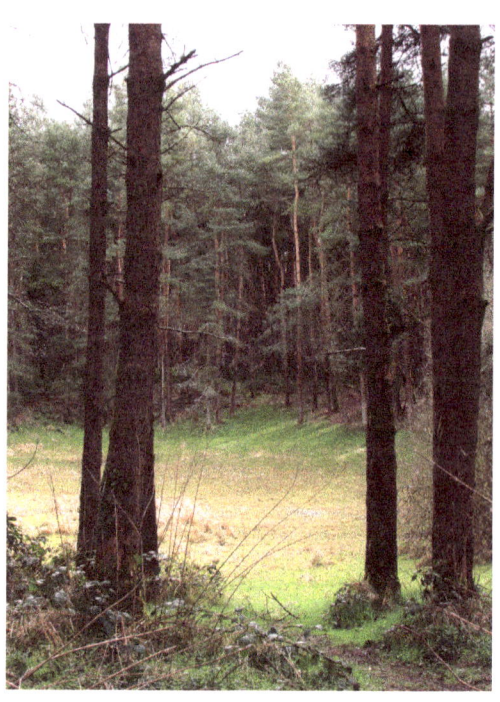

There is beauty to be found all around, if we can just take a few moments to look for it!

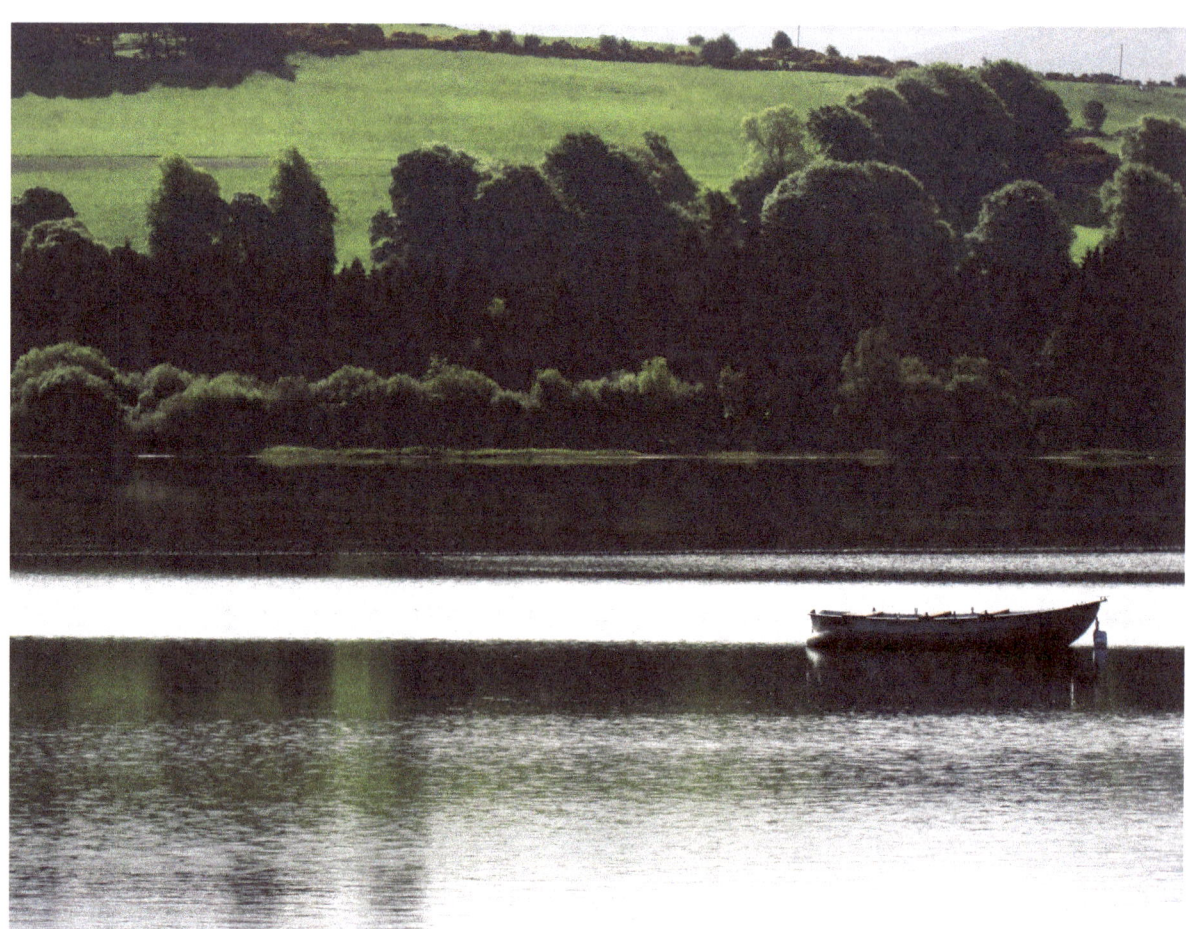

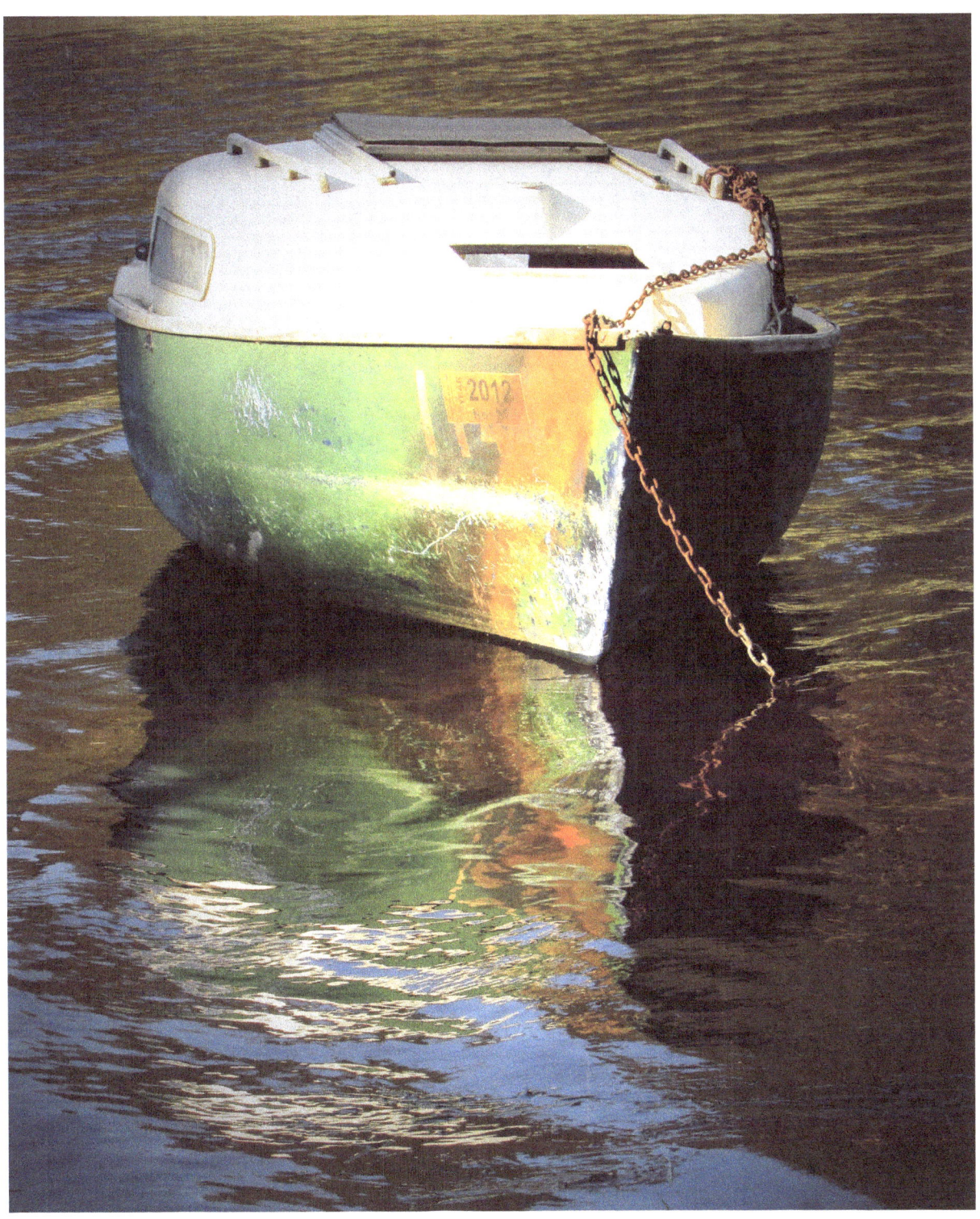
Rusty reflections can be very beautiful to look at.

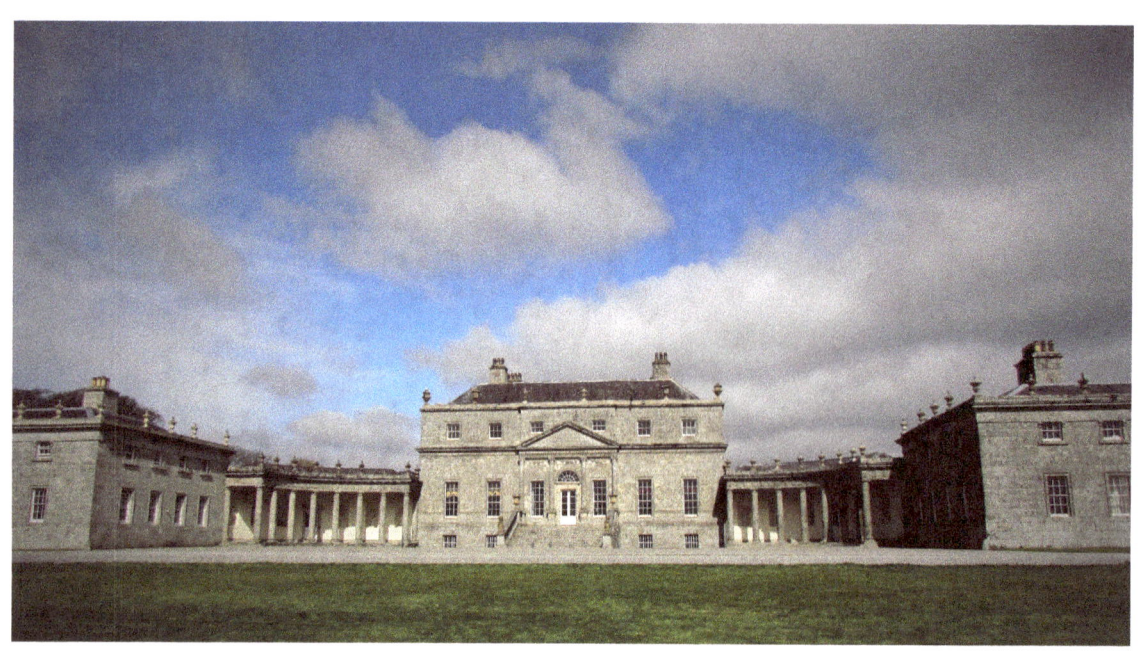

RUSSBOROUGH HOUSE

Russborough House is a Palladian Mansion, situated off the N81, near Blessington, Co. Wicklow, which has fabulous views of the Wicklow Mountains and Blessington Lakes. It was built between 1741 and 1748 from the designs of Richard Castle for the First Earl of Milltown, Joseph Leeson. It was sold in 1931 to Captain Denis Bowes Daly and then Sir Alfred Beit bought it in 1951 to house their extensive art collection. Sir Alfred and Lady Clementine Beit founded the Alfred Beit Foundation in 1976 and the house has been owned and managed by them since then. It was opened to the public in 1978.

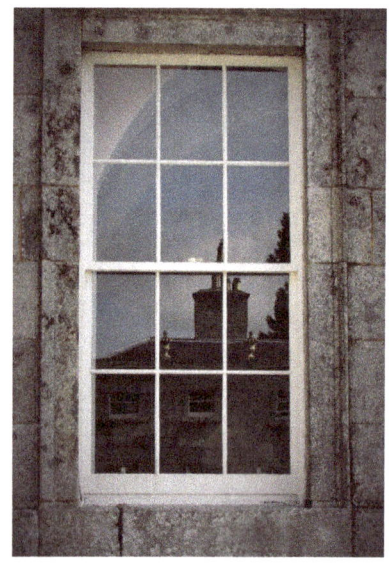
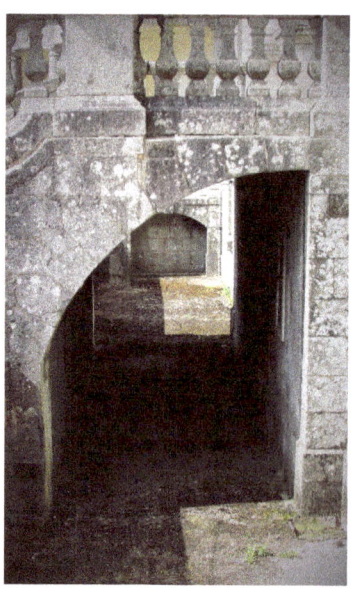
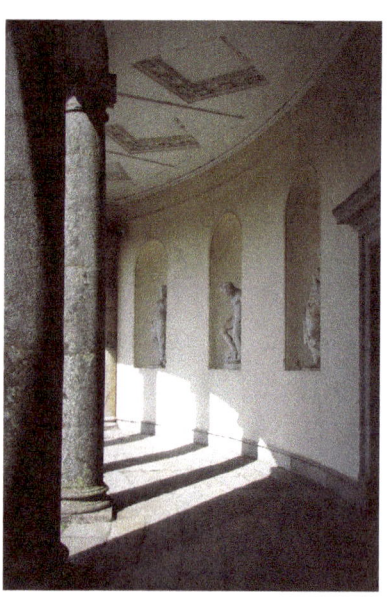

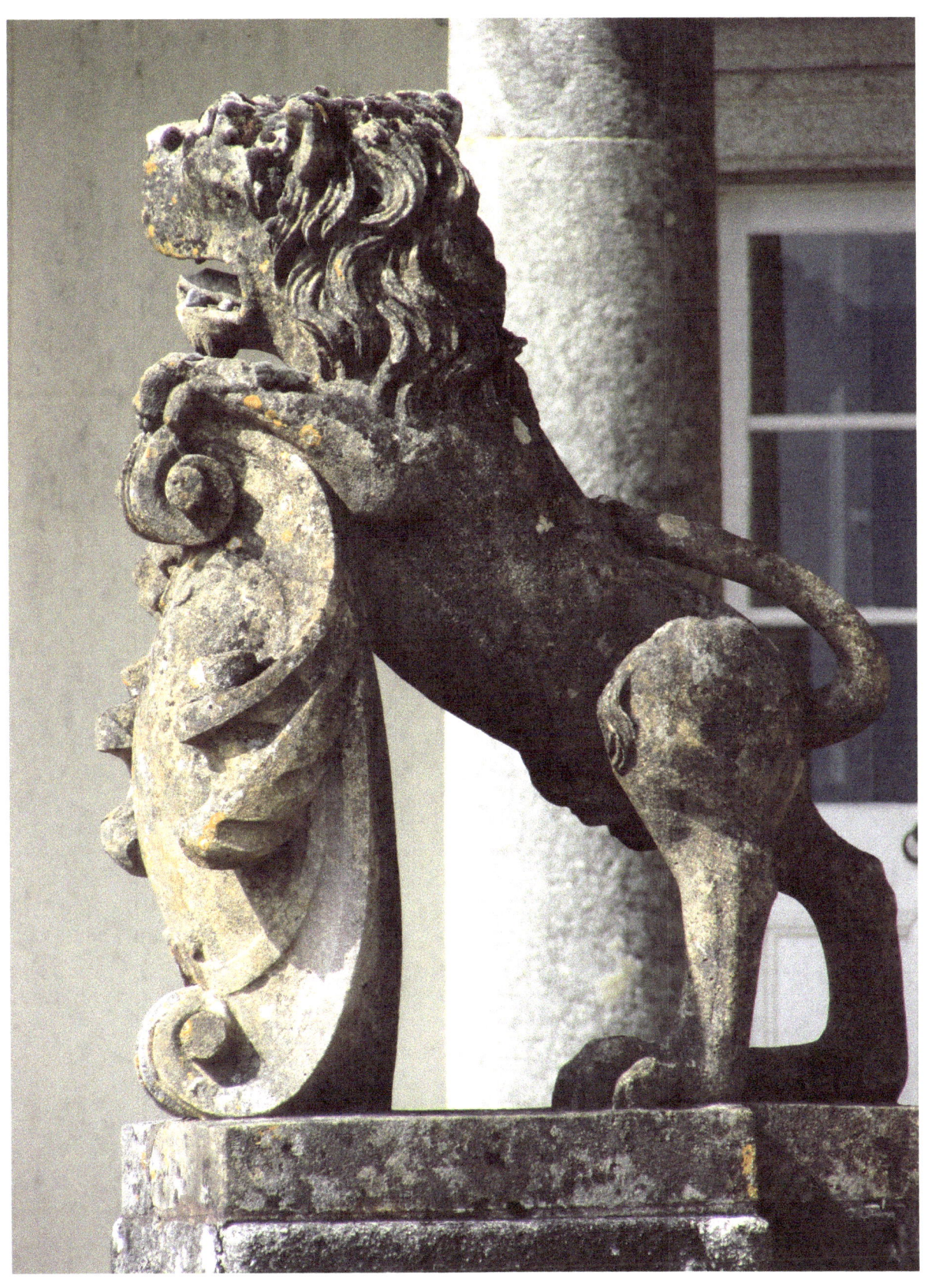

One of the pair of Heraldic Lions that are situated at the entrance
- they bear the Leeson Arms

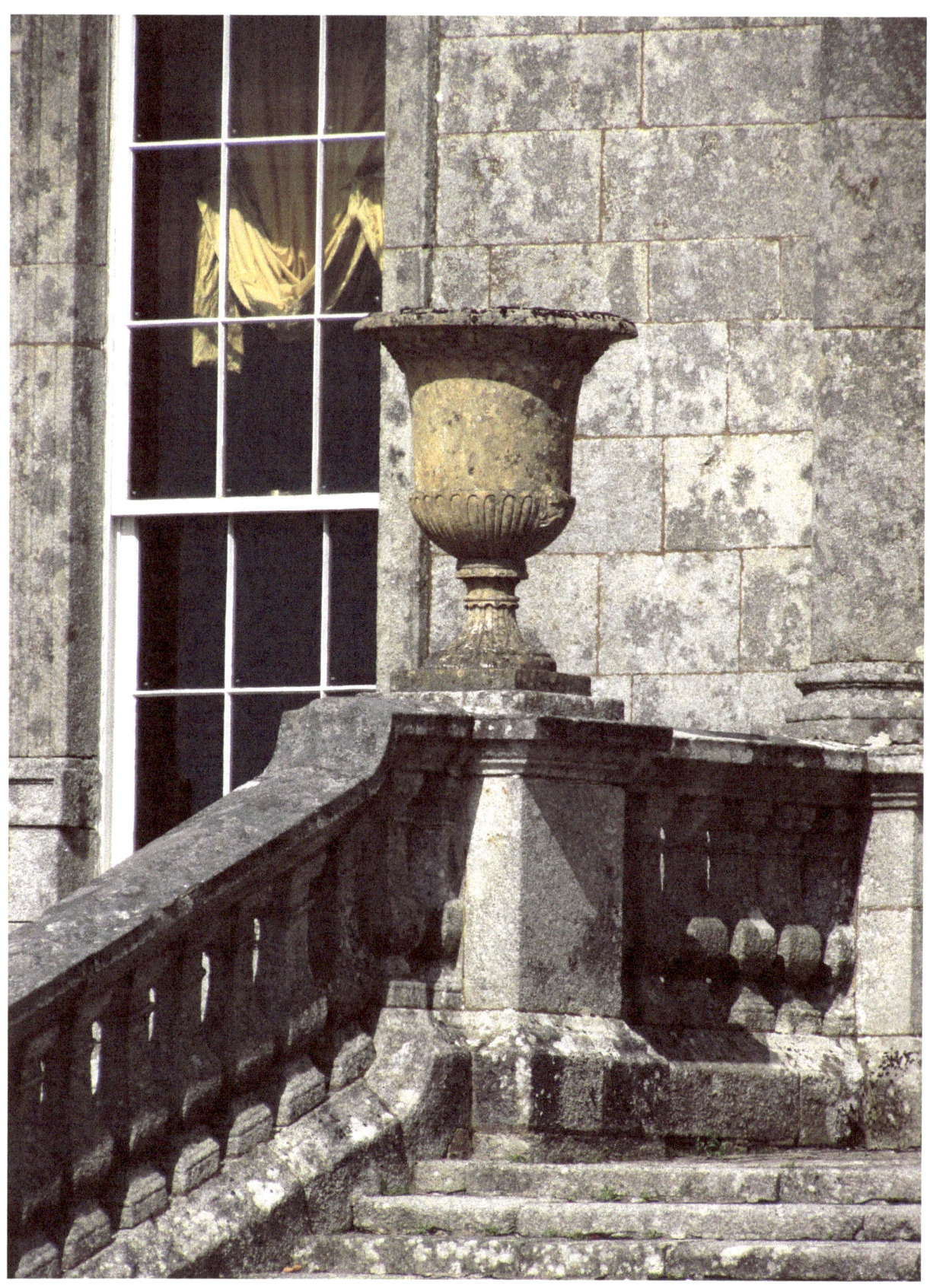

There are 76 ornamental urns in total, and there are five different designs

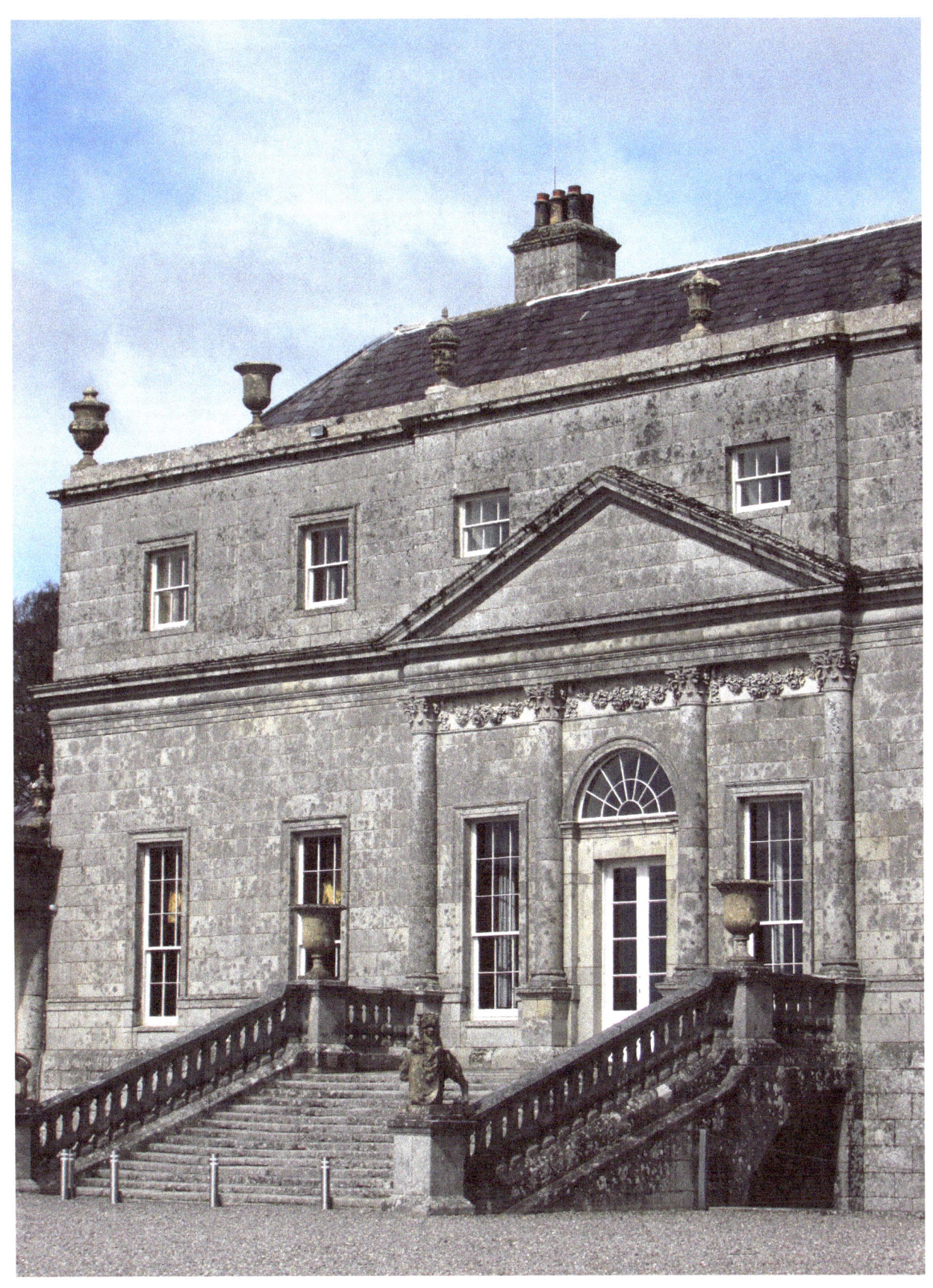

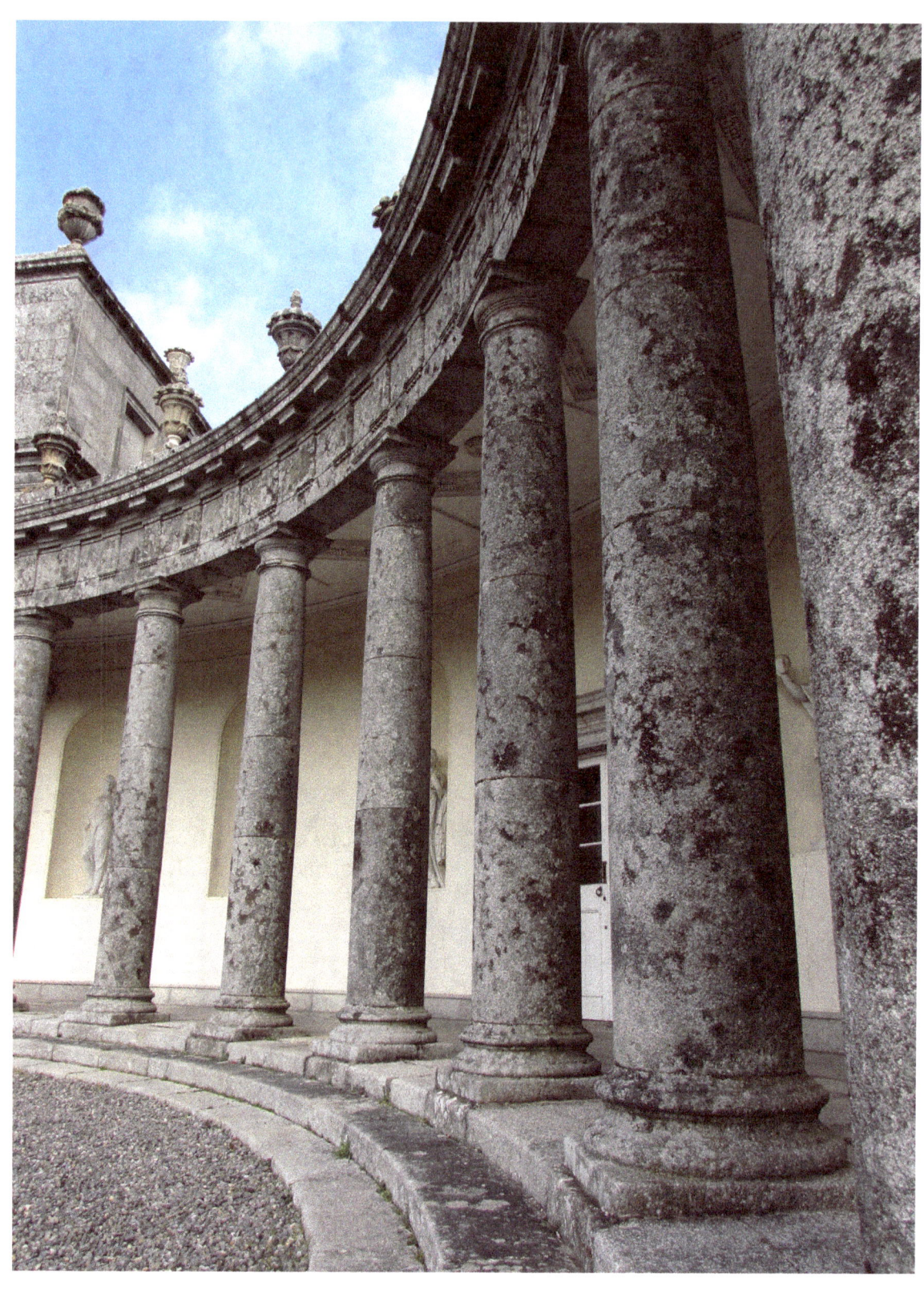

Russborough House is dressed granite and has a basement, two storeys and seven bays. The main house is linked to two pavilions with Doric colonnades.

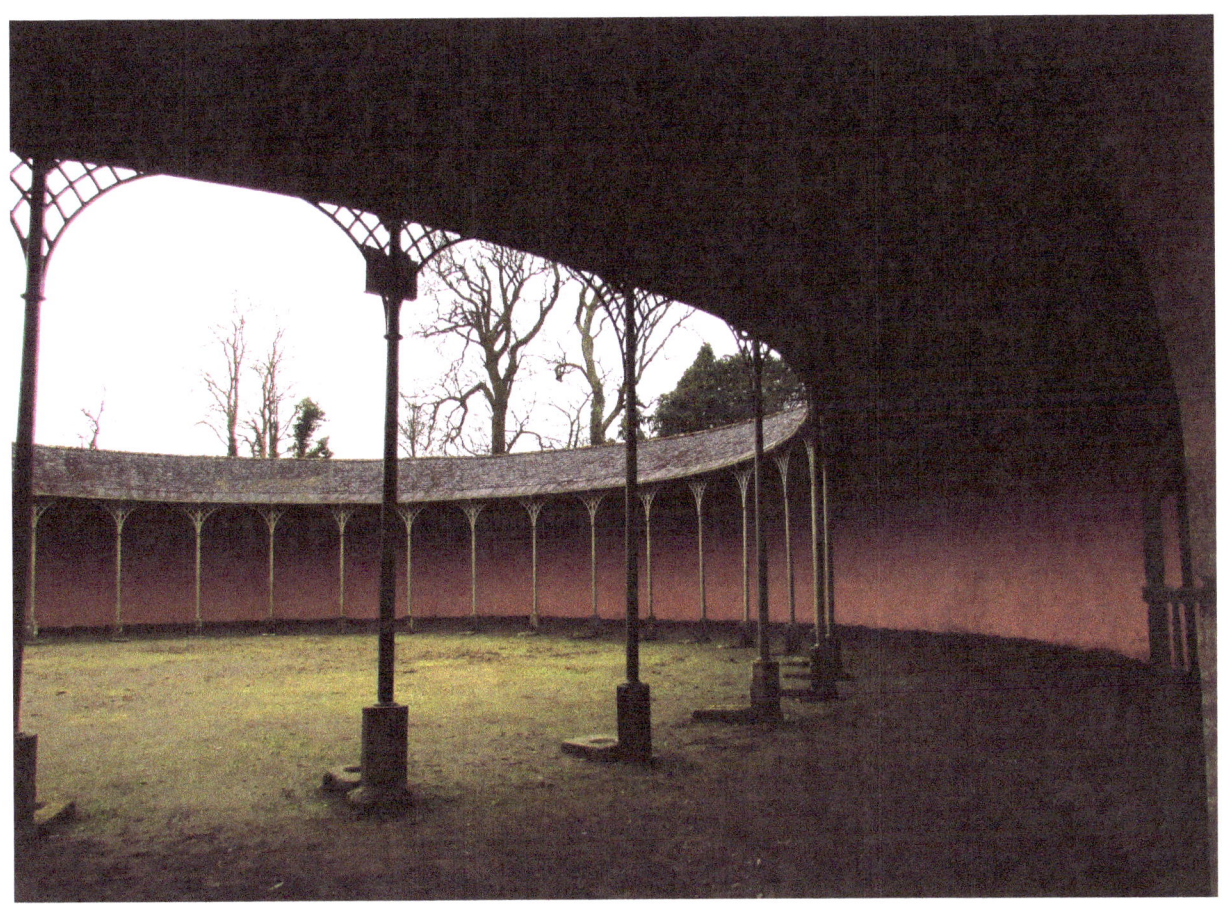

The Hippodrome is approximately 150 years old and was used for training horses

If you bring up the saturation when editing a photo, the Hippodrome looks like this! I thought it looked cool!

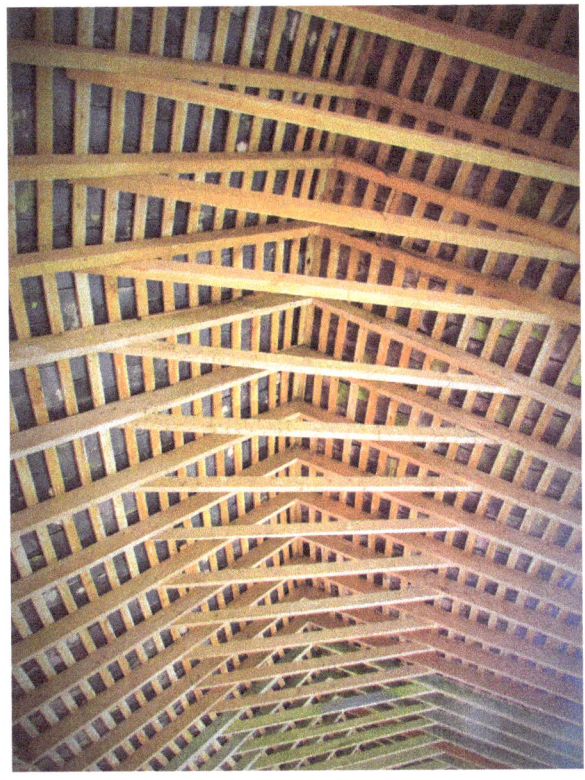
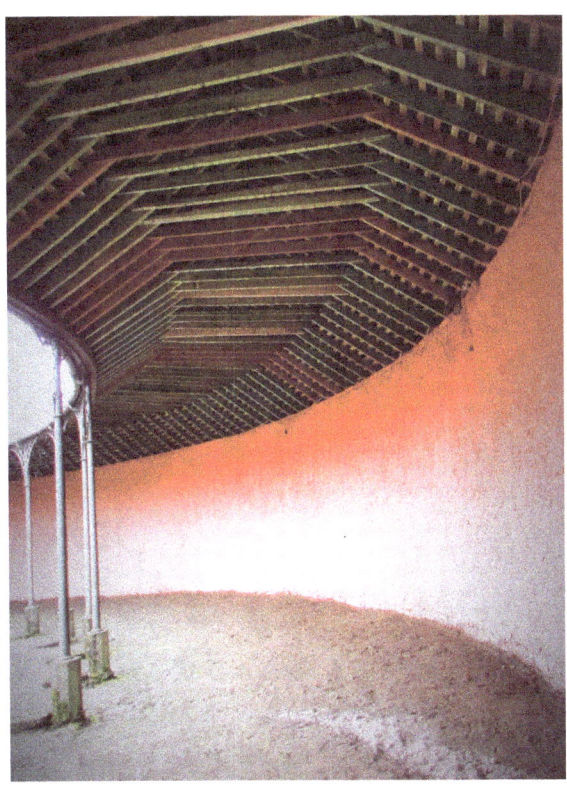

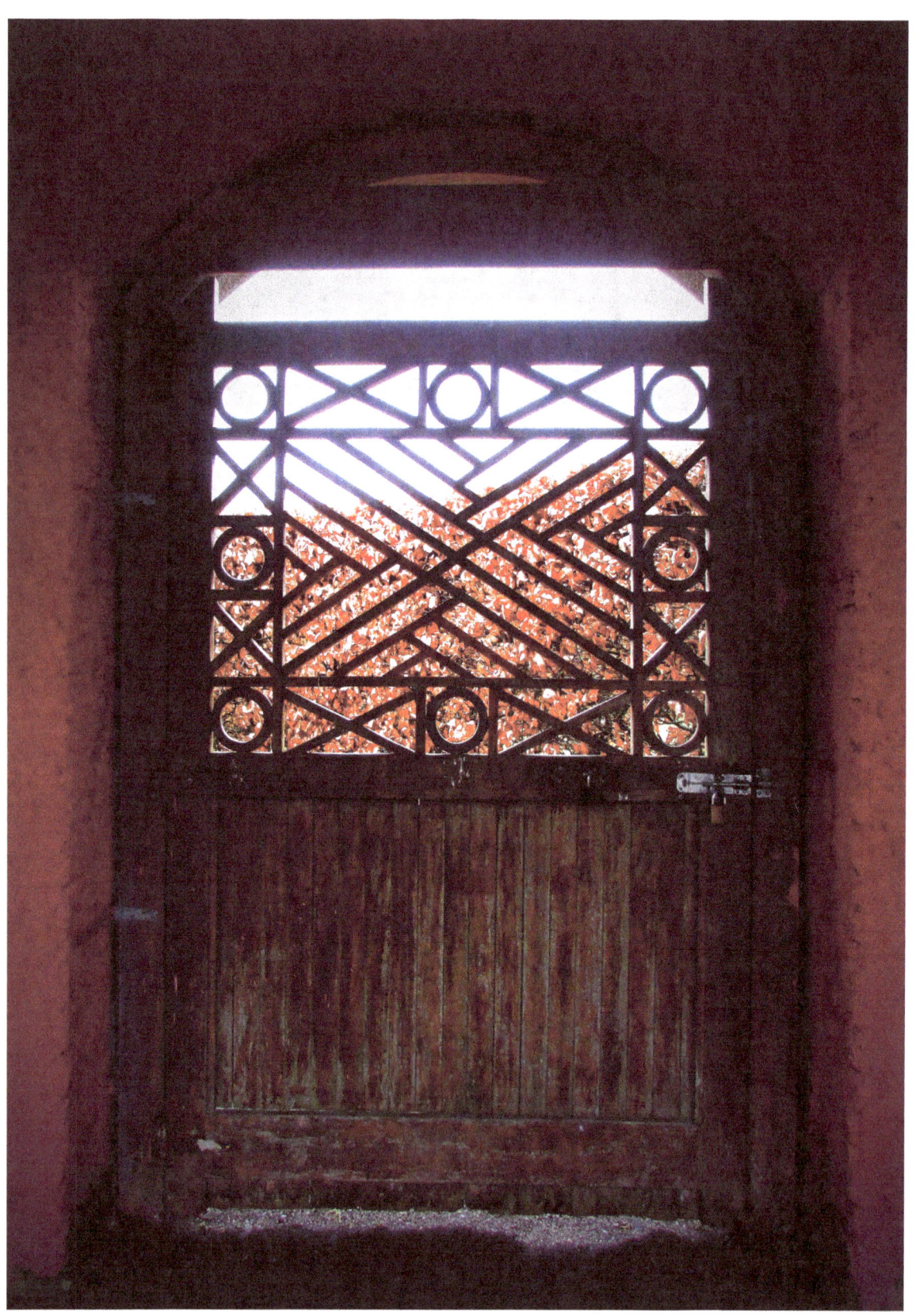

Beautiful door within the Hippodrome structure

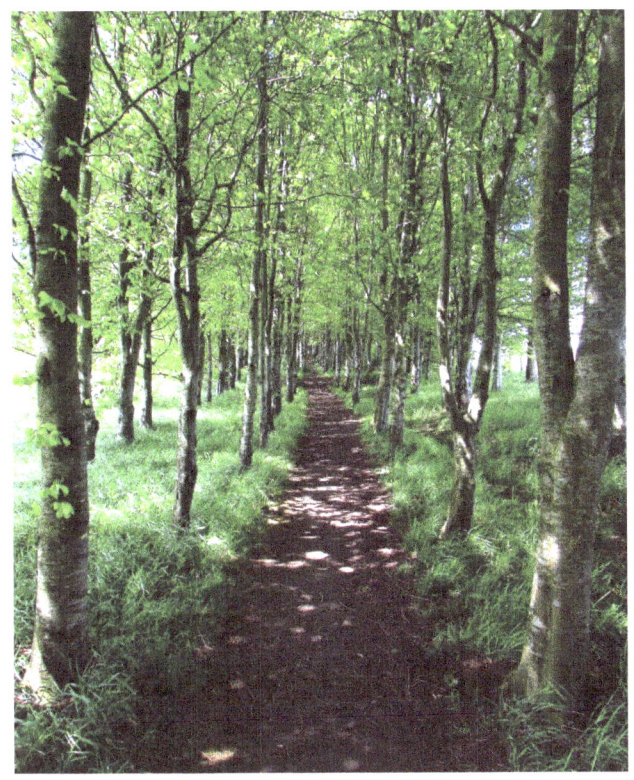
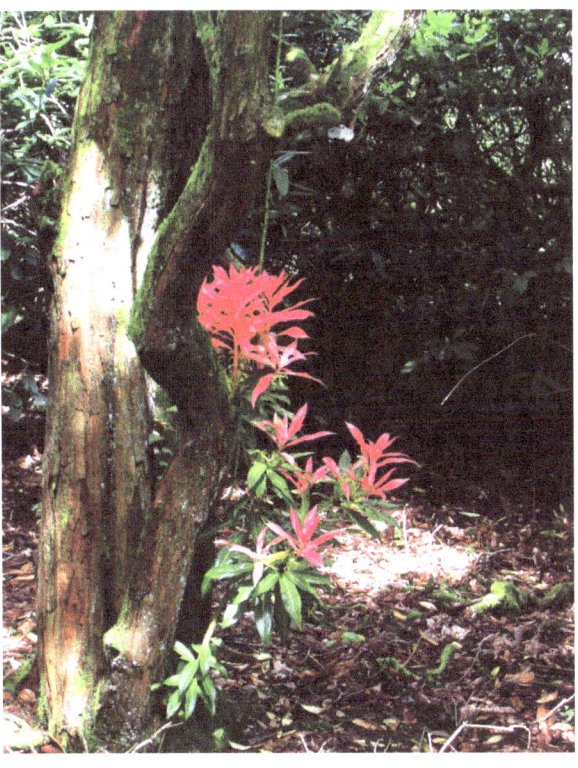

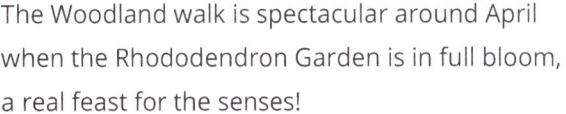

The Woodland walk is spectacular around April when the Rhododendron Garden is in full bloom, a real feast for the senses!

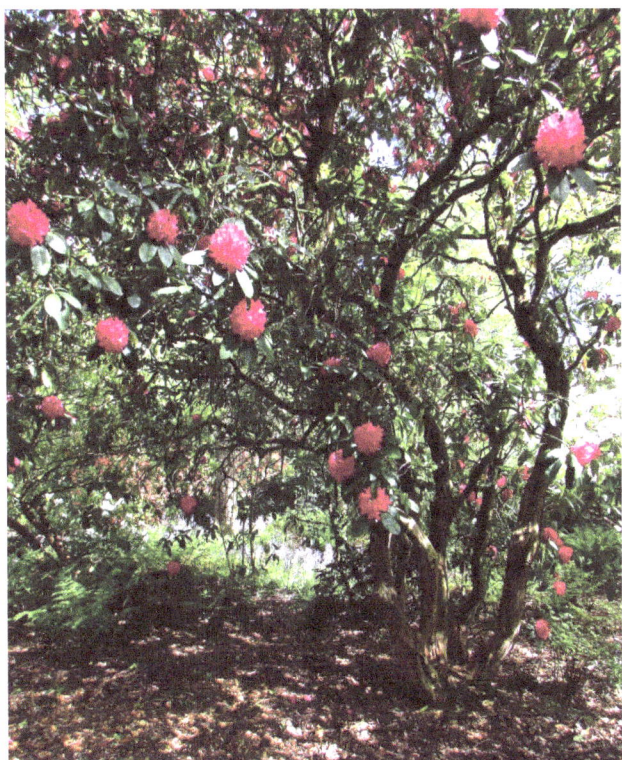

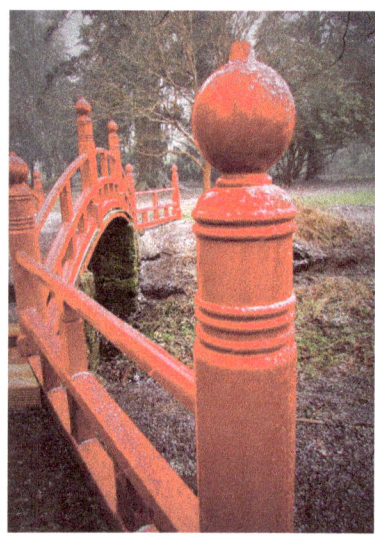 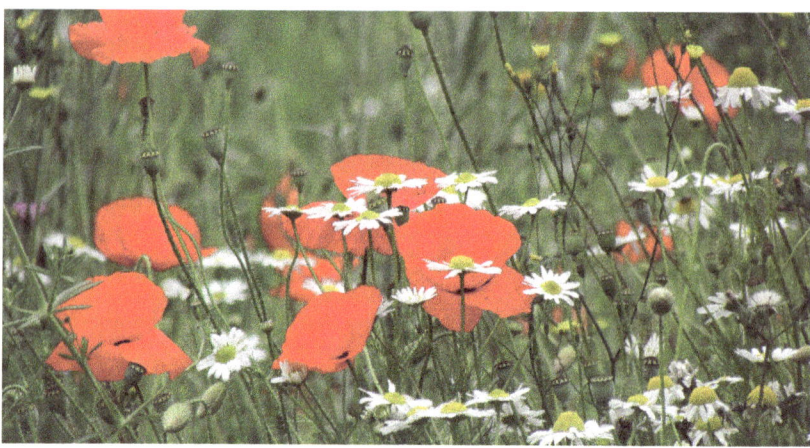

Wildflowers in the Walled Garden

The beautifully restored Japanese Style Bridge leading onto Lady's Island

Russborough House sits on a 200 acre site and still has many of its 18th century features including a maze, lime kiln, ice house, walled garden and serpentine lakes. It also includes extensive parklands, many lovely trails, a children's playground, coffee & gift shop, Lady's Island with its Japanese style bridge and Fairy Trail, The National Bird of Prey Centre, and Artisans Studios and Craft Courtyard.

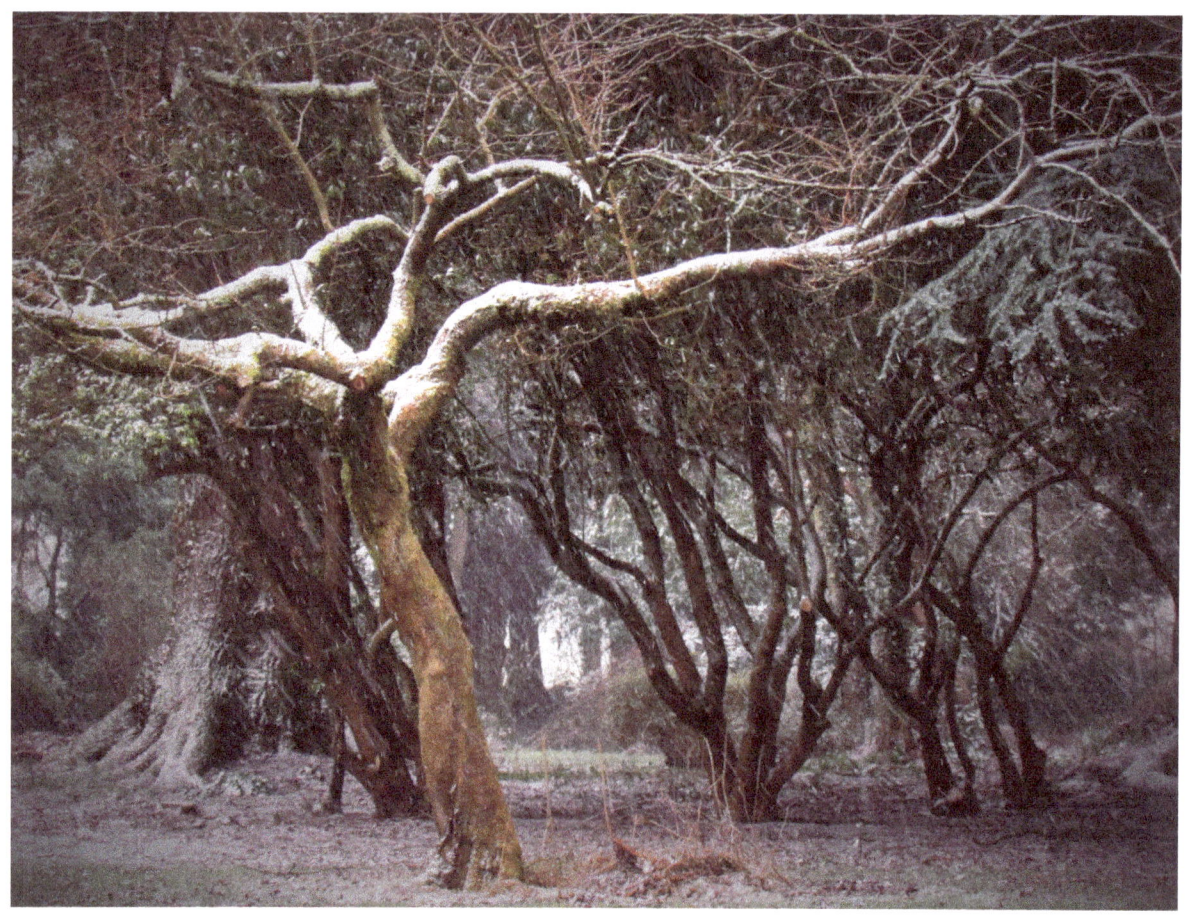

Beautiful trees on Lady's Island with a sprinkling of snow

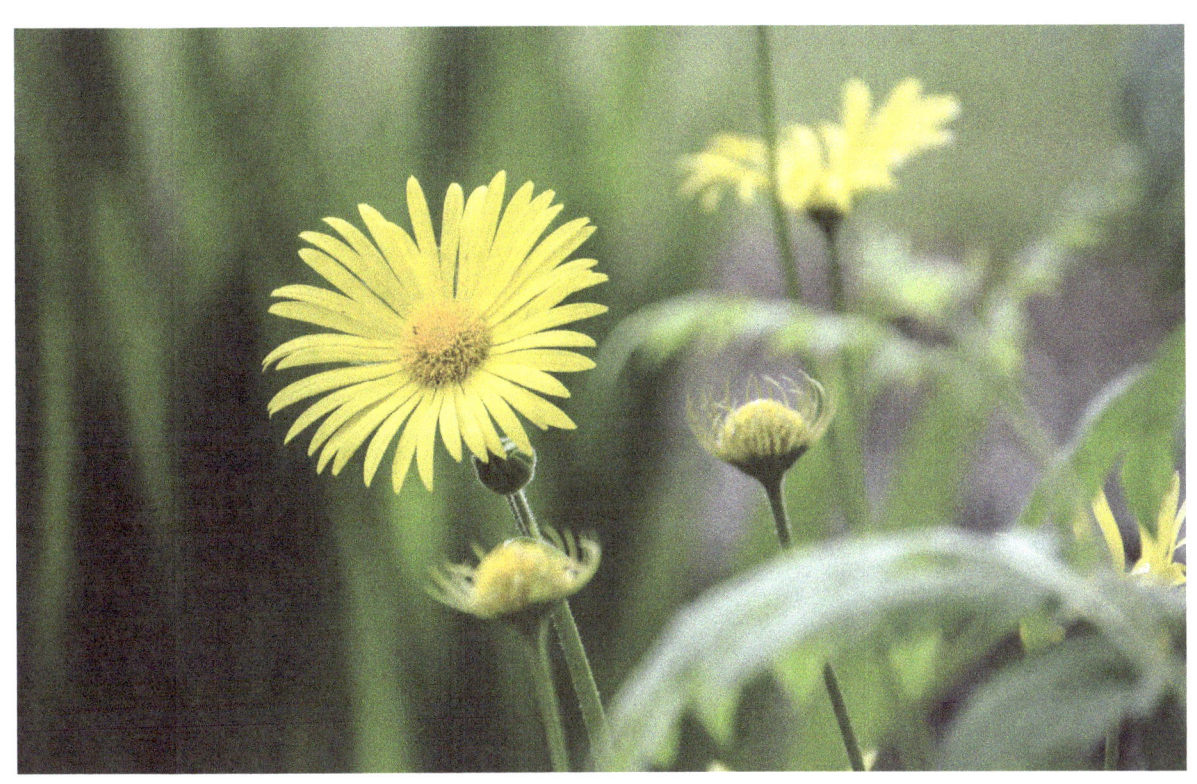
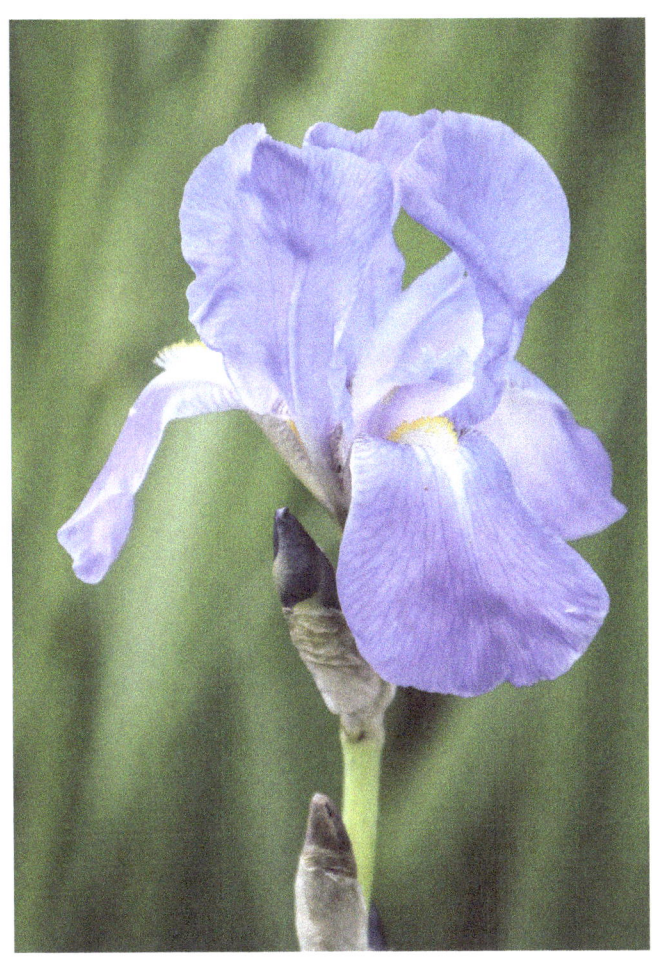
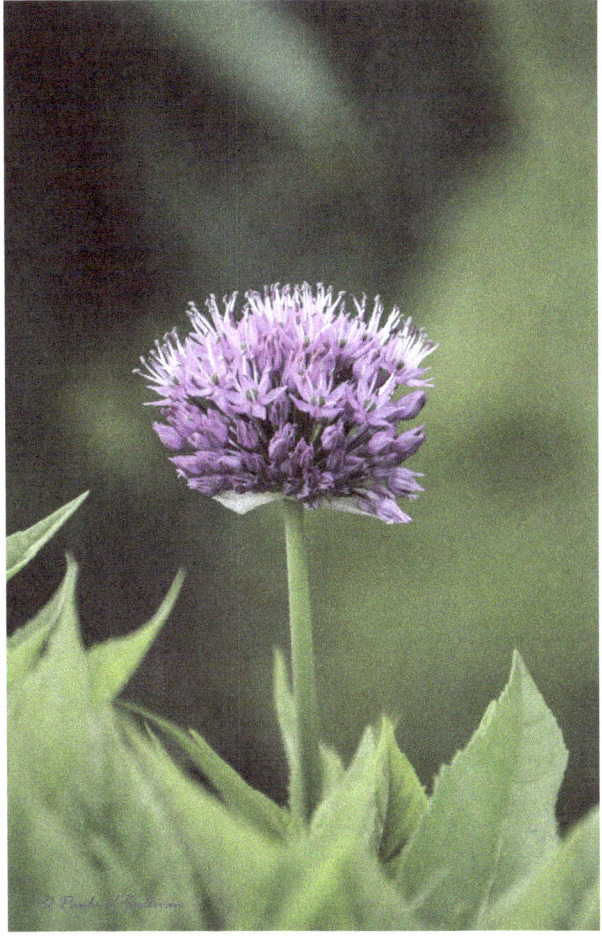

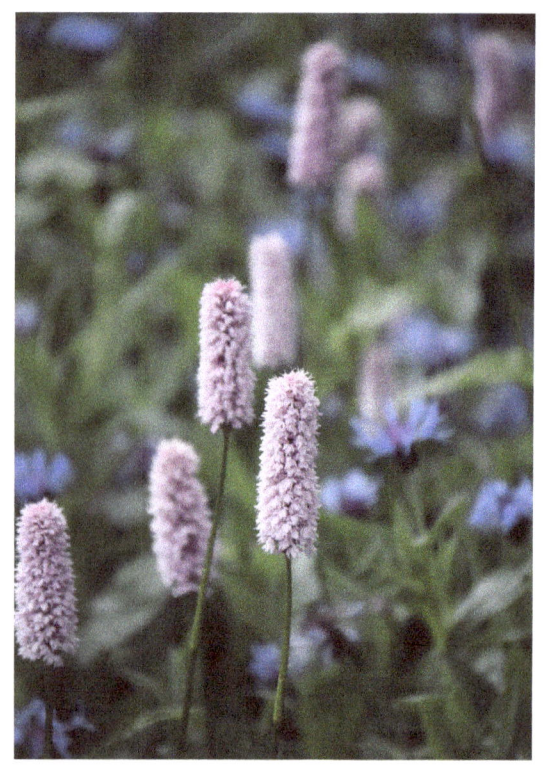
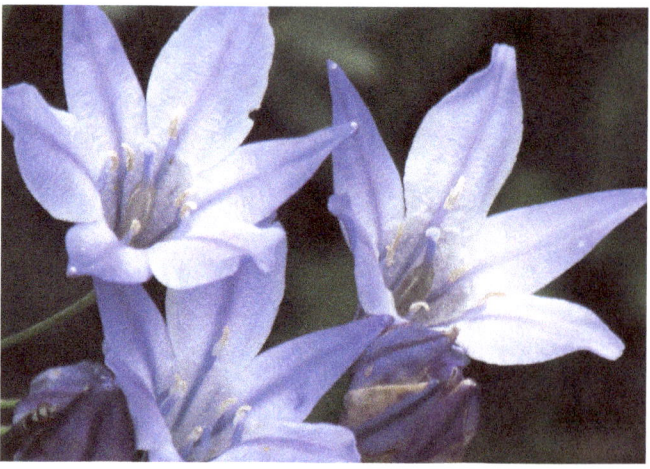

The Walled Garden is well worth a visit. I remember being like a kid in a candy shop when I first visited, I was greedily snapping photos, and the ladies who were gardening, were laughing at my oooh's and aaaah's as I snapped away happily!

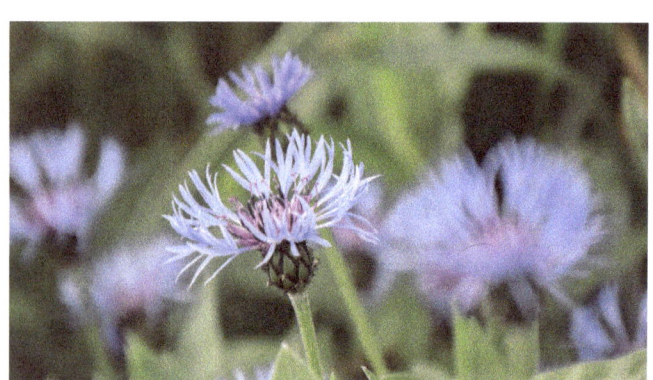
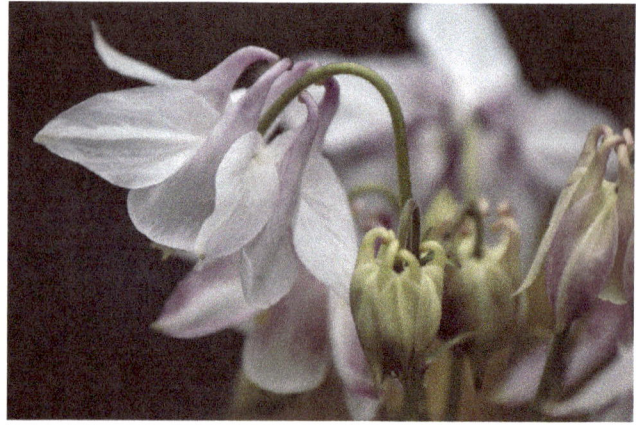
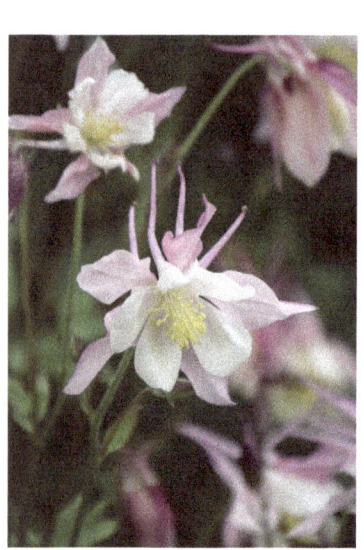
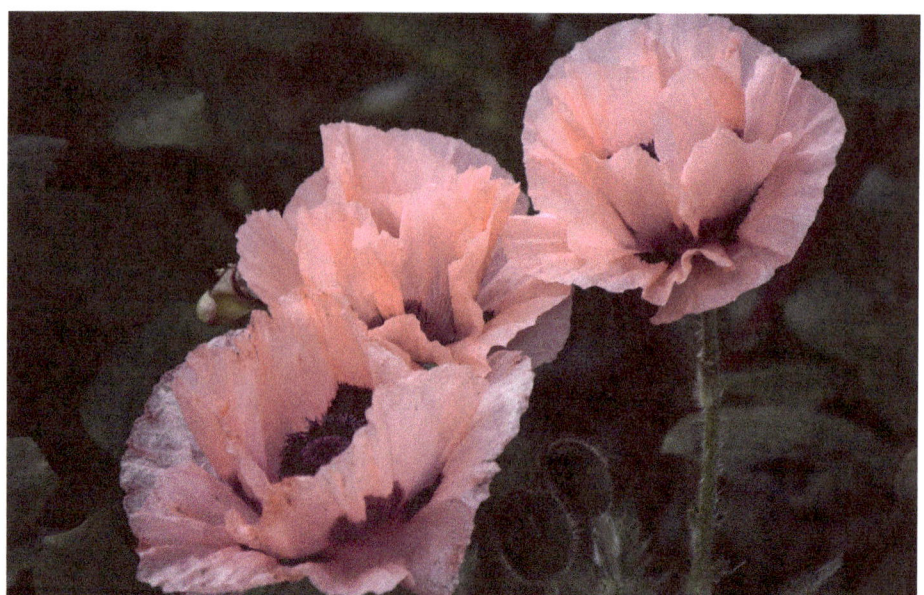

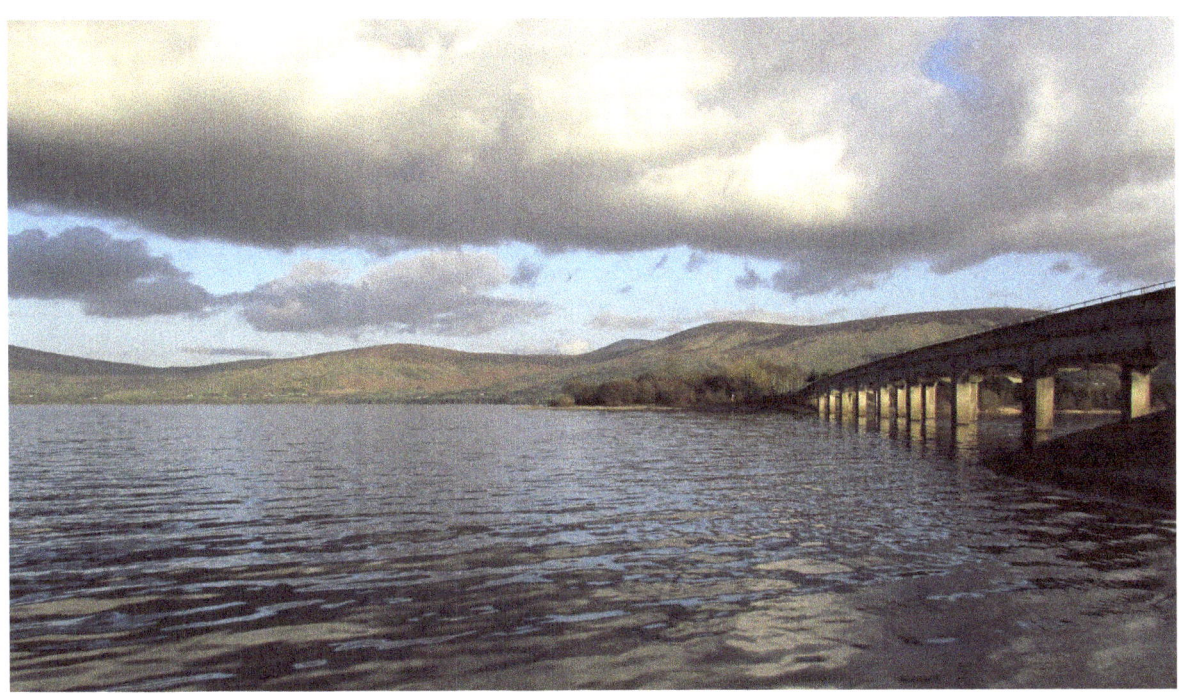

VALLEYMOUNT

Being on the Facebook groups as I mentioned earlier was exciting. Word got around quickly if the lakes were high or low, all giving great photo opportunities for those who wanted something different and historical to capture. Also occasionally someone would tell me about a little known pathway onto a shoreline, and off I'd go in a furry of anticipation. And so it was that I heard about Valleymount. And oh boy was it worth it!

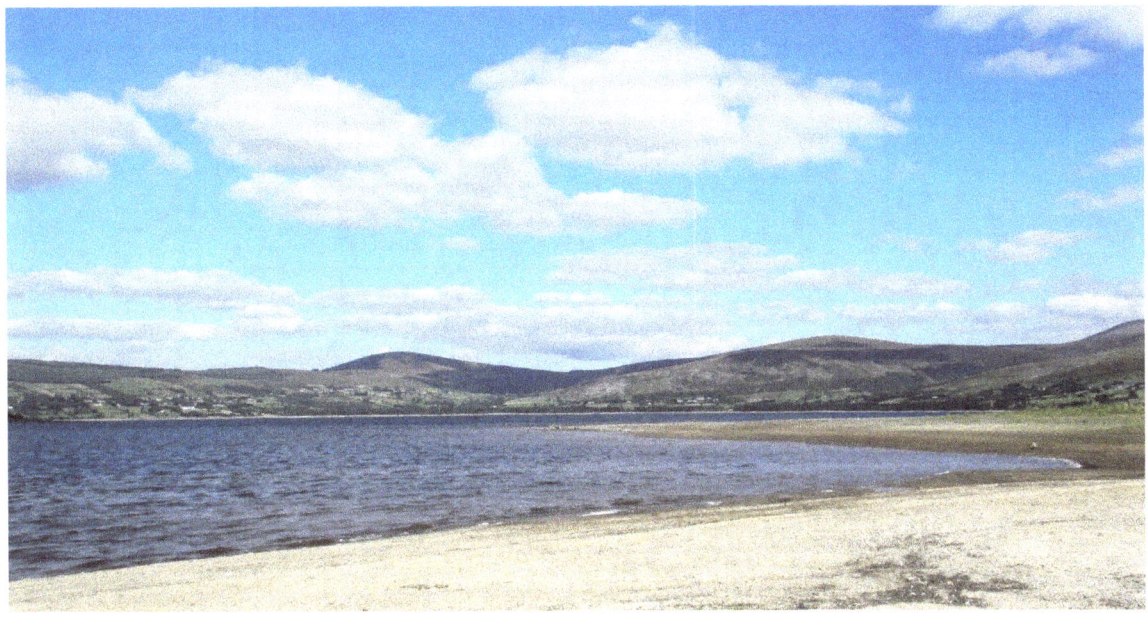

On Valleymount shoreline

On Valleymount shoreline looking over to Ballyknockan

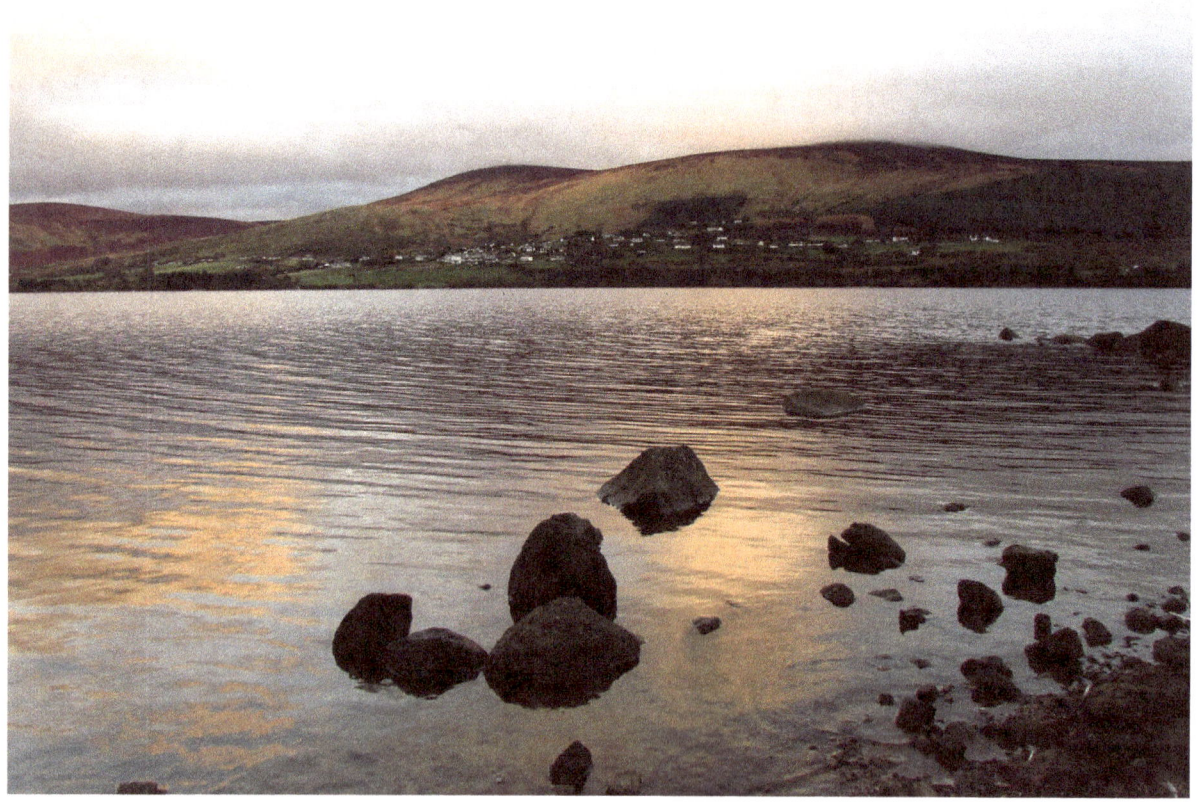

The evening sun lights up the hills of Ballyknockan

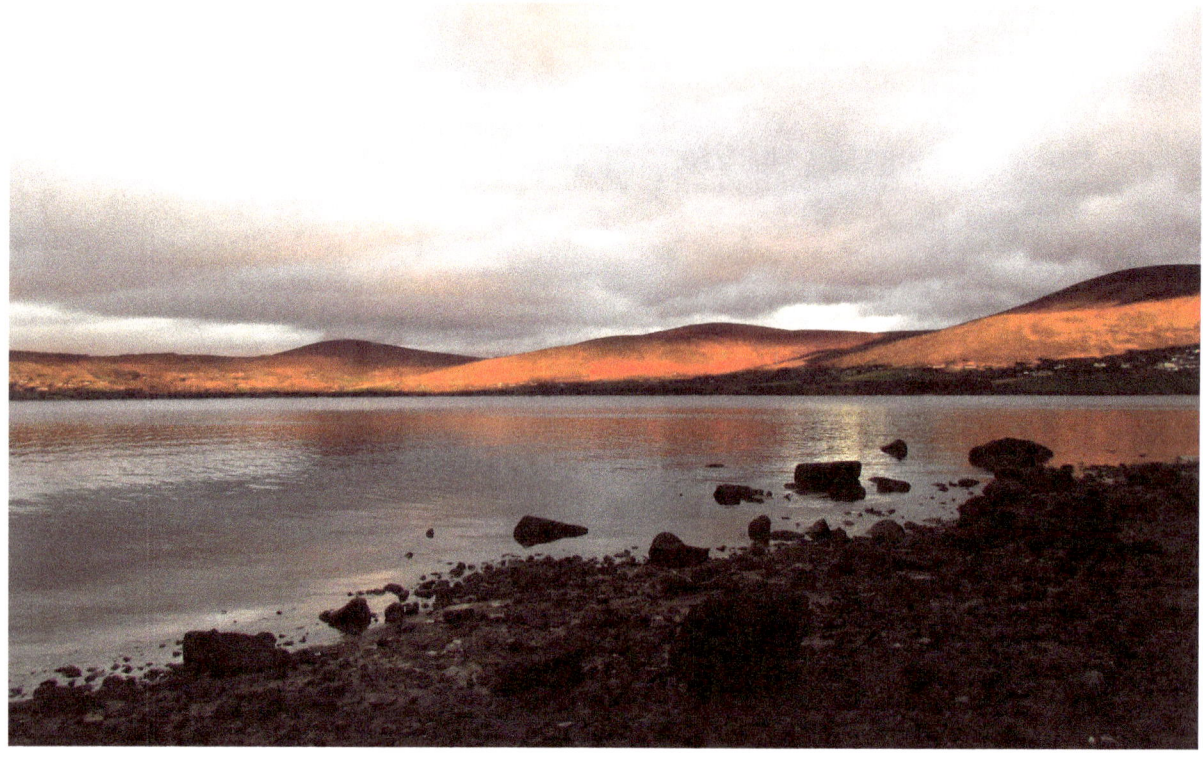

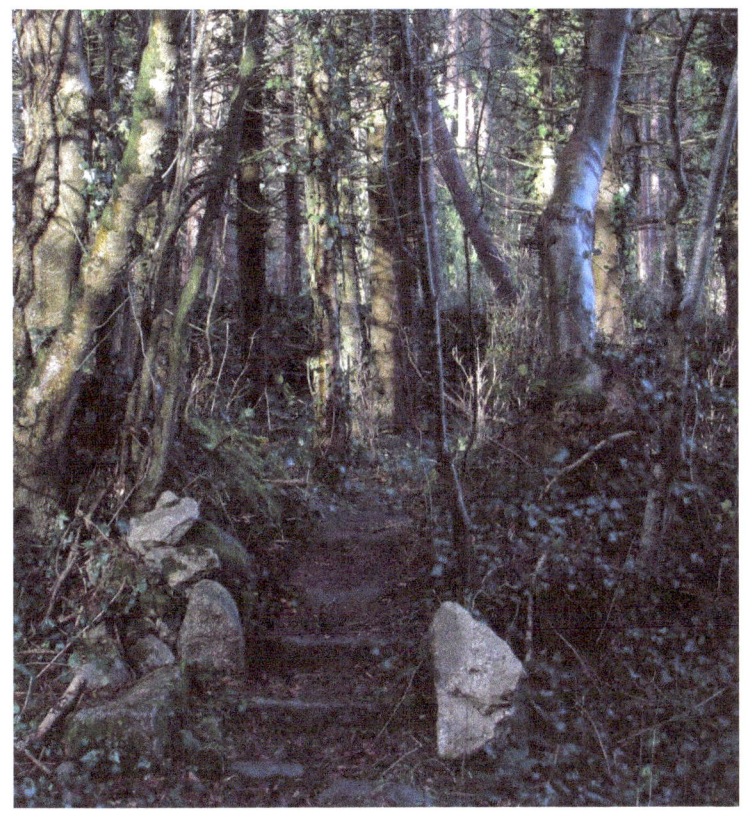

There is a lovely little trail that runs parallel to the shoreline on the right in Vallymount, when you go through the initial barrier, its a bit uneven with various tree roots and can be a bit slippery, but its lovely all the same.

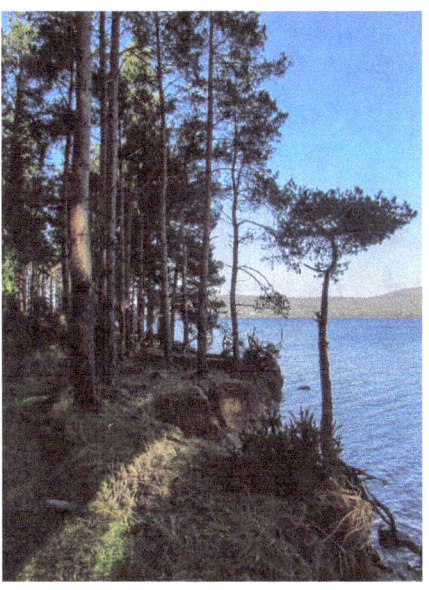

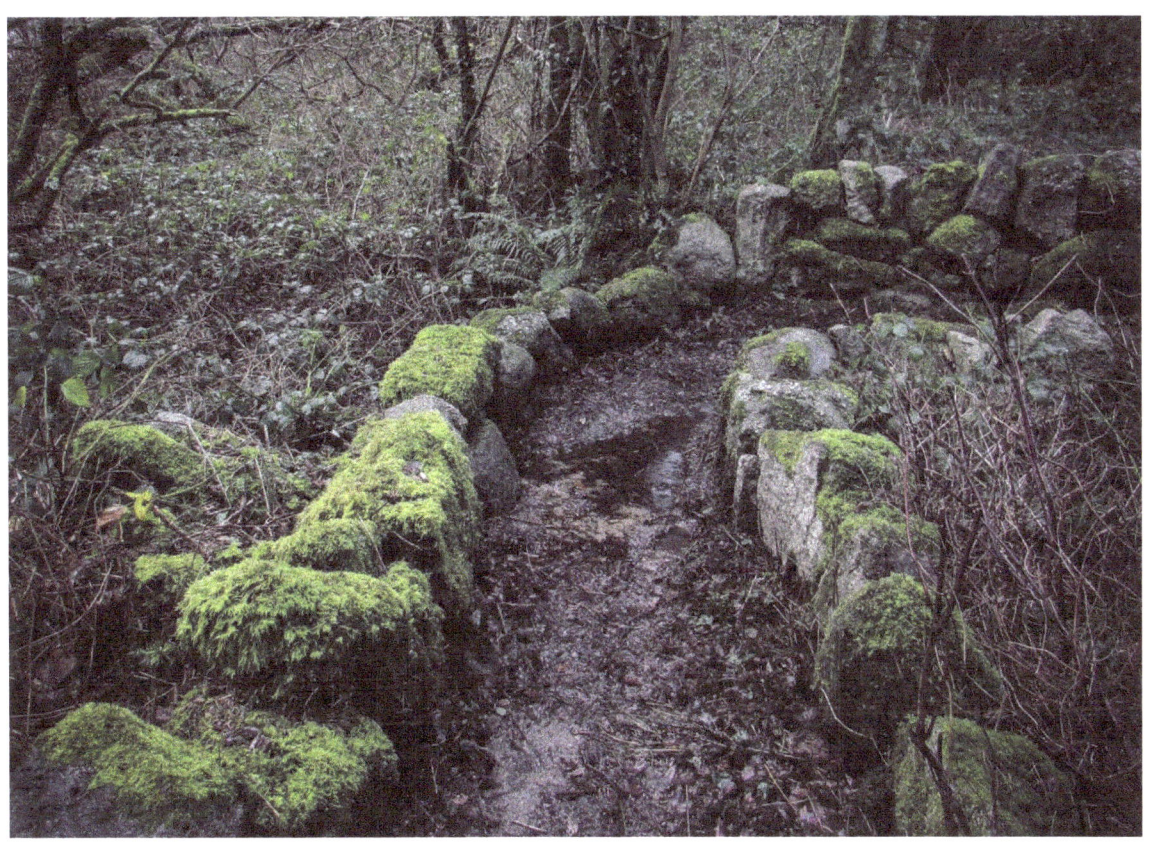

There are lots of very large boulders on Valleymount shoreline. I called this one 'Rock Bottom!'

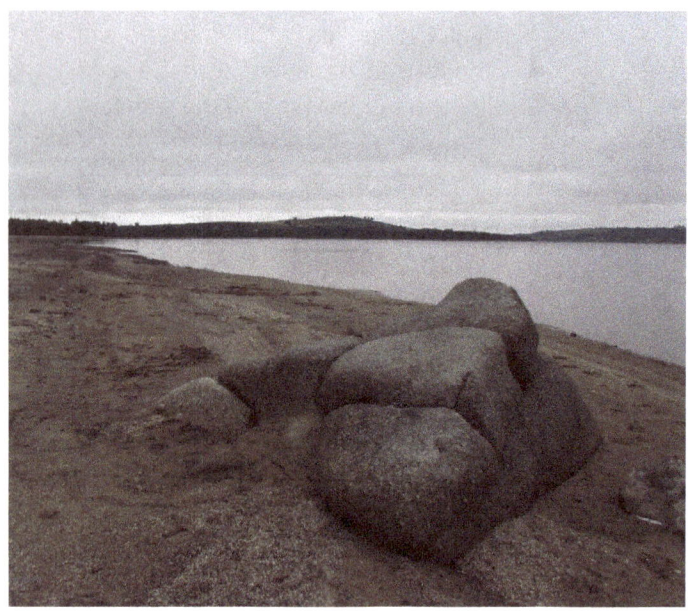

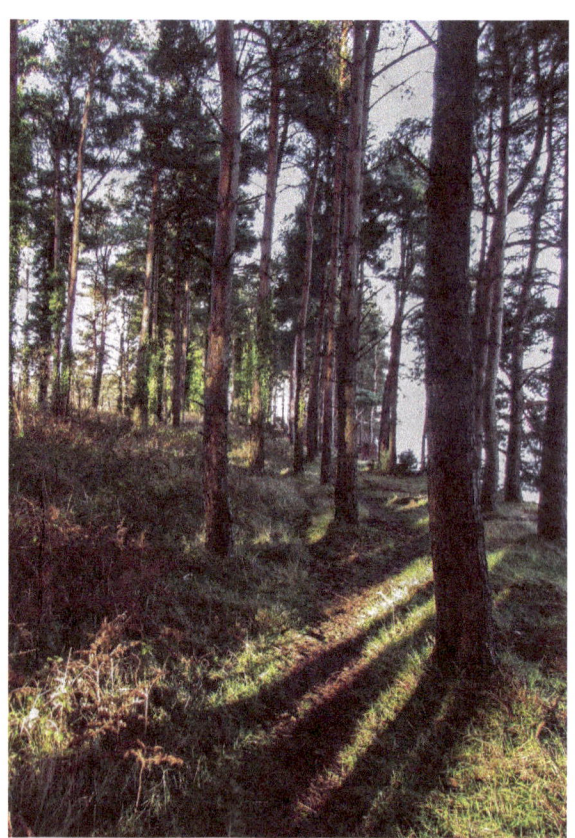

Lovely woodland trail

I see shapes in everything - anyone else see a sloth crouching?

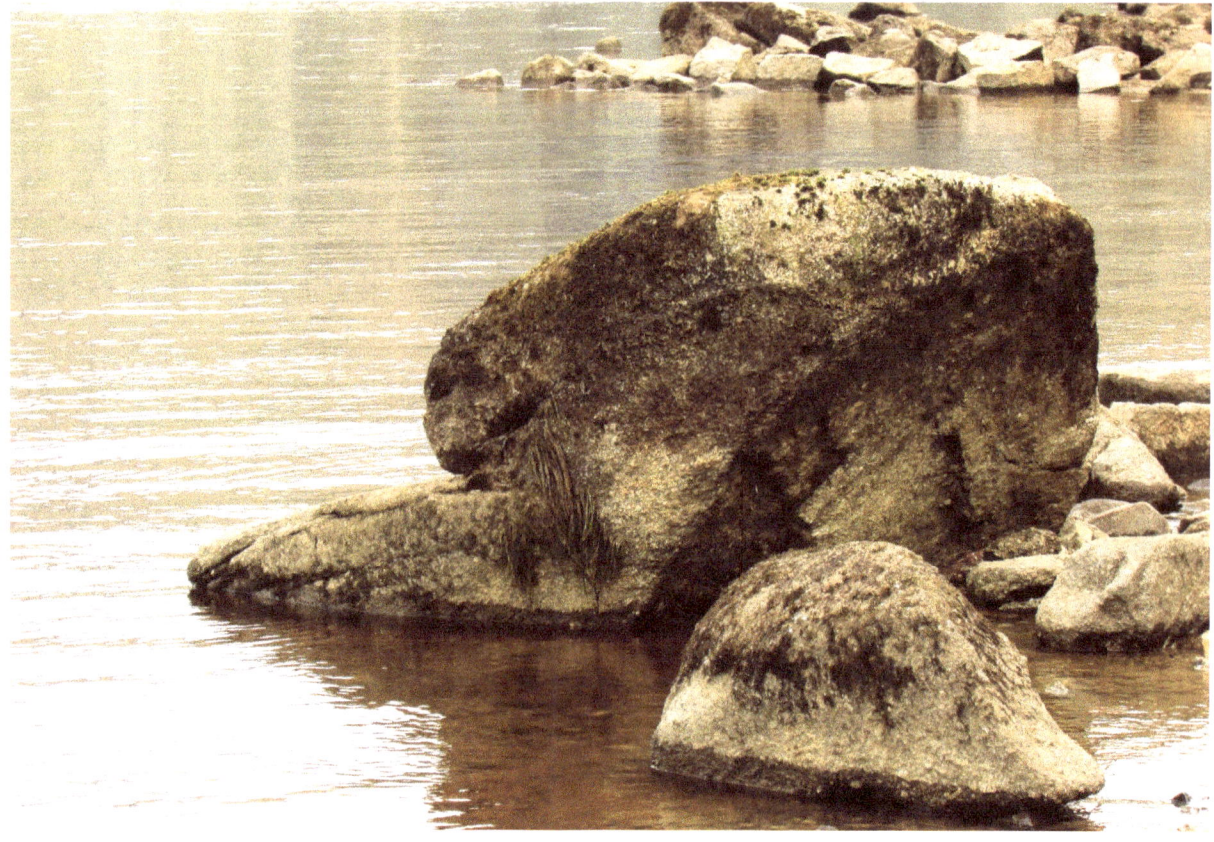

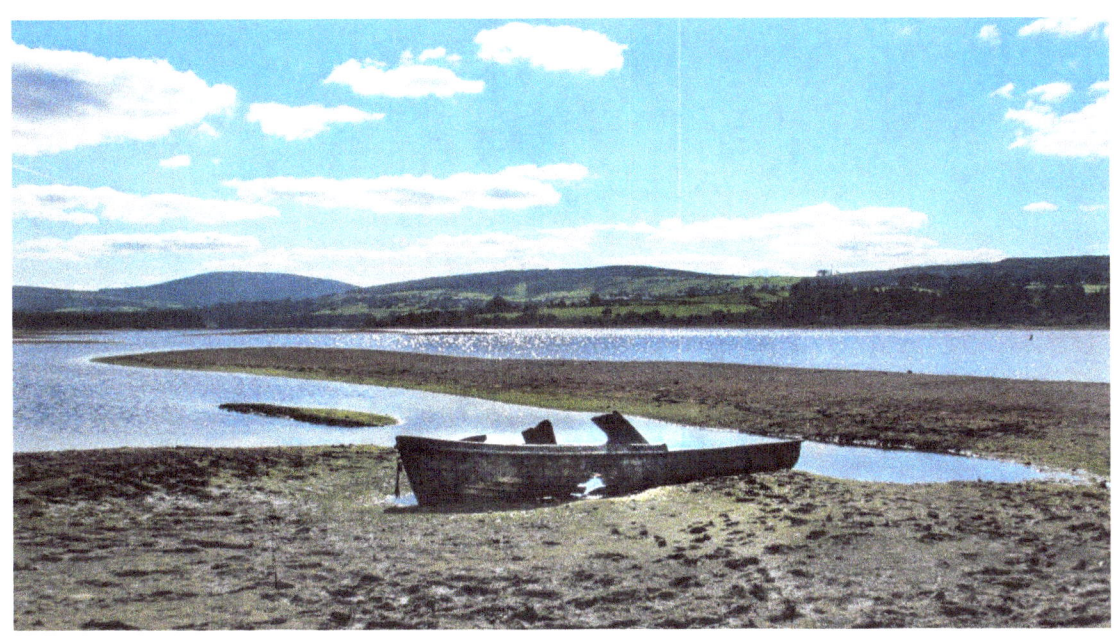

This old boat resurfaced after about 40 years of being hidden in the mud near Valleymount 2018

Word was out that the Lakes were at an all time low in 2018, and that some things had started to resurface. I didn't have as much free time as I had at the beginning of my adventures, but I managed to get a few shots.

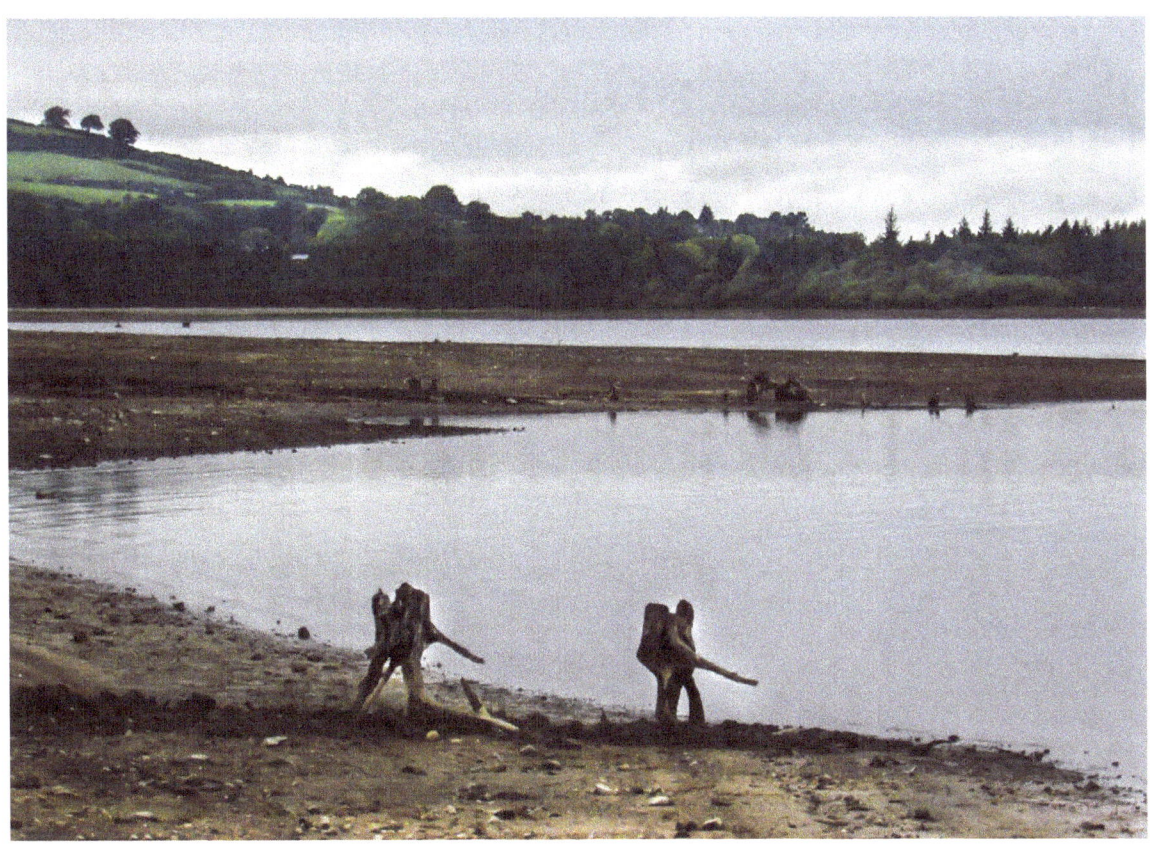

Valleymount - tree stumps try to make their way back into the depths of the lakes 2018 - Reconnaissance mission!

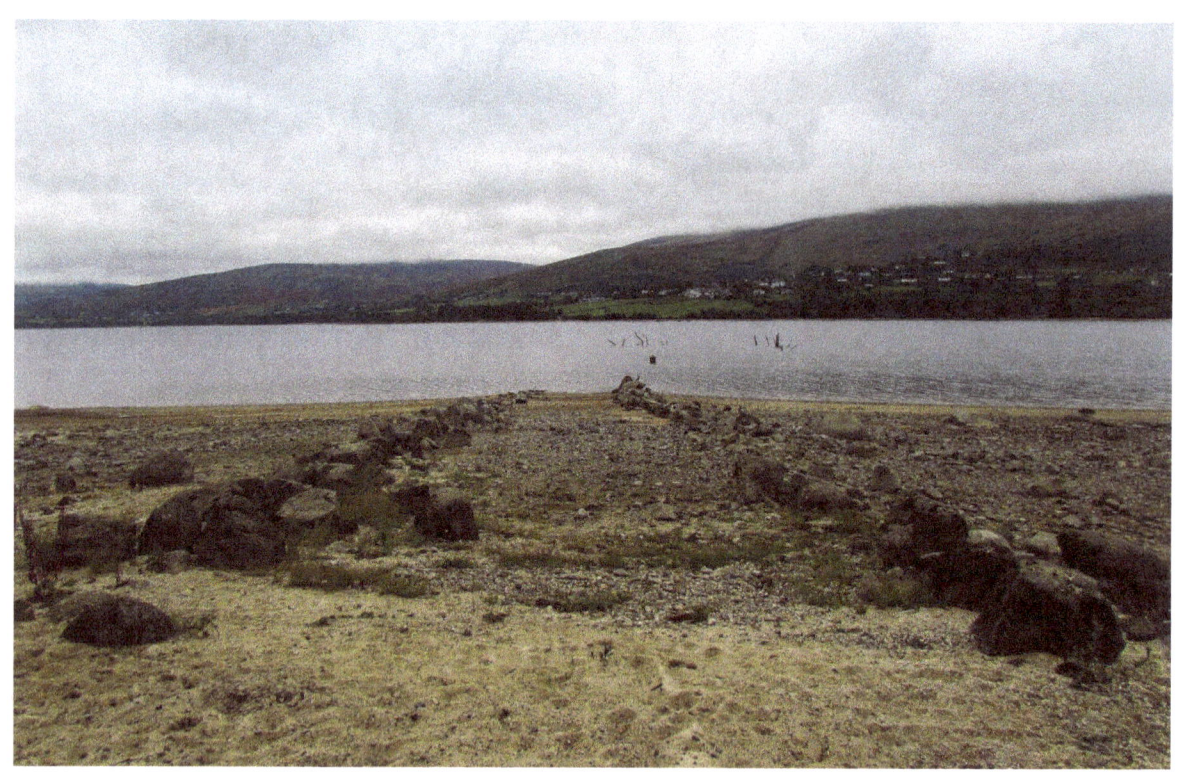

An old roadway appears as the lake levels drop in Valleymount 2018

Old crockery and containers are found as the waters recede - Valleymount 2018

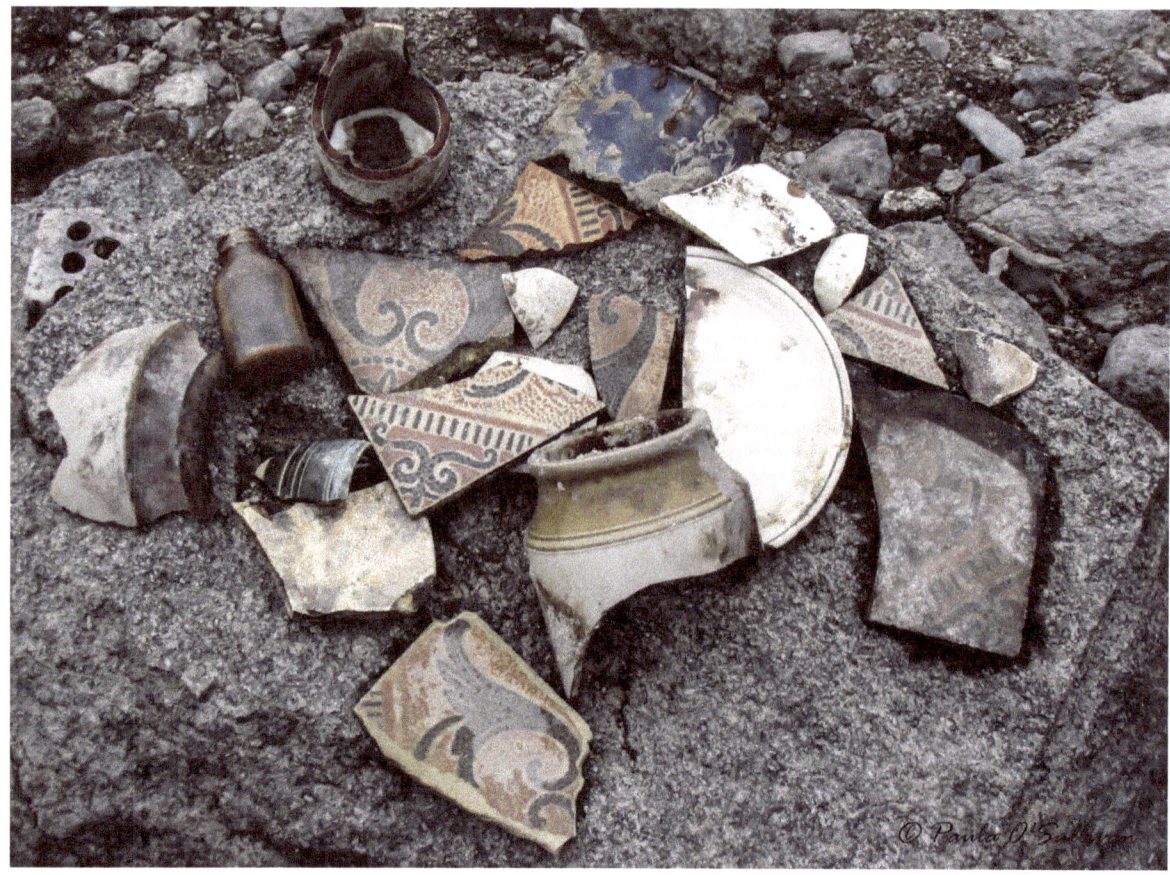

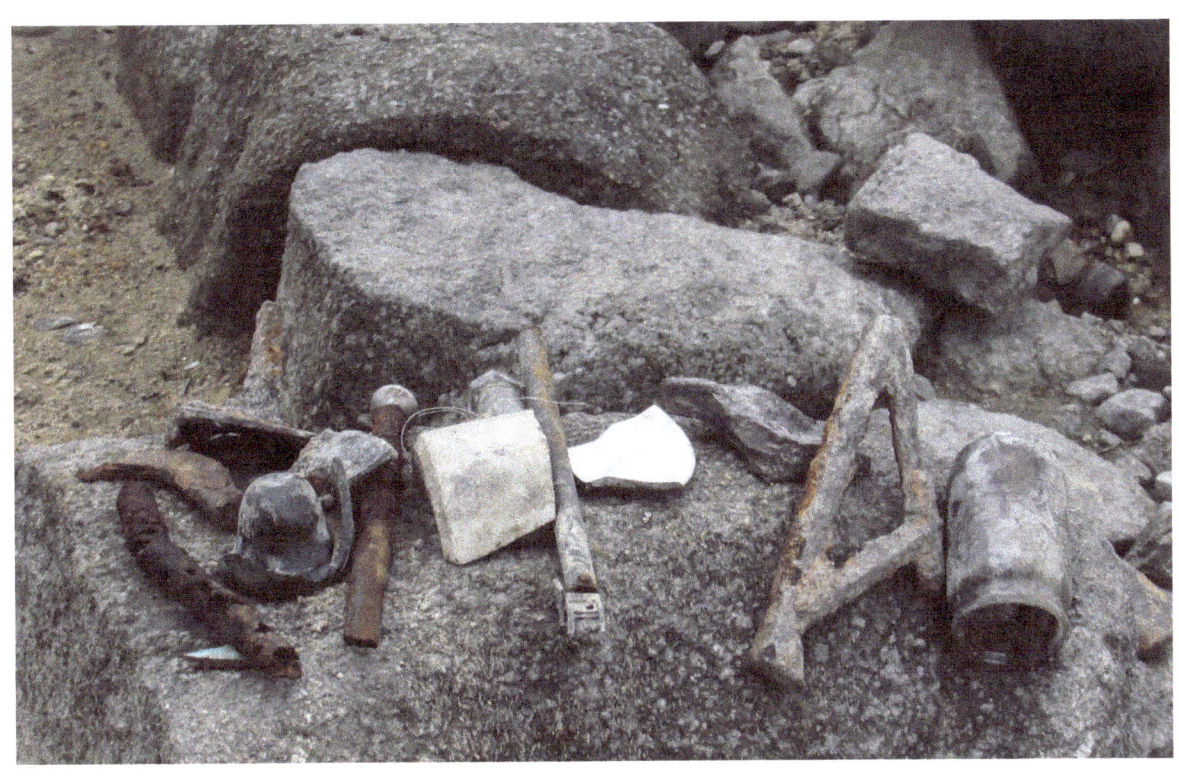

More interesting finds are left by locals on rocks for all to see - Valleymount 2018

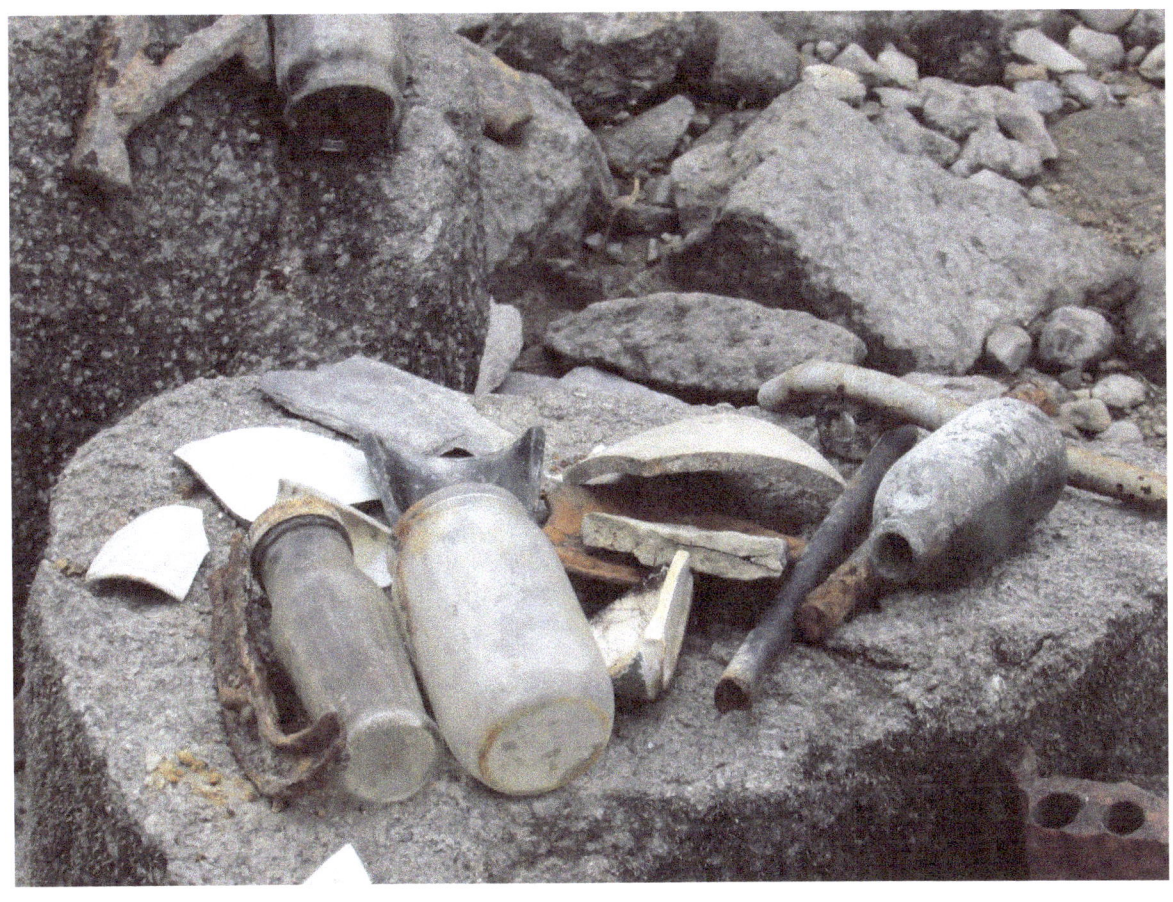

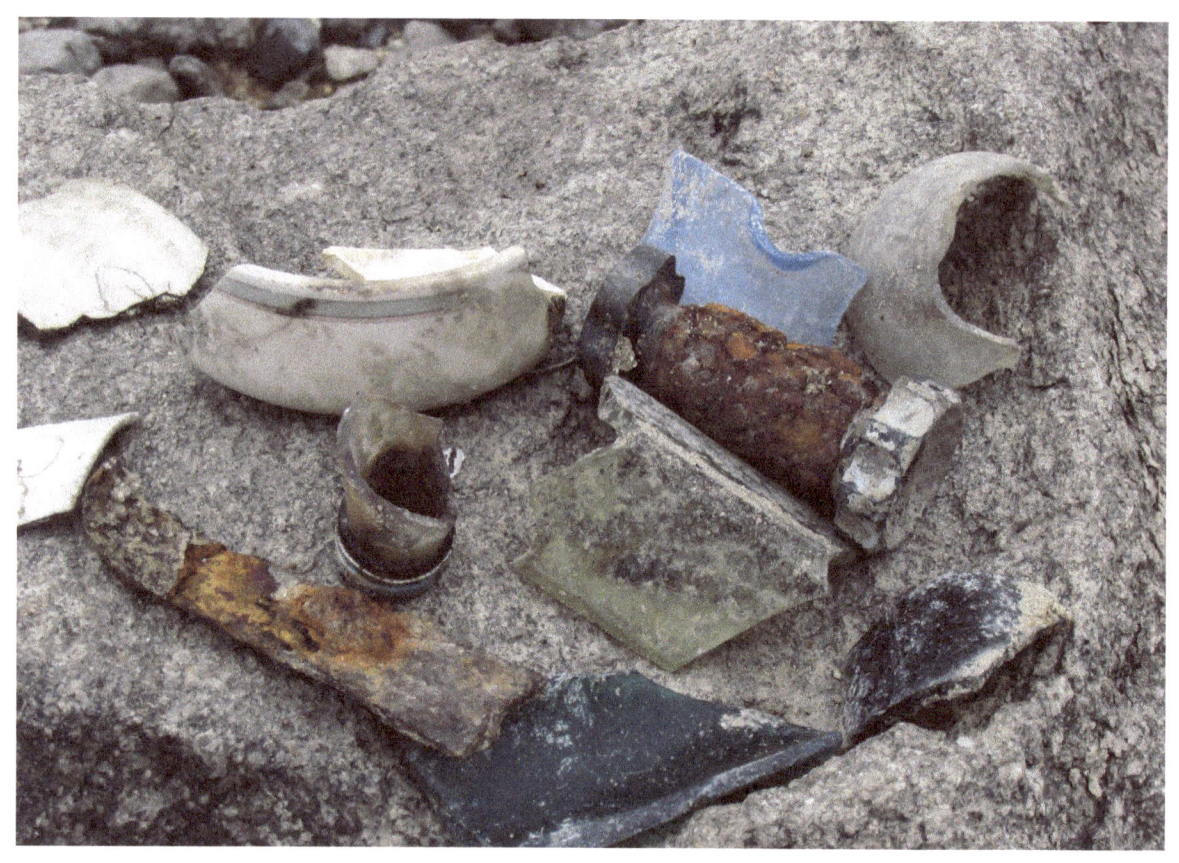

Valleymount before the lakes dropped really low, beautiful reflections facing Ballyknockan

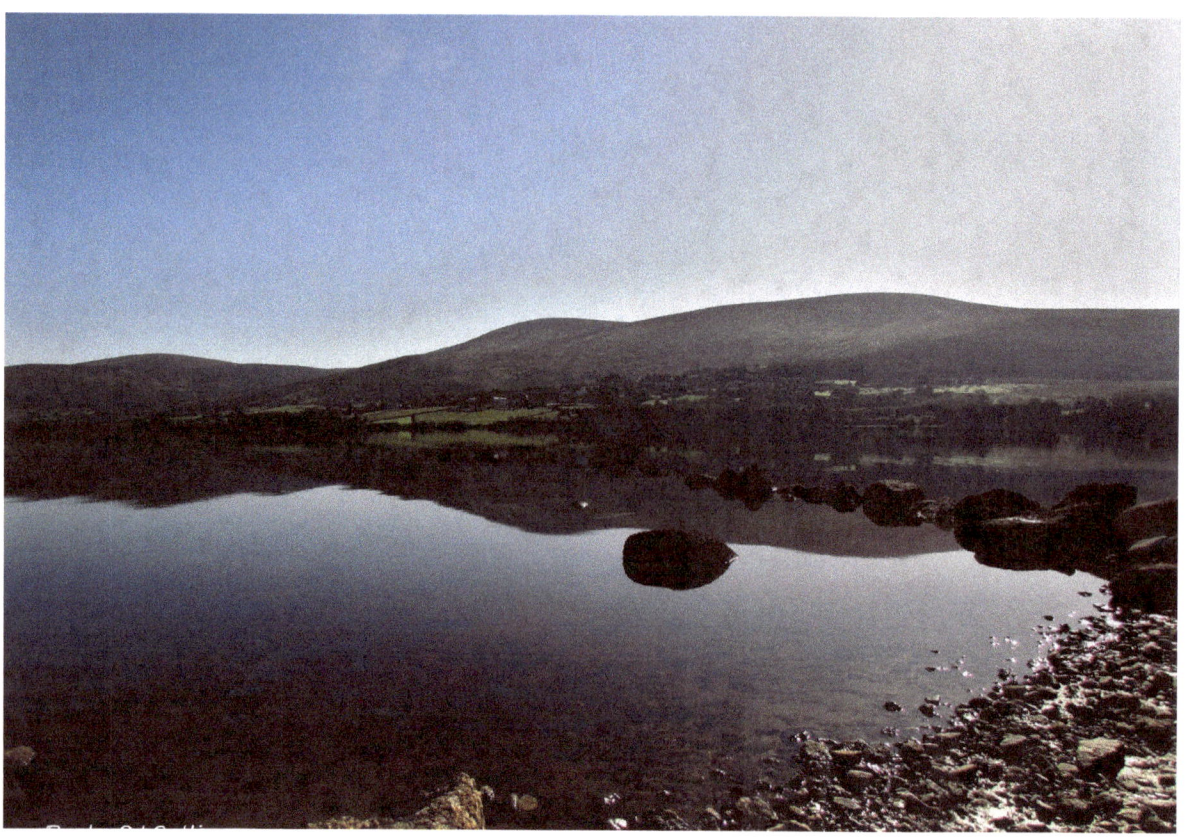

BRIDGES

In the mid 1930's some rather beautiful bridges were demolished because of the creation of the reservoir, which would become known as the Blessington Lakes. The replacement bridges, while not as attractive, can be quite photogenic, especially when the lakes are reflective.

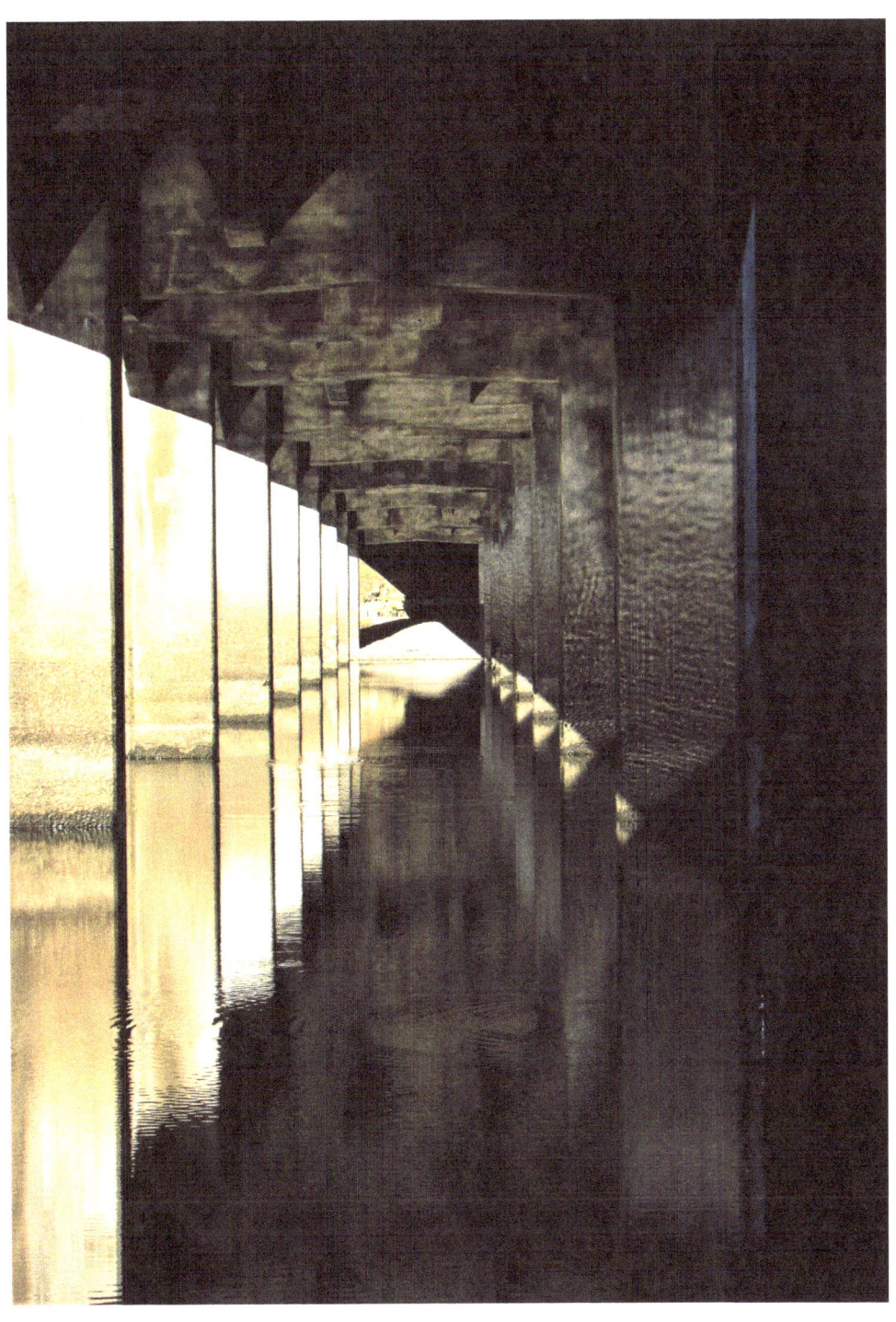

Morning sun highlights under Burgage Bridge

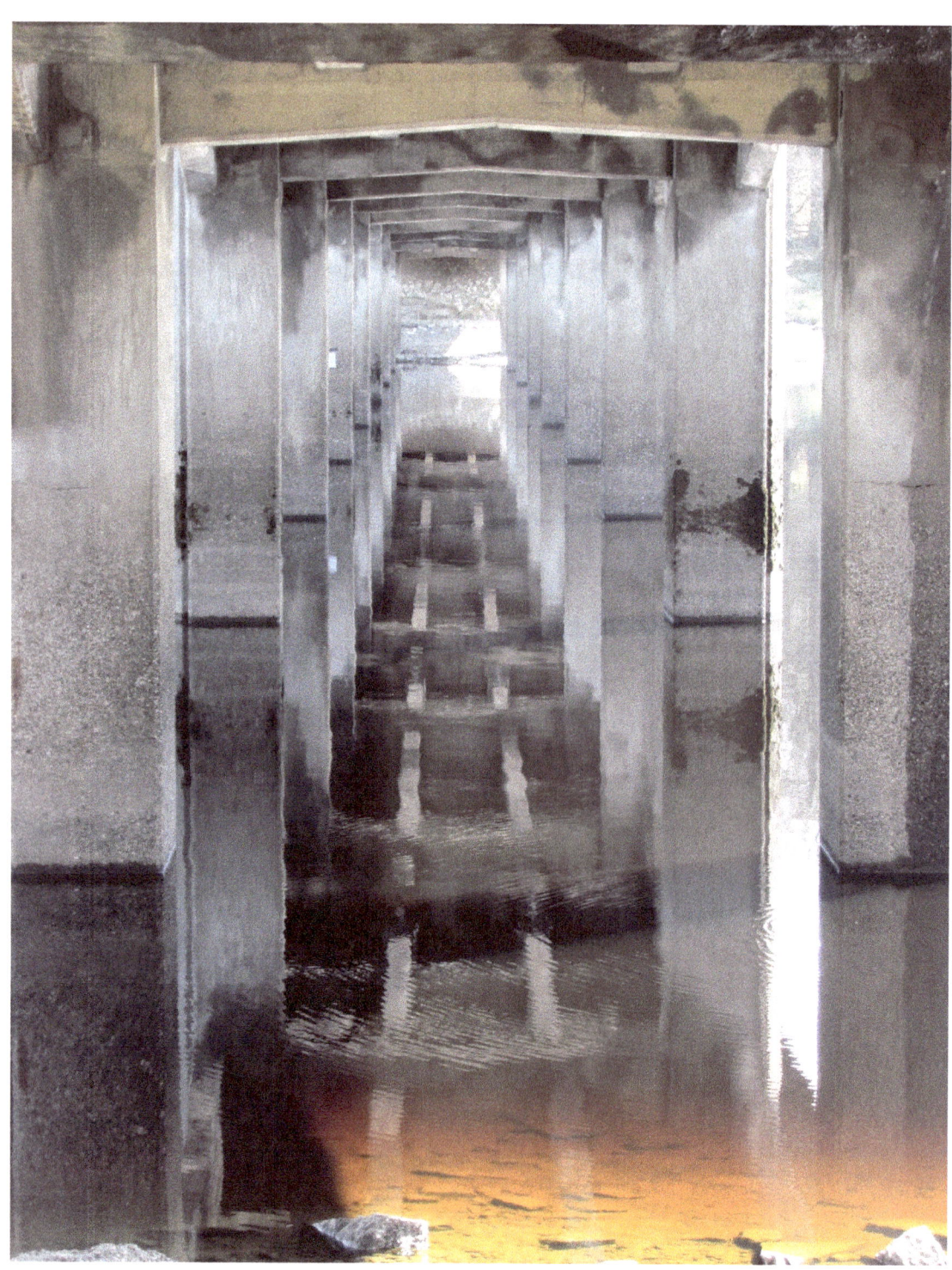

Another shot from under Burgage Bridge the opposite side to the previous photo.

I'm always amazed at how different the bridges can look based on which side I take it from and the availability of light and calm waters.

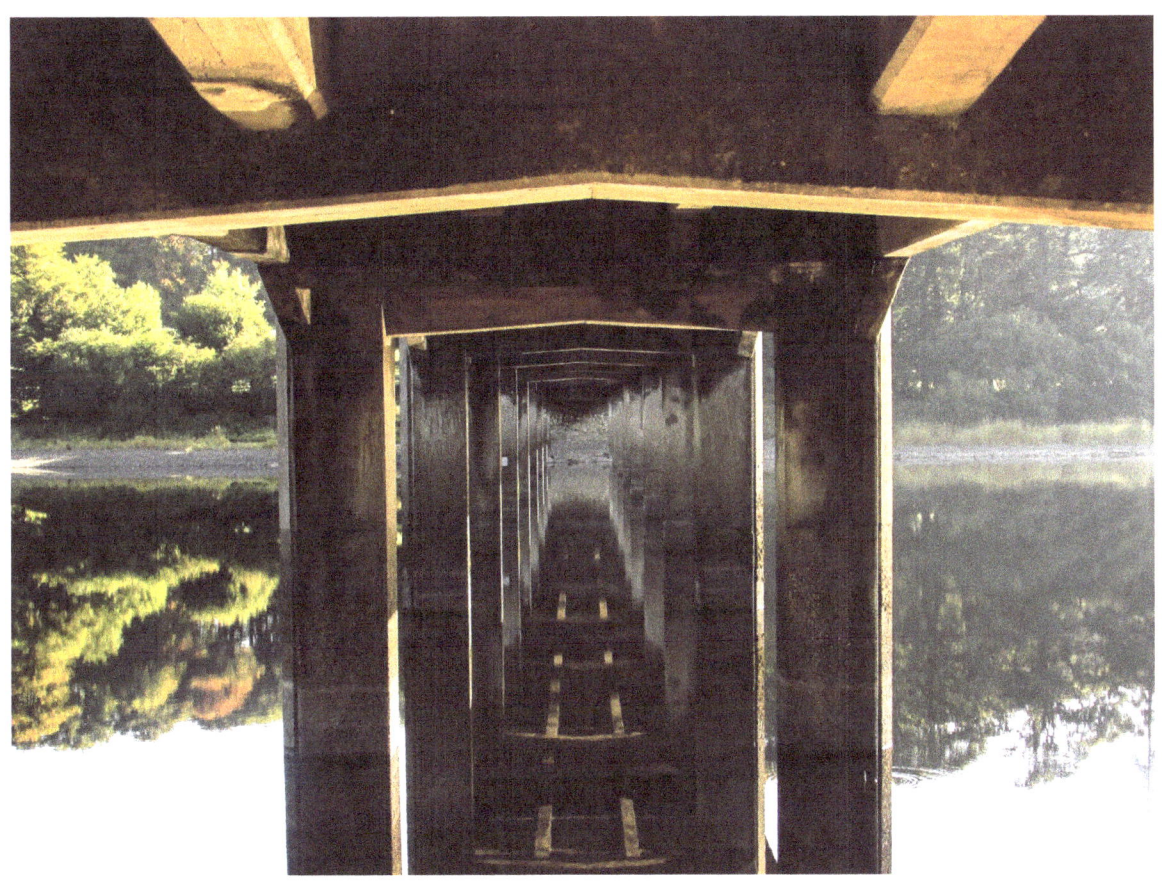

Burgage Bridge on a reflective day!

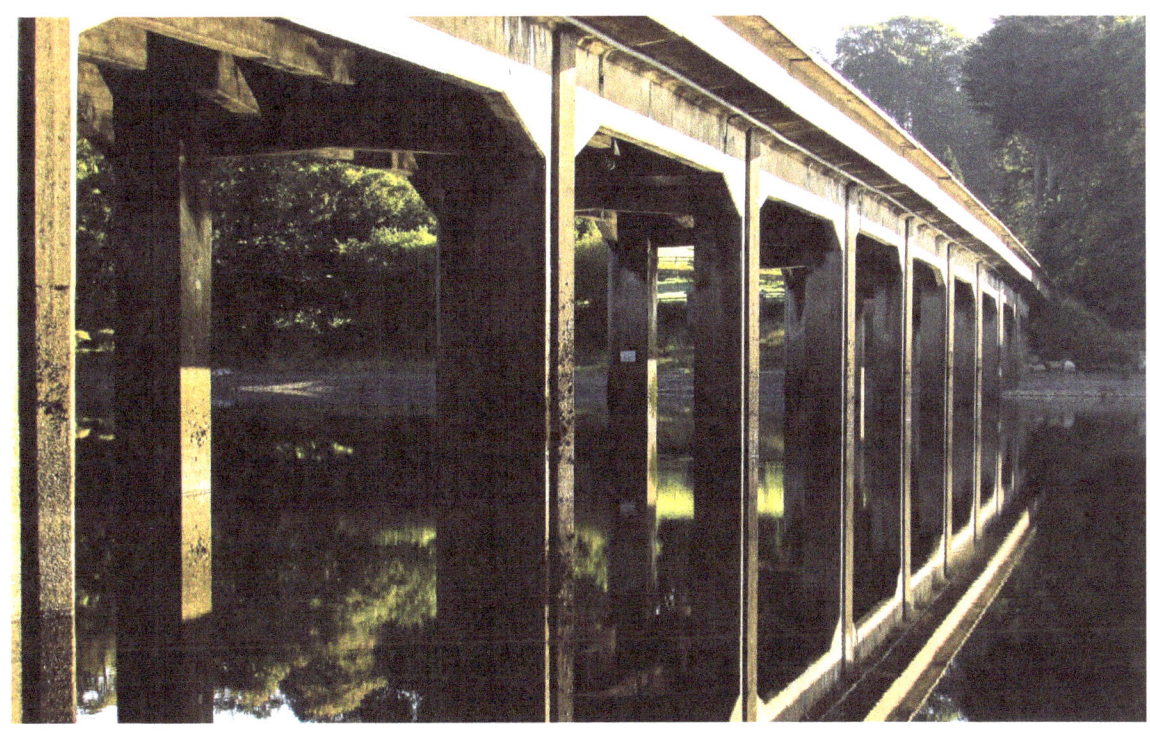

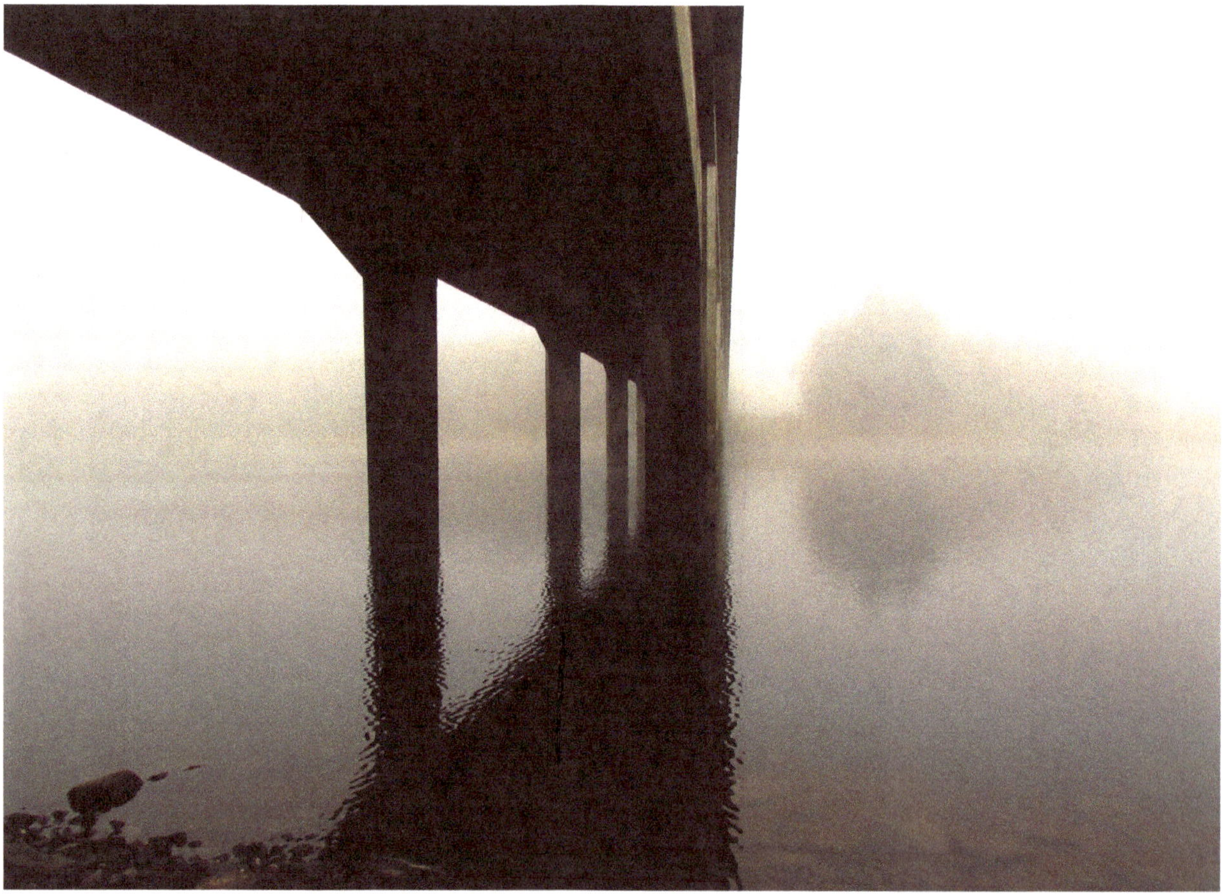

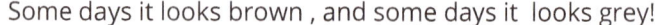

Even the mist can't keep me away!

Some days it looks brown, and some days it looks grey!

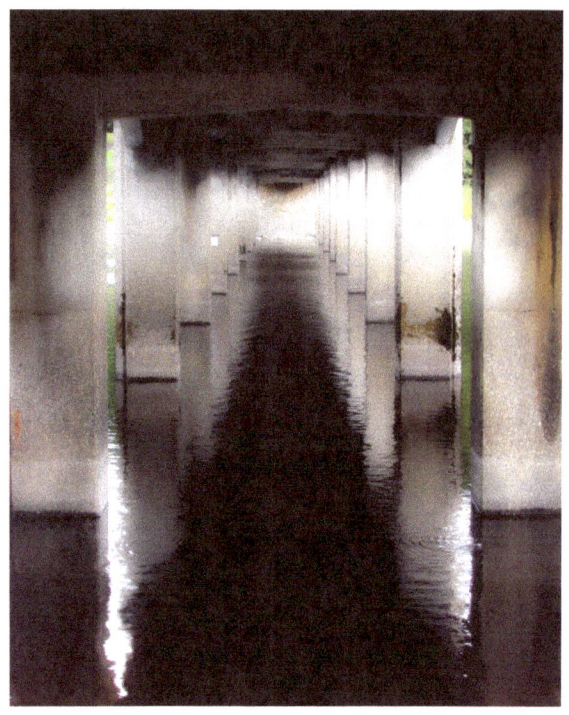
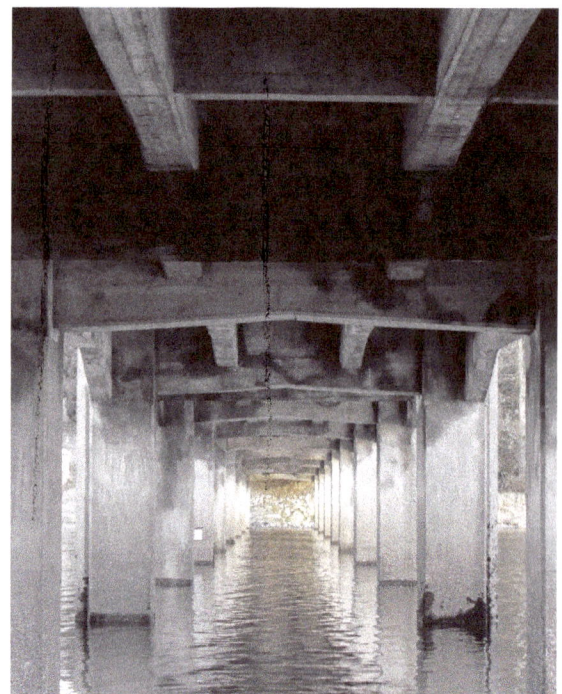

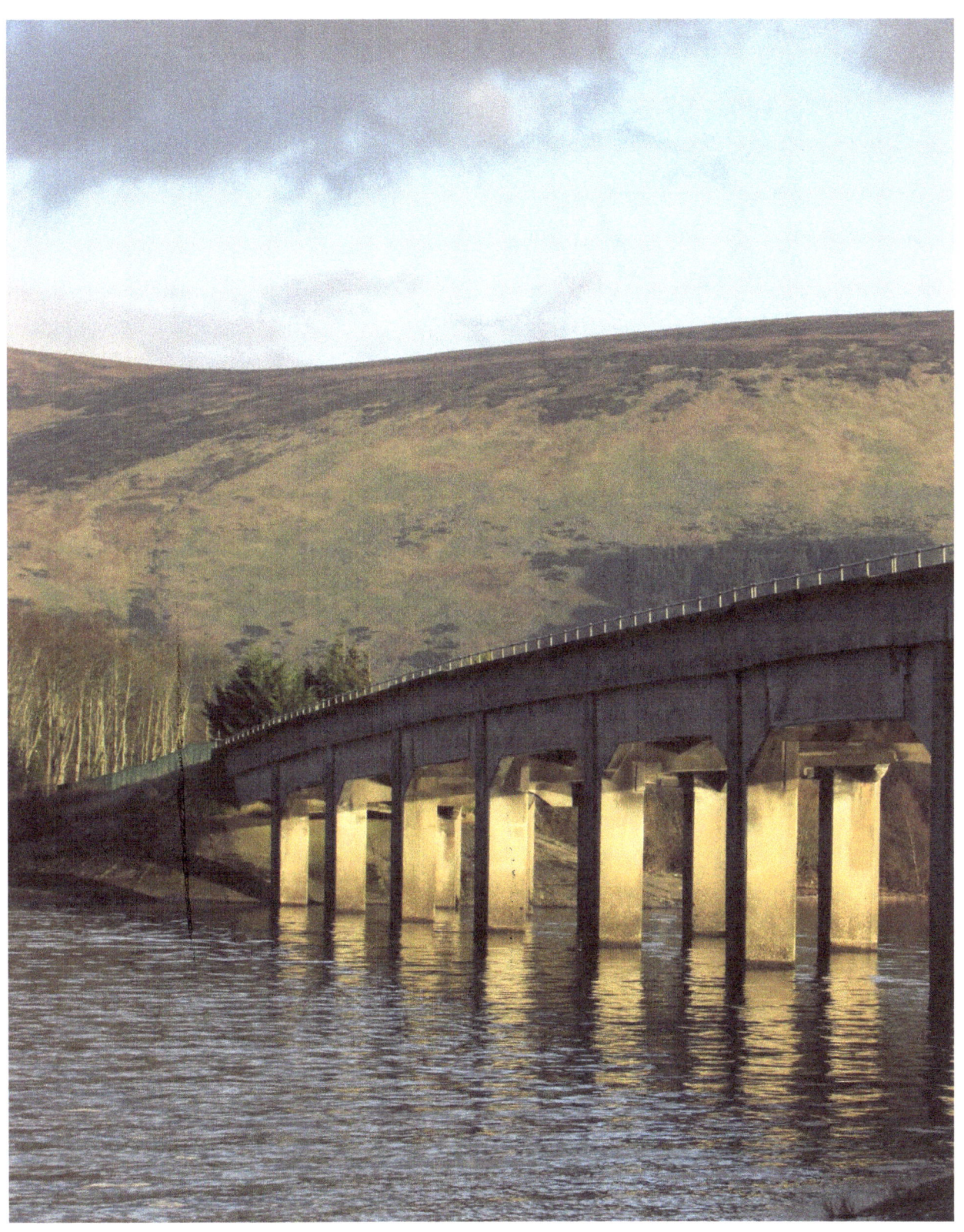
Valleymount Bridge in the evening sunlight looks beautiful

WINTERY DAYS

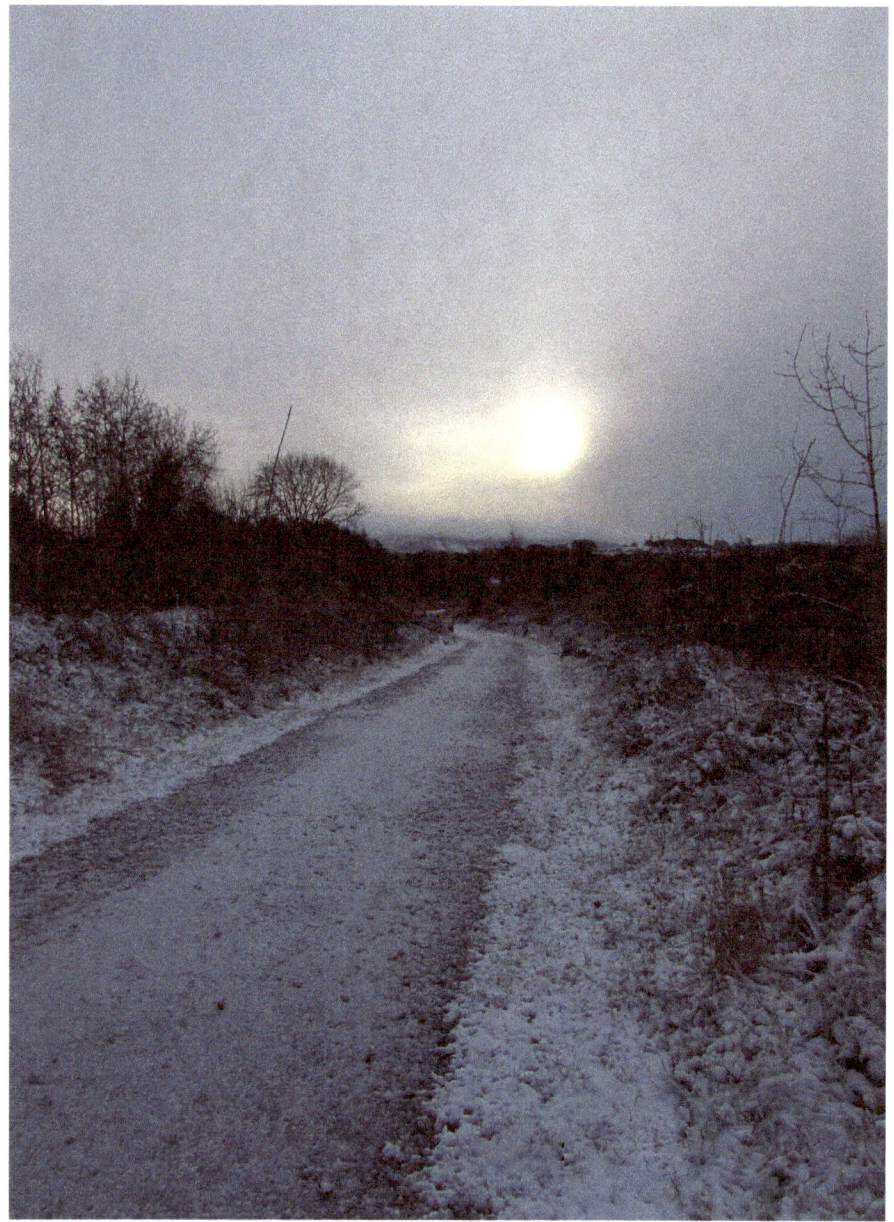

A sprinkling of snow on the Greenway at Burgage

Oh the excitement amongst the local photographers when it snowed. There were days when I'd travel around to several locations and keep meeting the same people either arriving or departing as we all tried to get a great shot! Great fun!

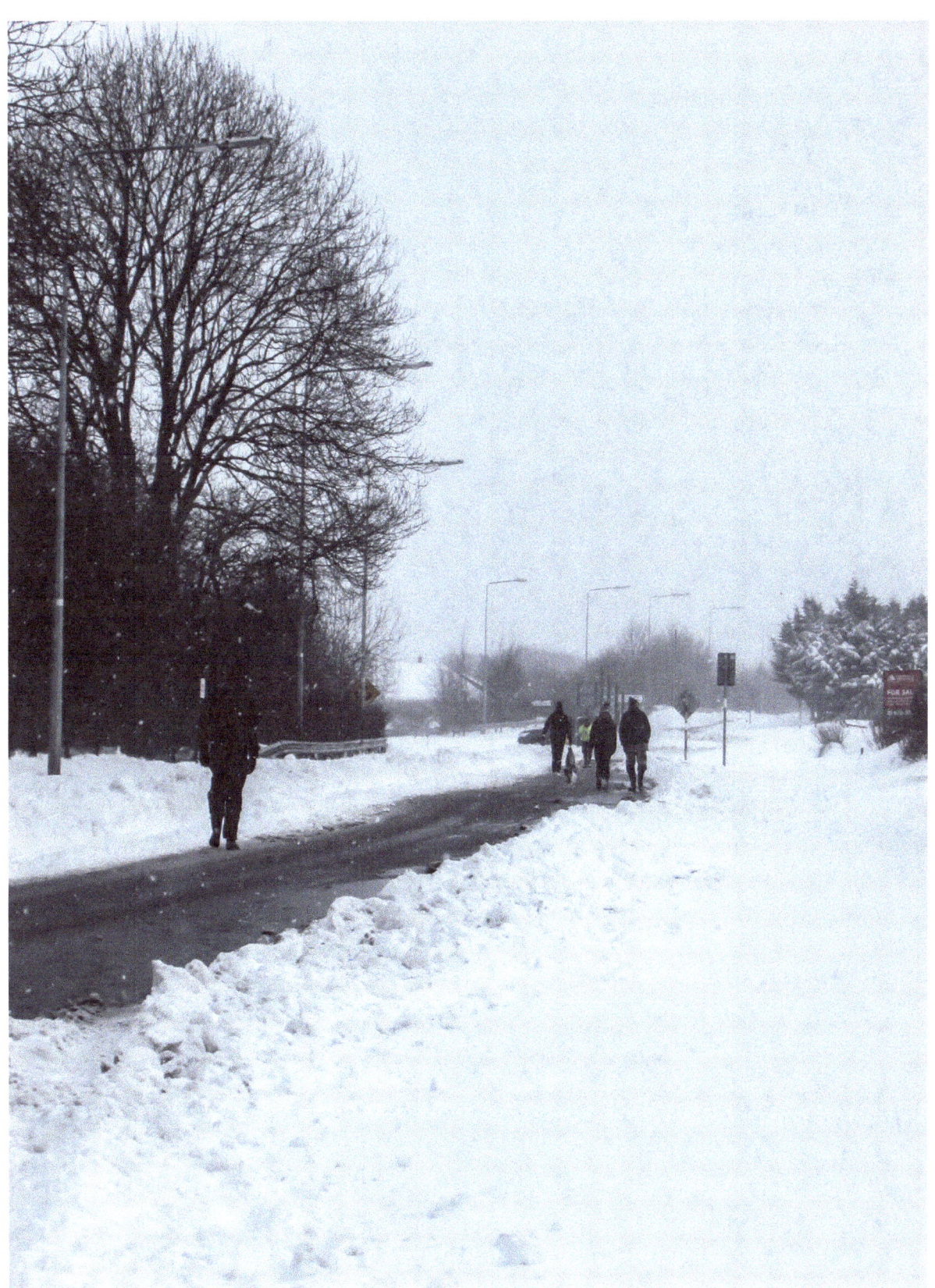

Pilgrimage for bread and milk on N81 near Burgage - Heavy Snow 2018

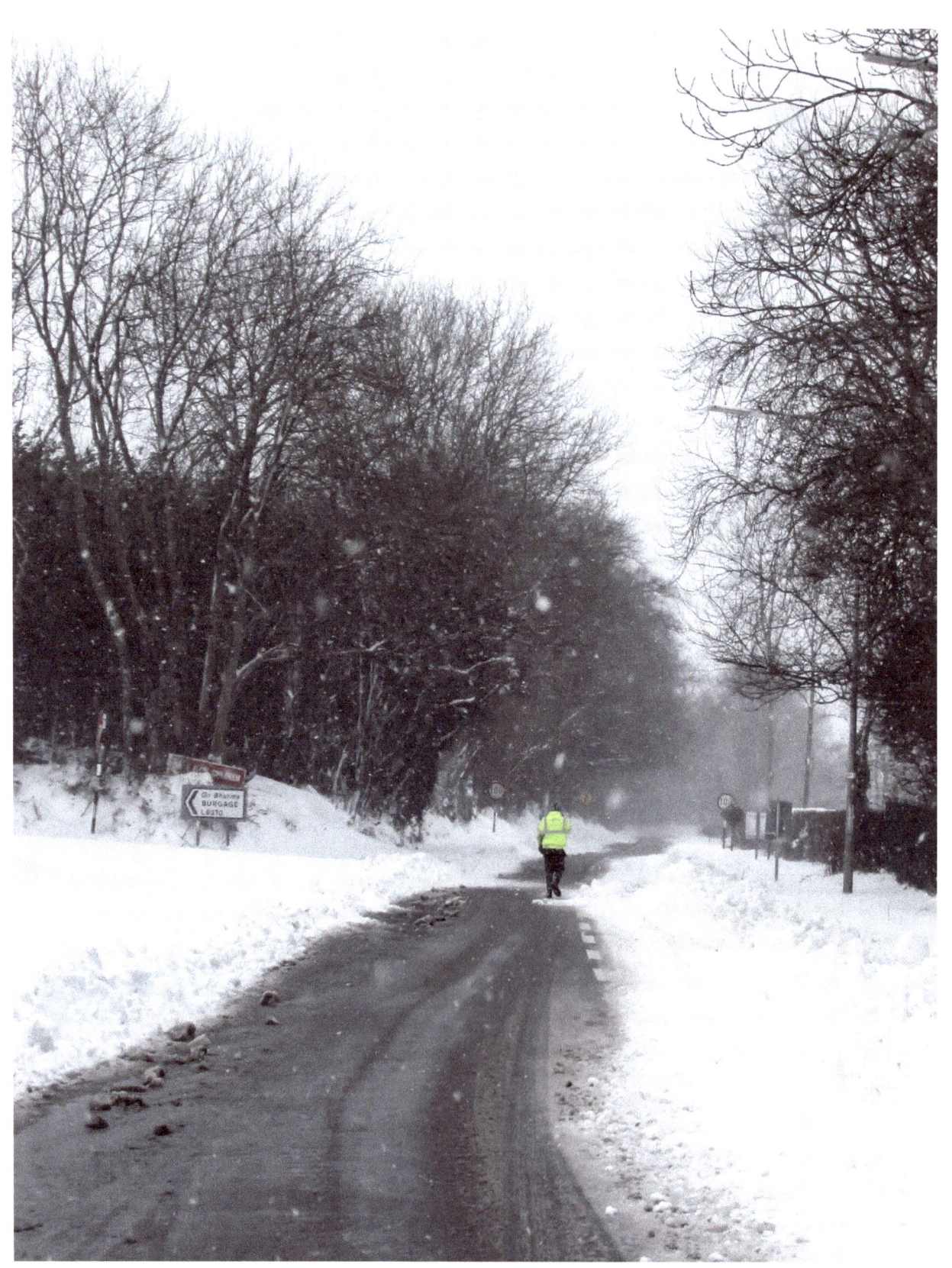

The Long Walk Home - N81 near Burgage - Heavy Snow 2018

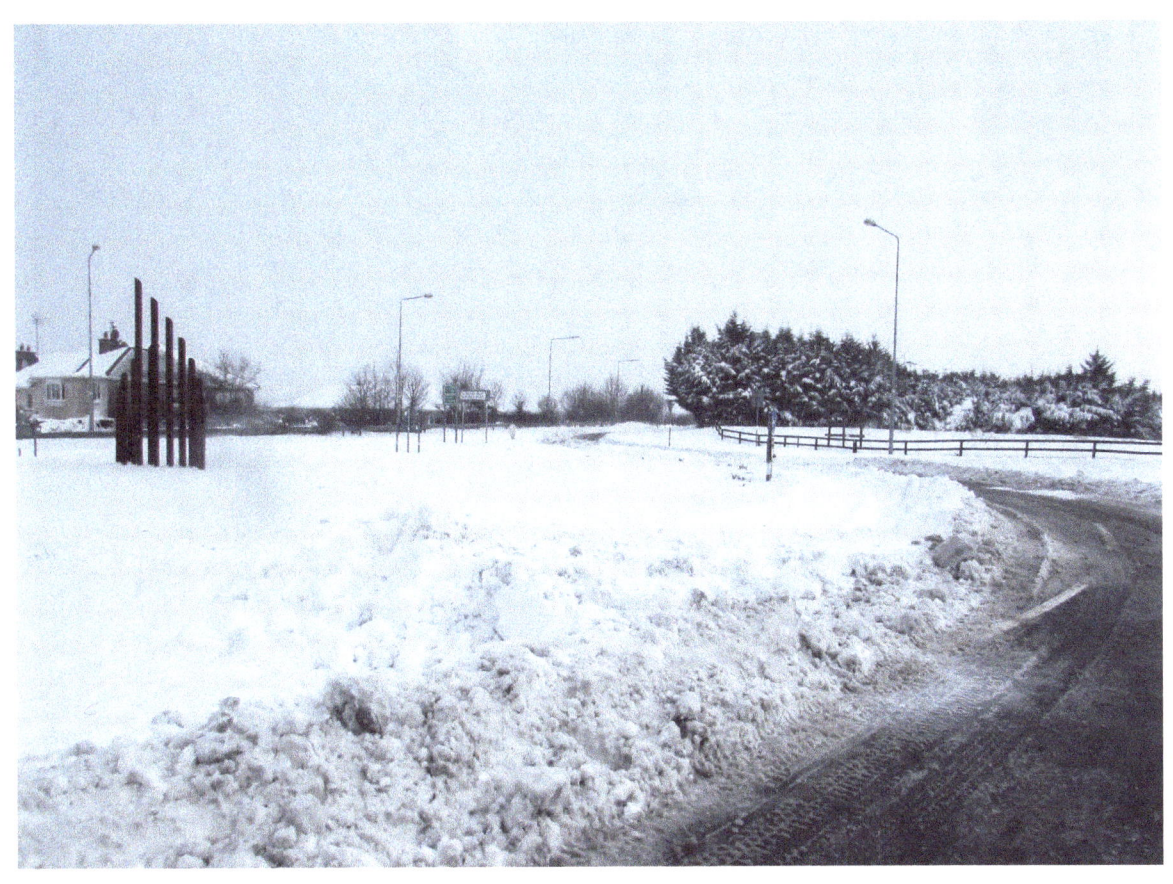

Roundabout on N81 near Burgage - Heavy Snow 2018

Entrance to The Avon - Heavy Snow 2018

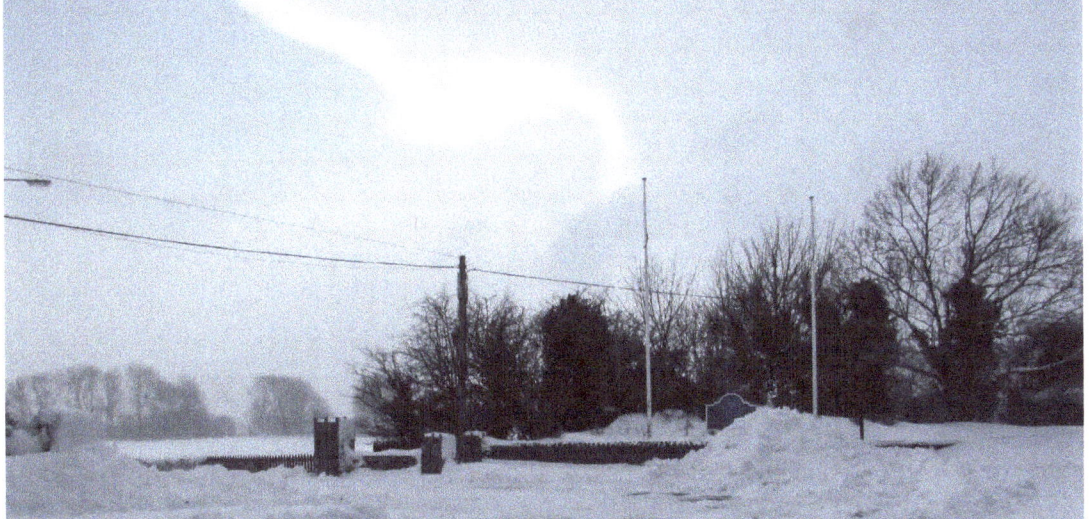

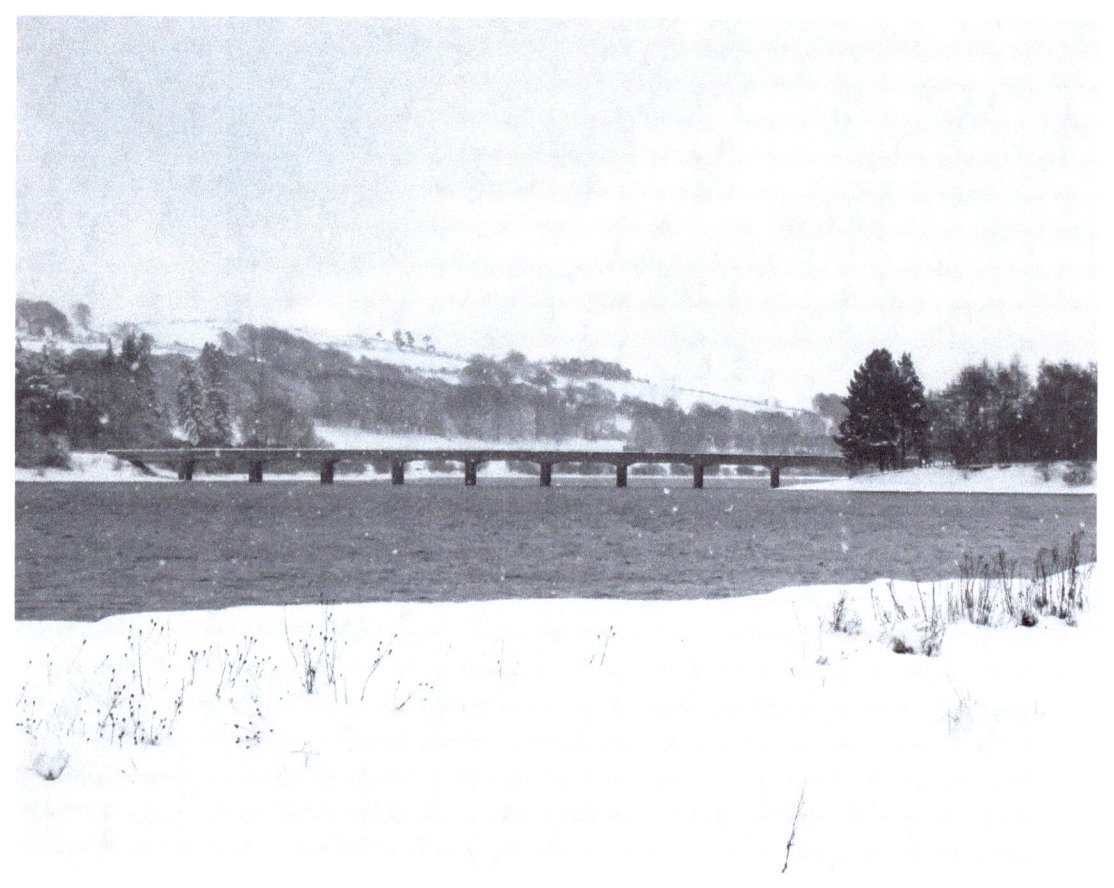

Burgage Bridge and Burgage shoreline - Heavy Snow 2018

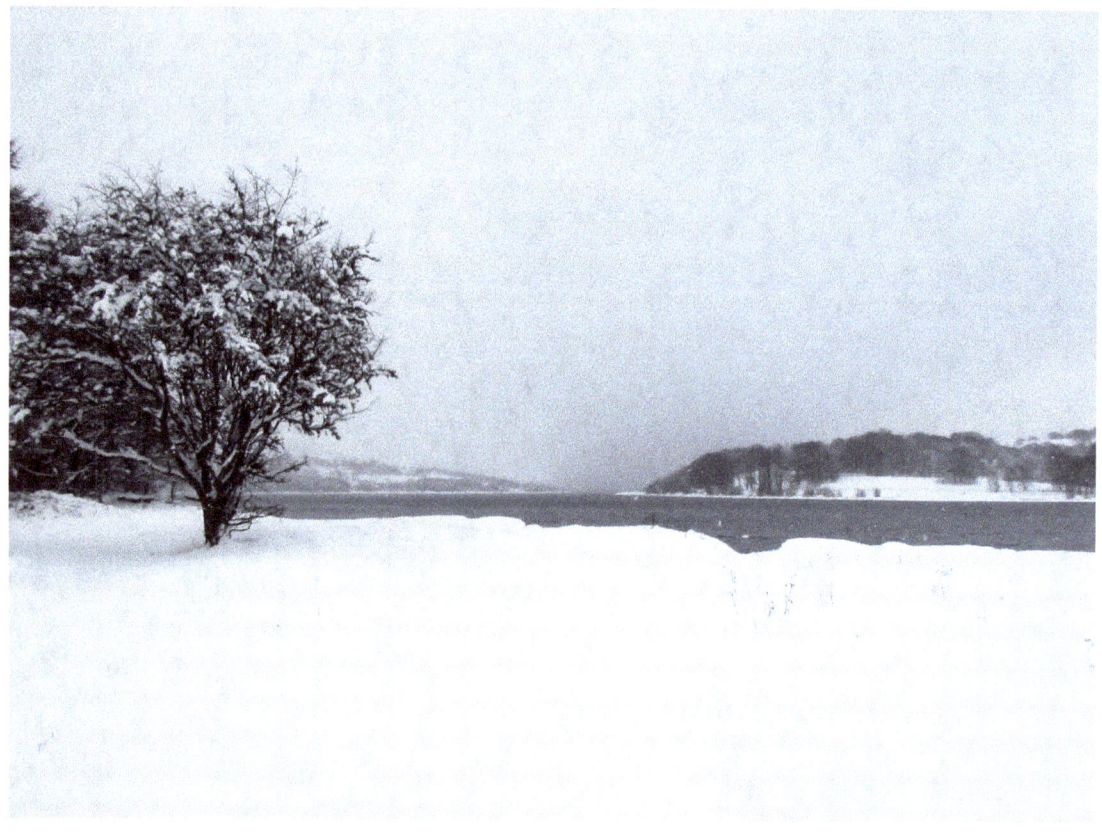

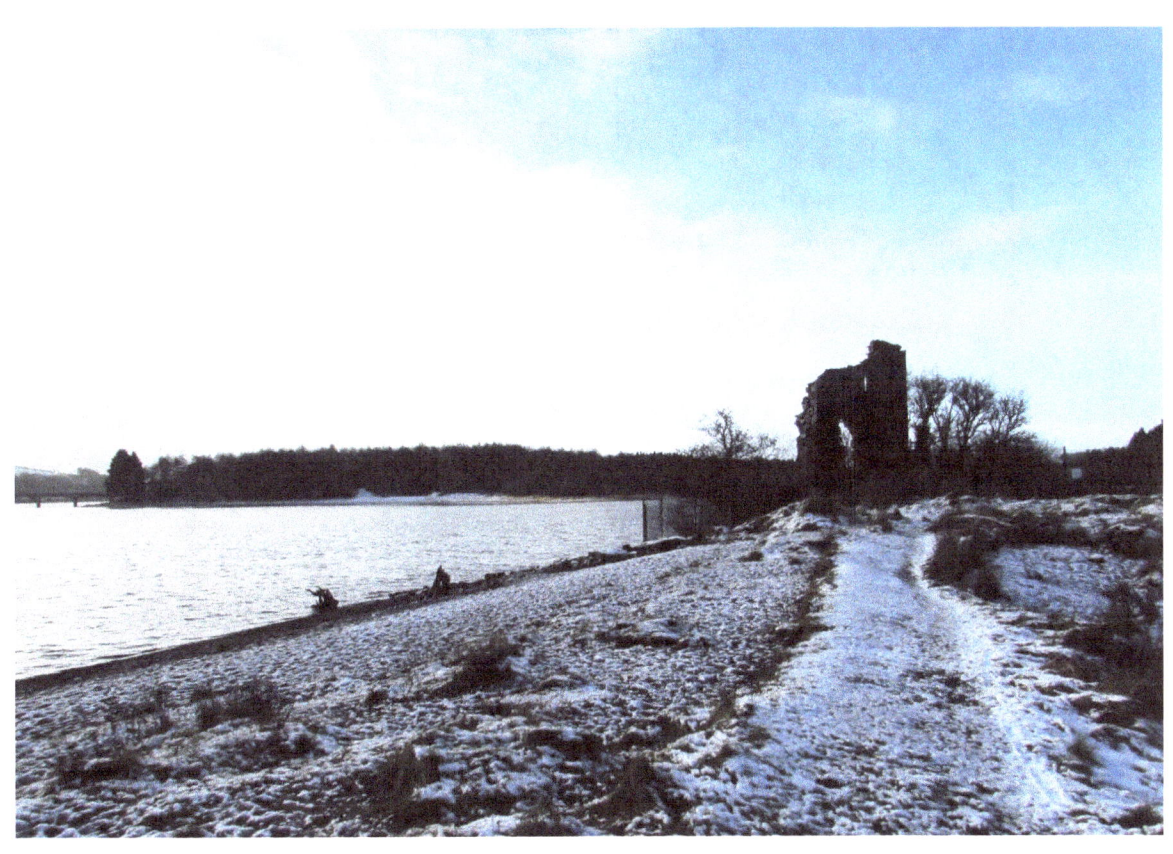
Burgage Tower with a dash of snow - even a hint of it was enough to get me out with the camera!

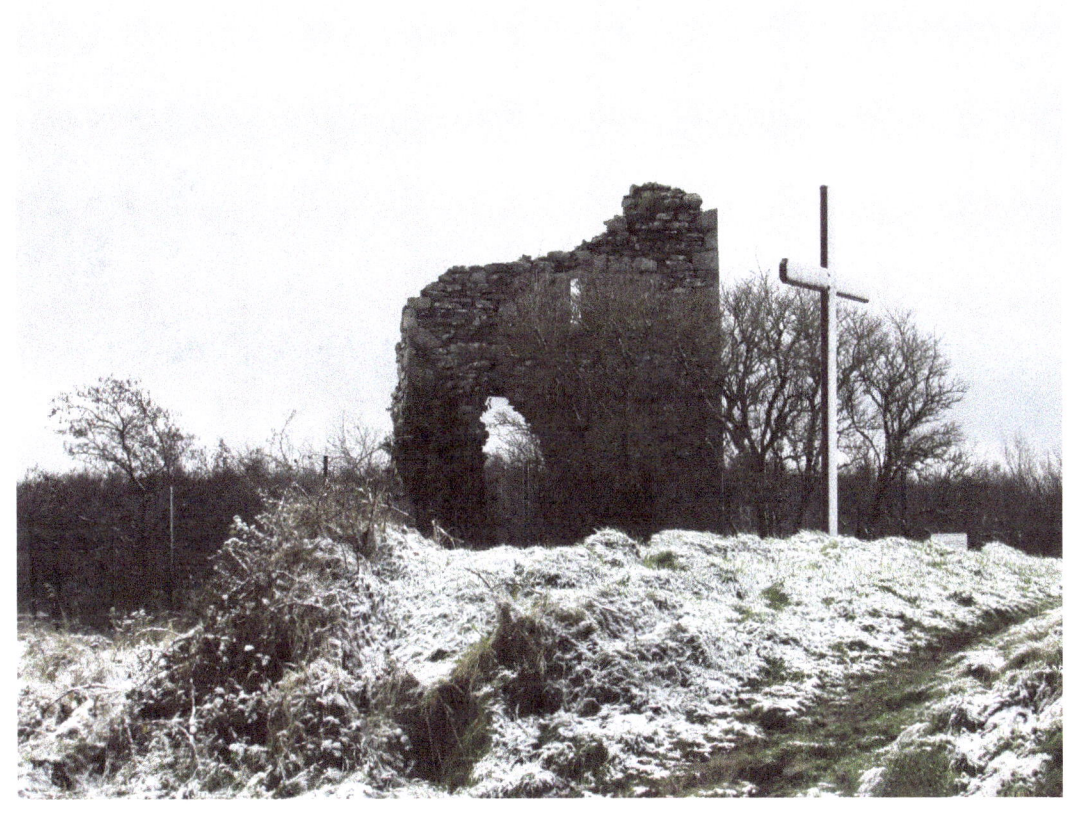

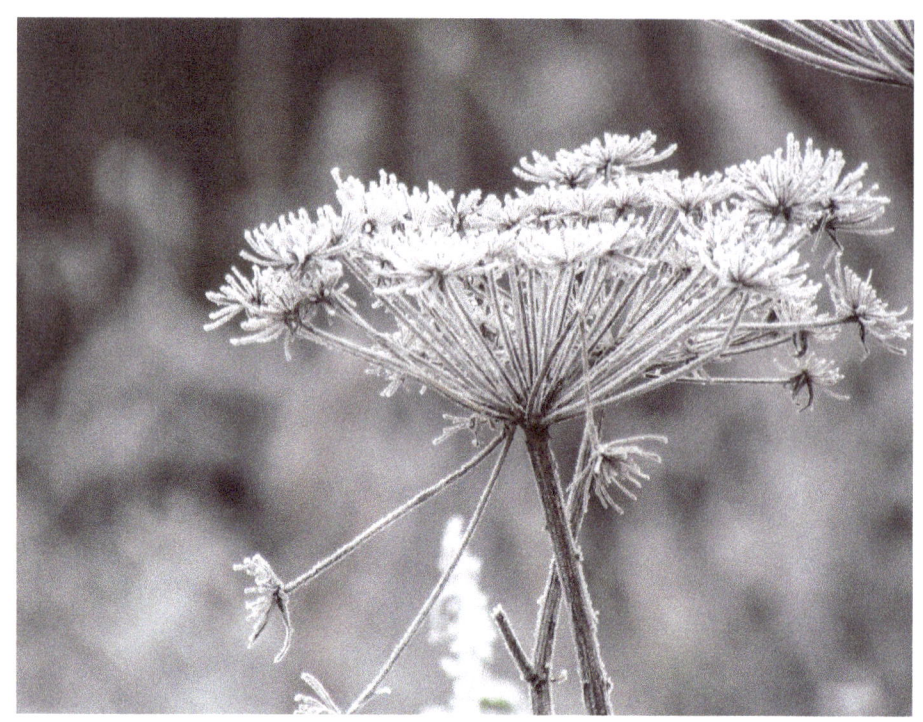

Frozen Hogweed and a frosty leaf, so beautiful to look at.

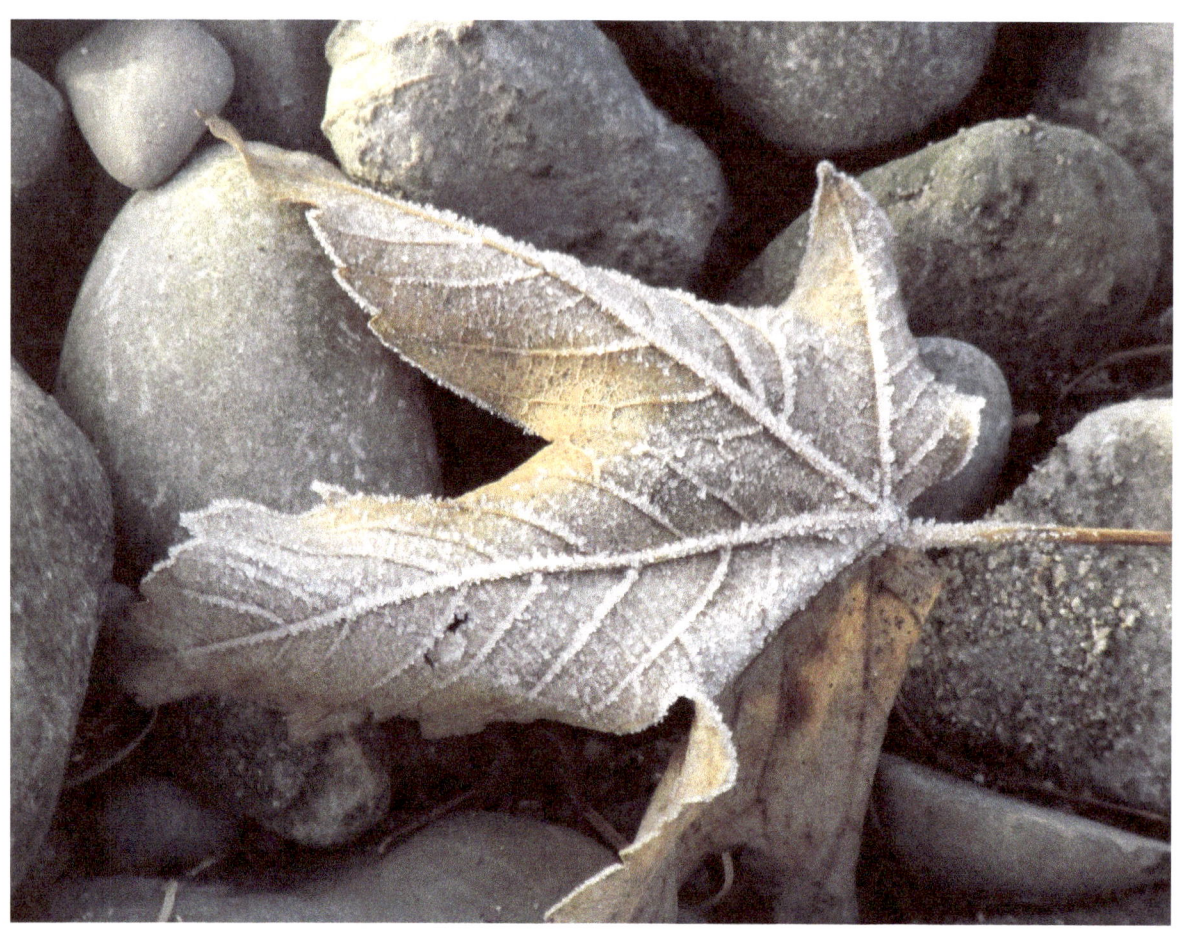

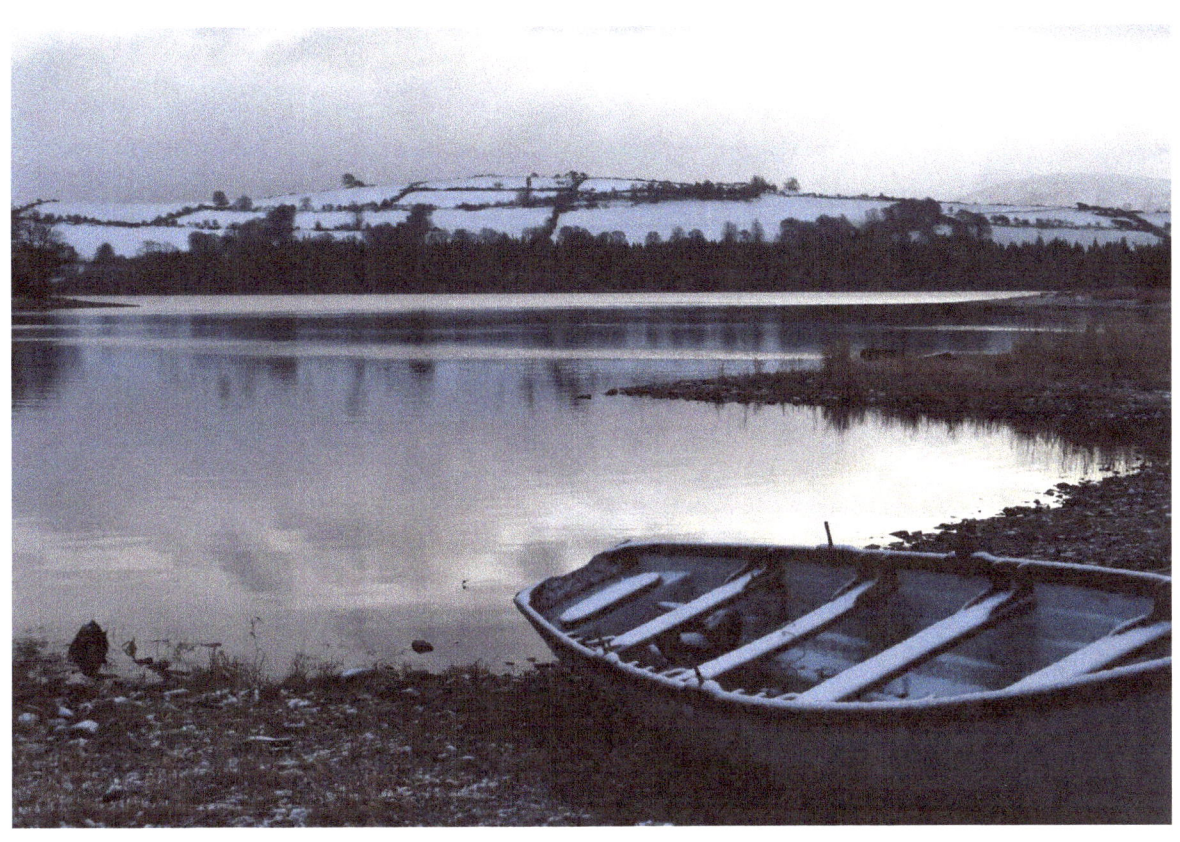

Russellstown is amazing when there is snow or frost

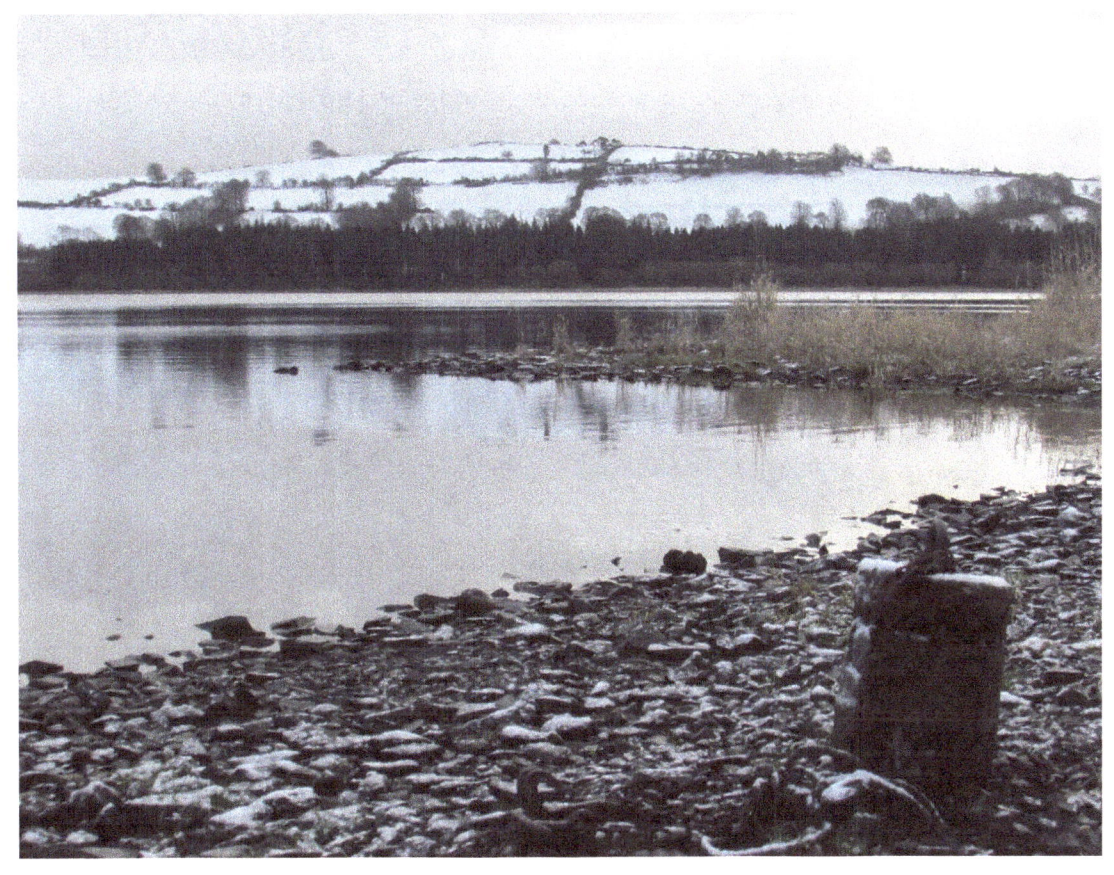

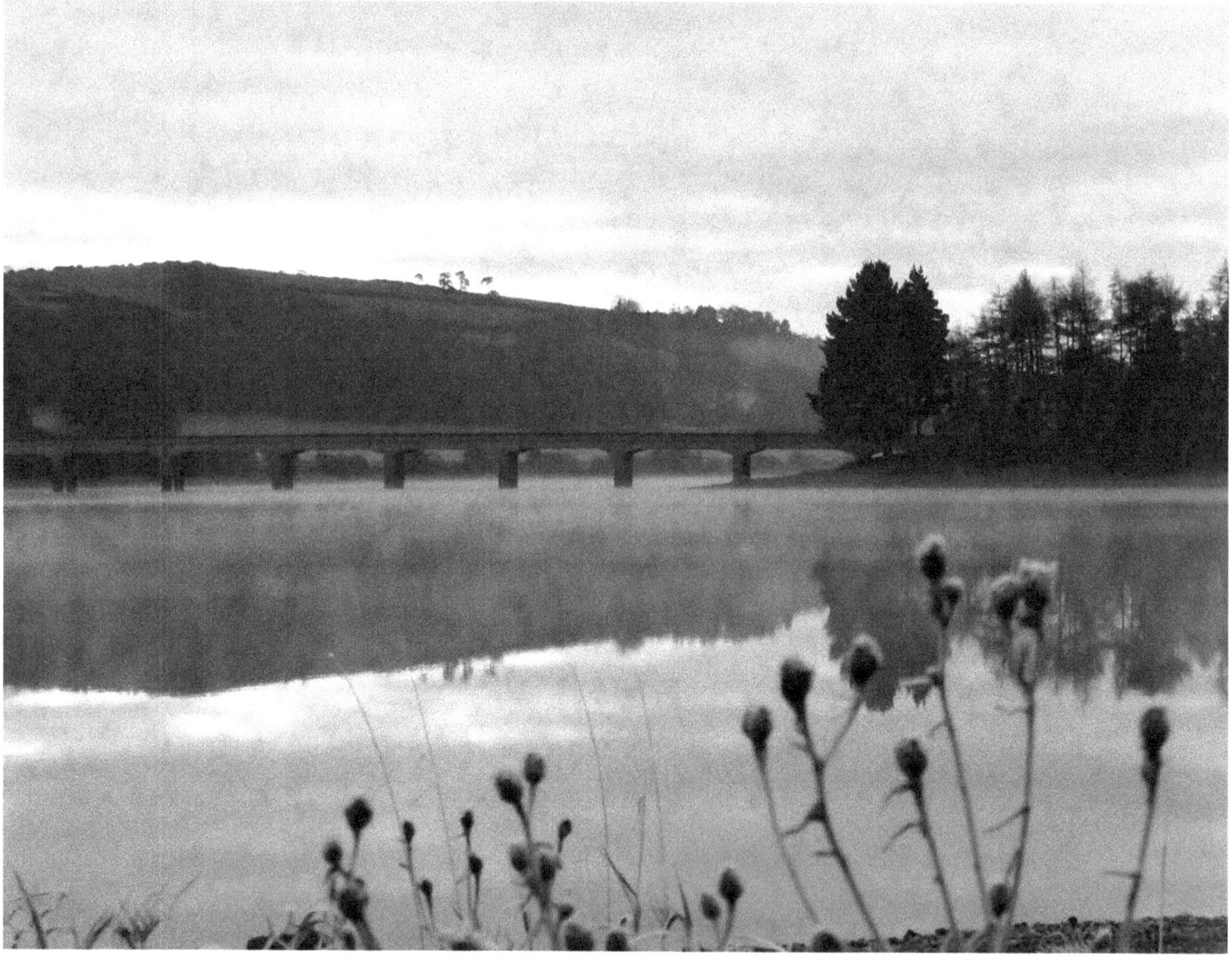

A cold morning looking over at Burgage Bridge and Baltyboys area

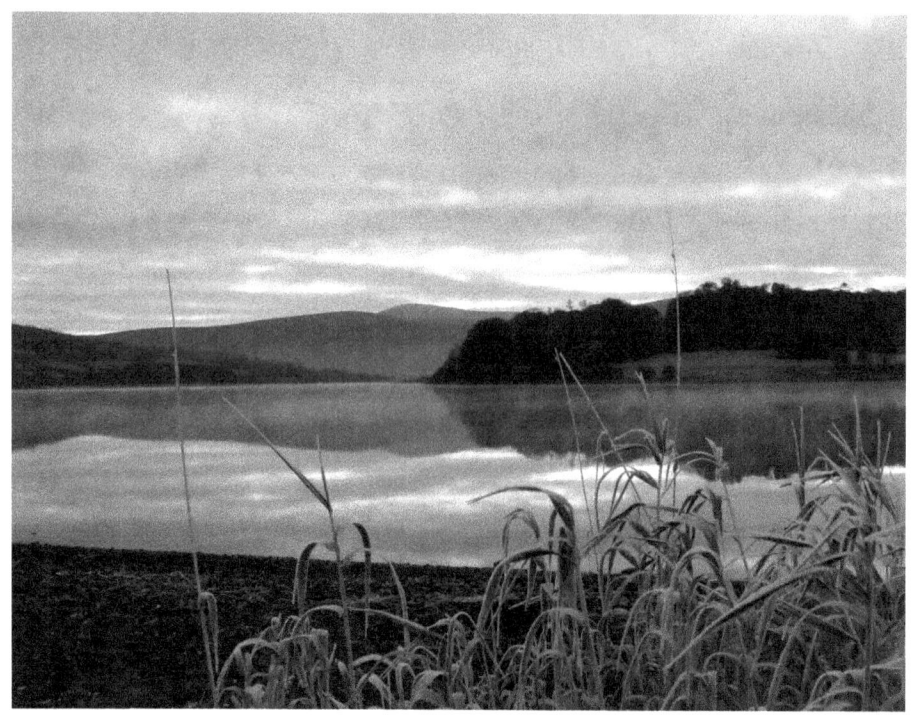

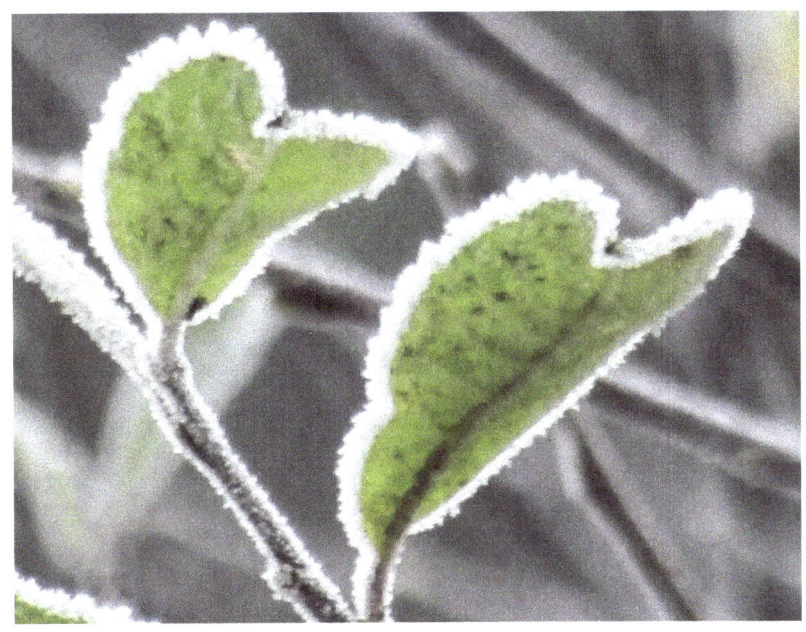

Love is all around me - even in the leaves!

View from the N81 - The lakes looking lovely on this chilly morning!

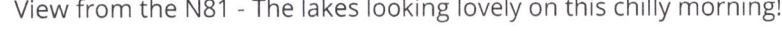

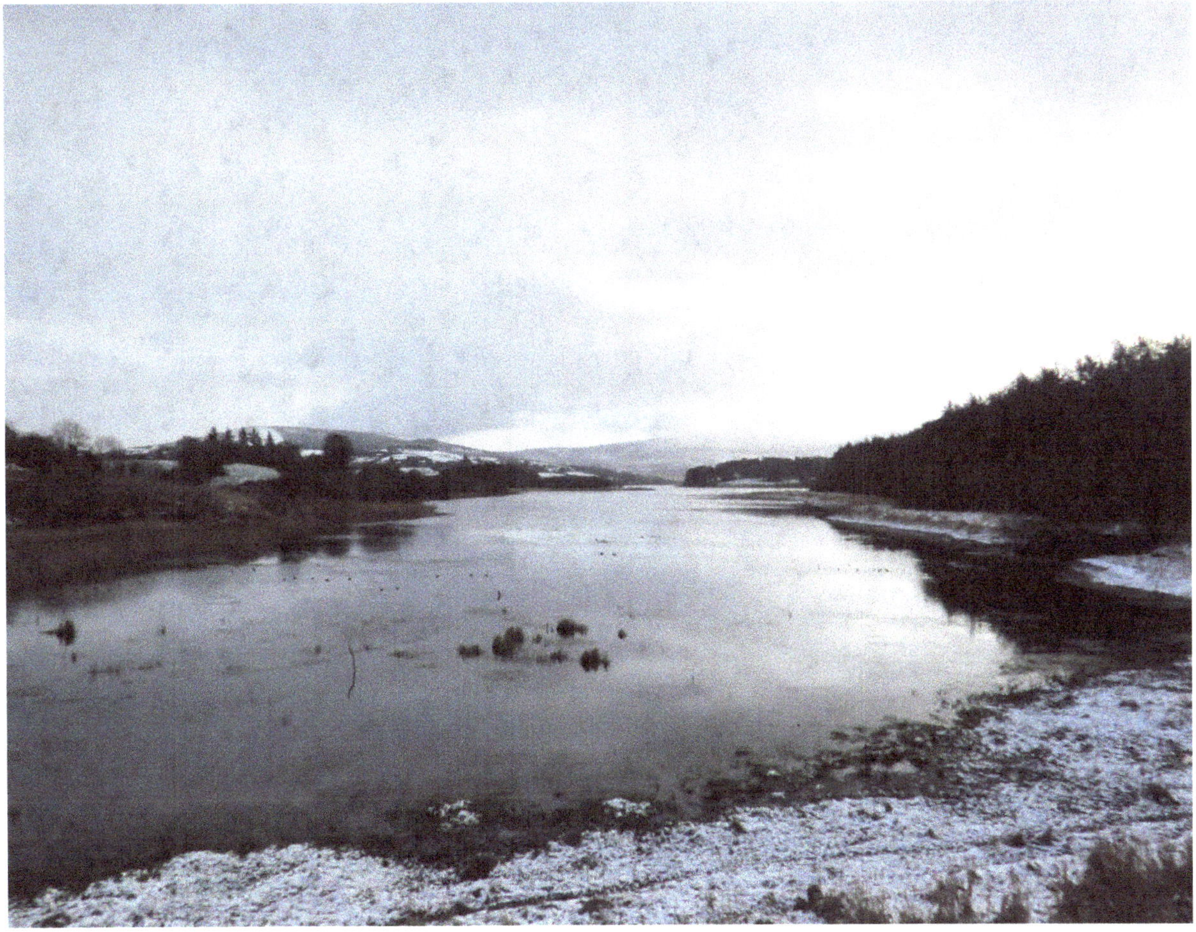

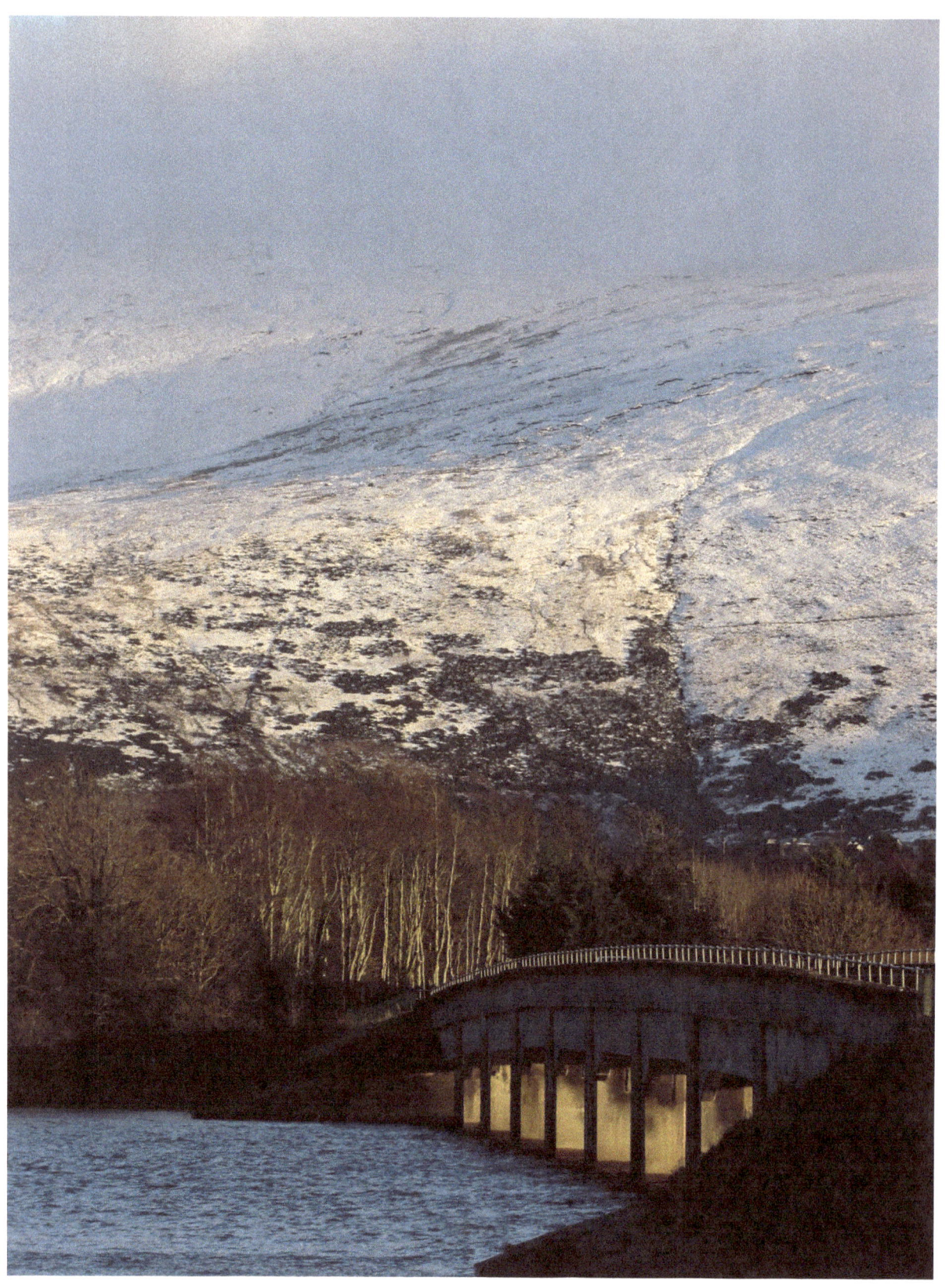

The evening sun highlights Valleymount Bridge and there's a beautiful backdrop of snow

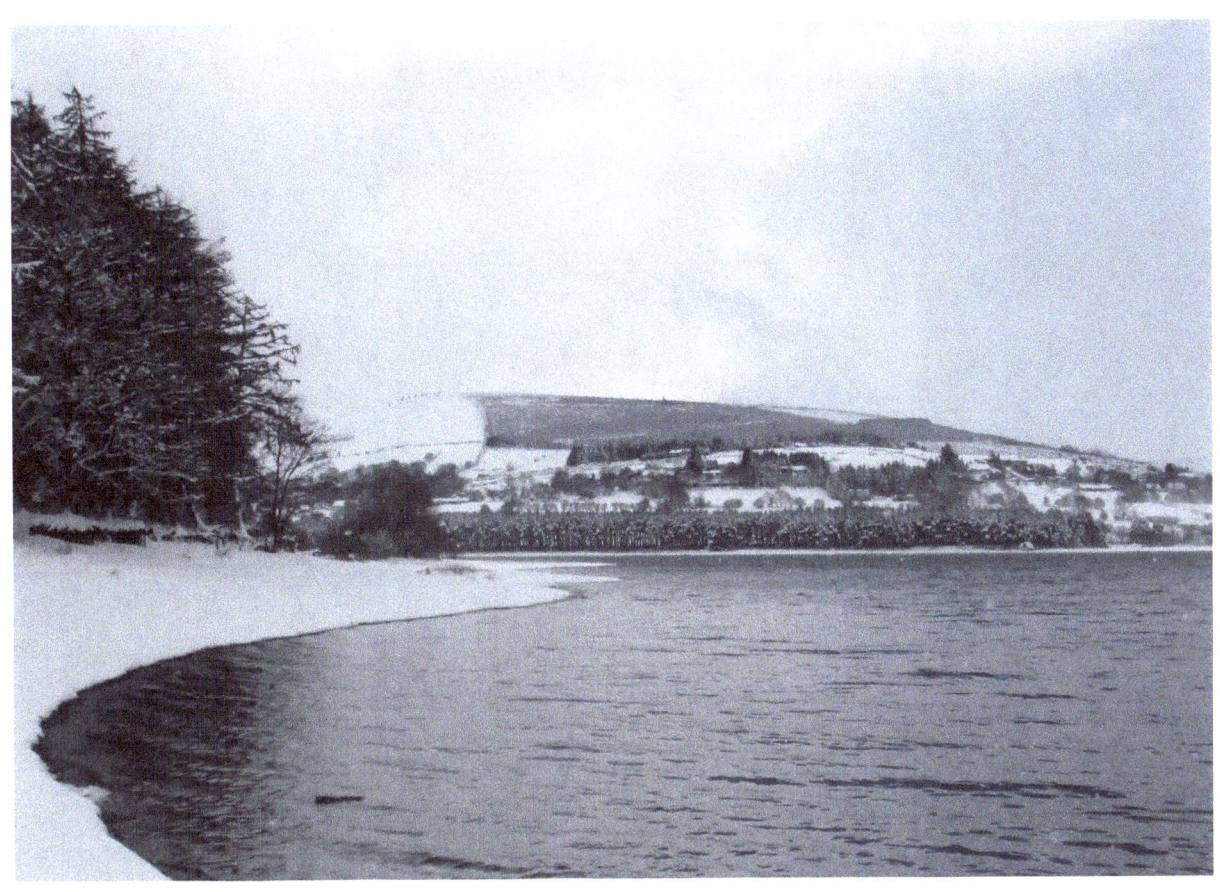

Burgage Shoreline with a dash of snow - facing Lackan

The reeds add a splash of colour in the snowy landscape - near The Avon

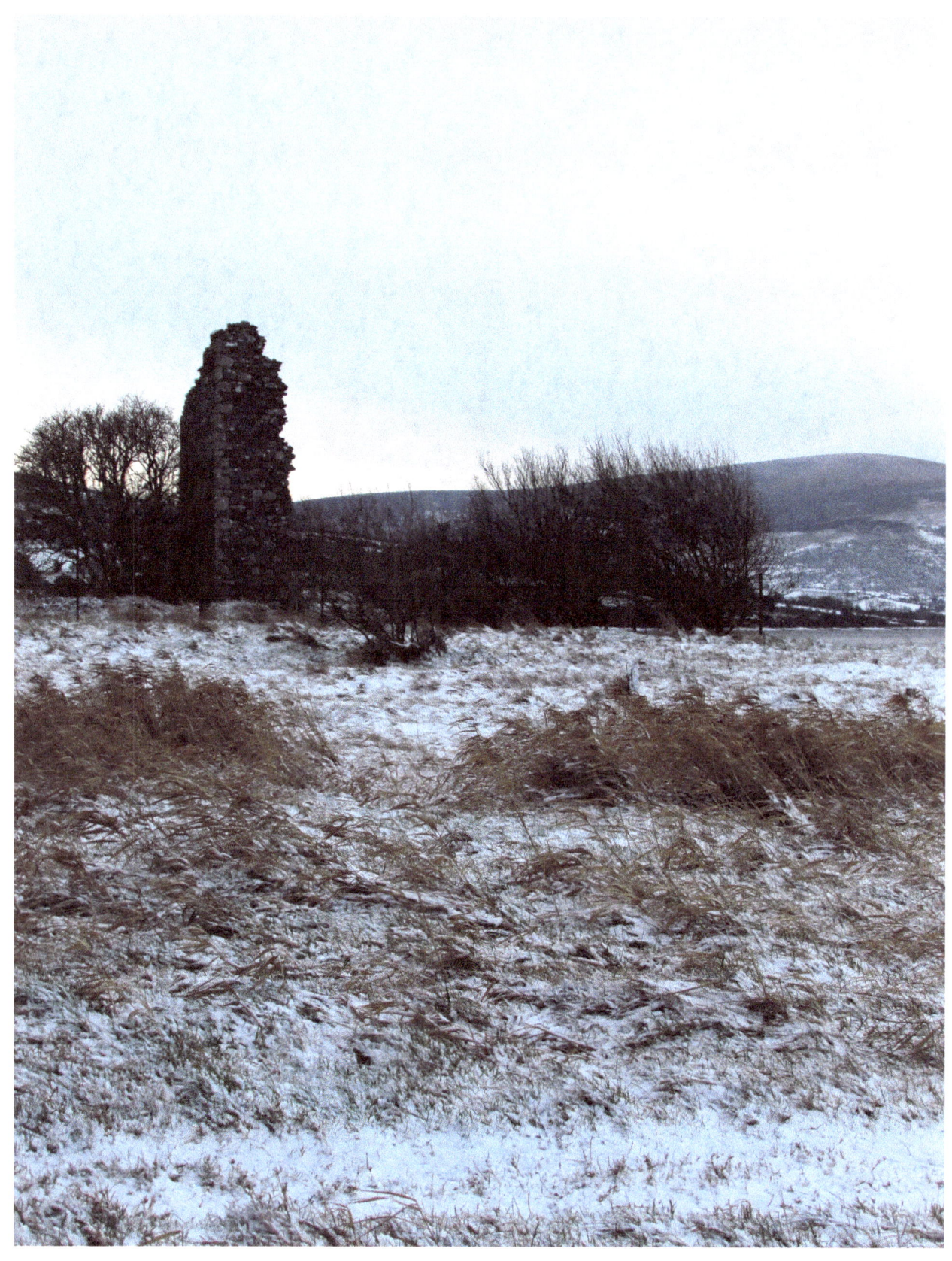

Burgage Tower on a cold day

ARTWORK VS PHOTOGRAPHY

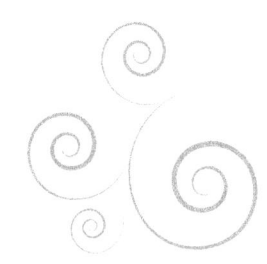

Besides from having a love of photography, my first love was painting and drawing. For a long time I longed to paint what I was seeing on my rambles.

But the energy wasn't there, and I wasn't sure about techniques as I'm self taught. It was easier to just snap a photo, do a little editing when I got home, and then share the photos.

However there came a time when that was no longer enough for me, and so I set myself an Art vs Photography Challenge. Mostly it was a photo I had taken locally, then I would try to recreate it . Then I decided to try some historic work based on old photos I found on internet searches.

I thoroughly enjoyed this and have continued doing this. I paint in acrylics and sometimes mixed media. I had this very odd notion as I was growing up that mixing media was somehow breaking a rule, I've no idea where that came from, but if there are rules, I now do try to break them, where painting is concerned anyway!

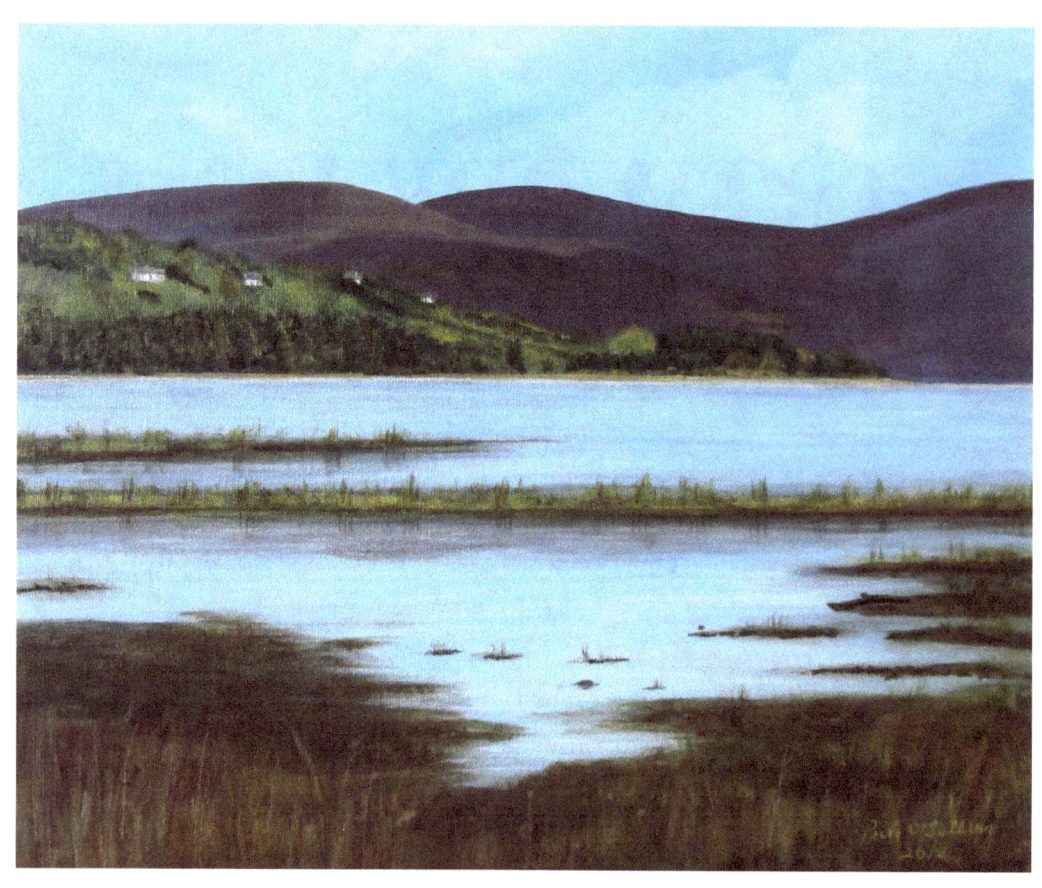

Blessington Greenway between the Avon and Burgage - top artwork - below the photo I took

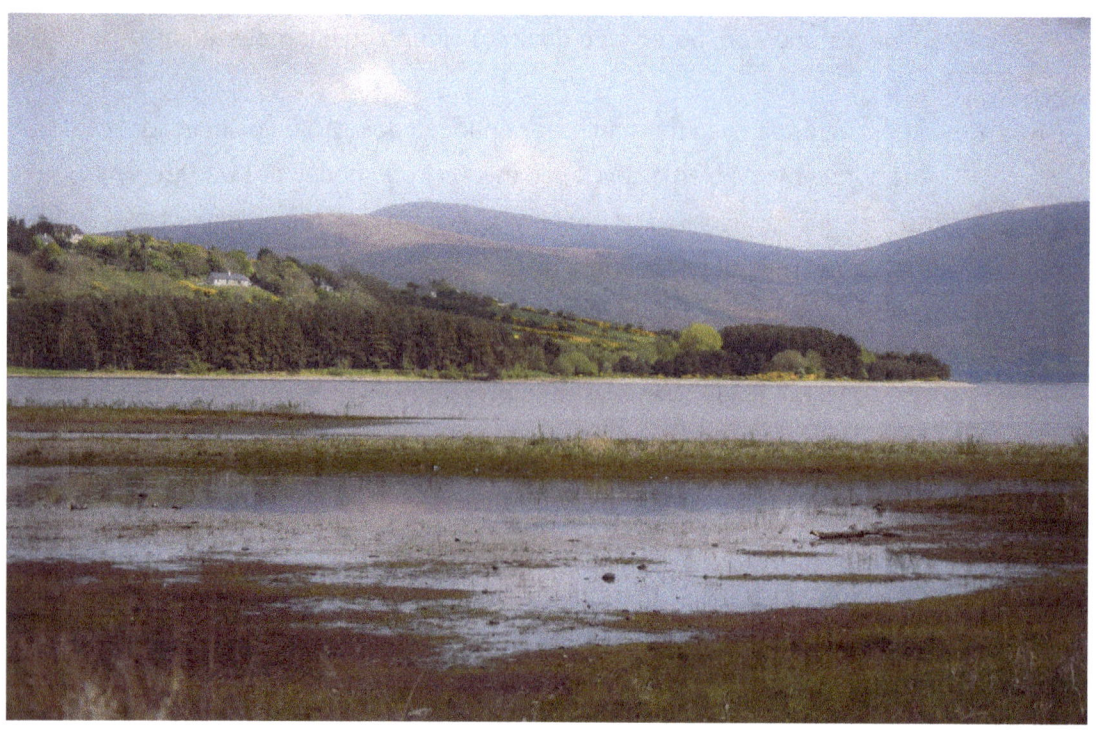

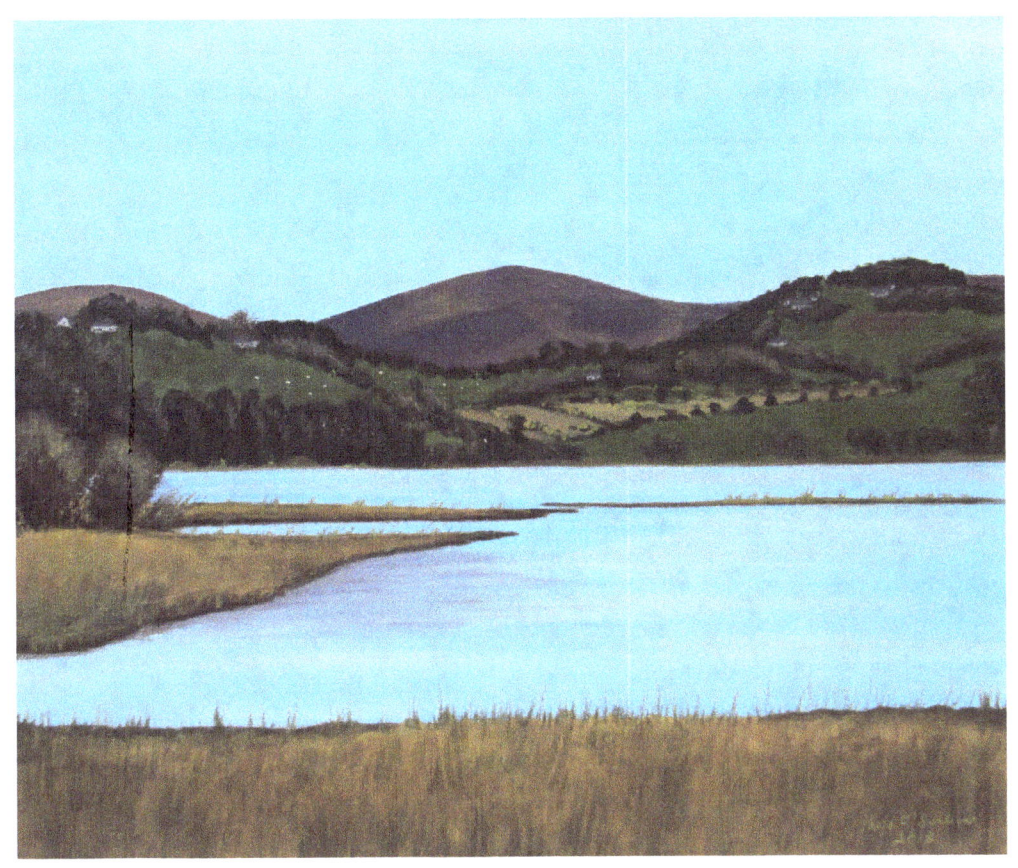

Between The Avon and Burgage on The Greenway - My artwork, top is not always an exact copy of the photo I took, below

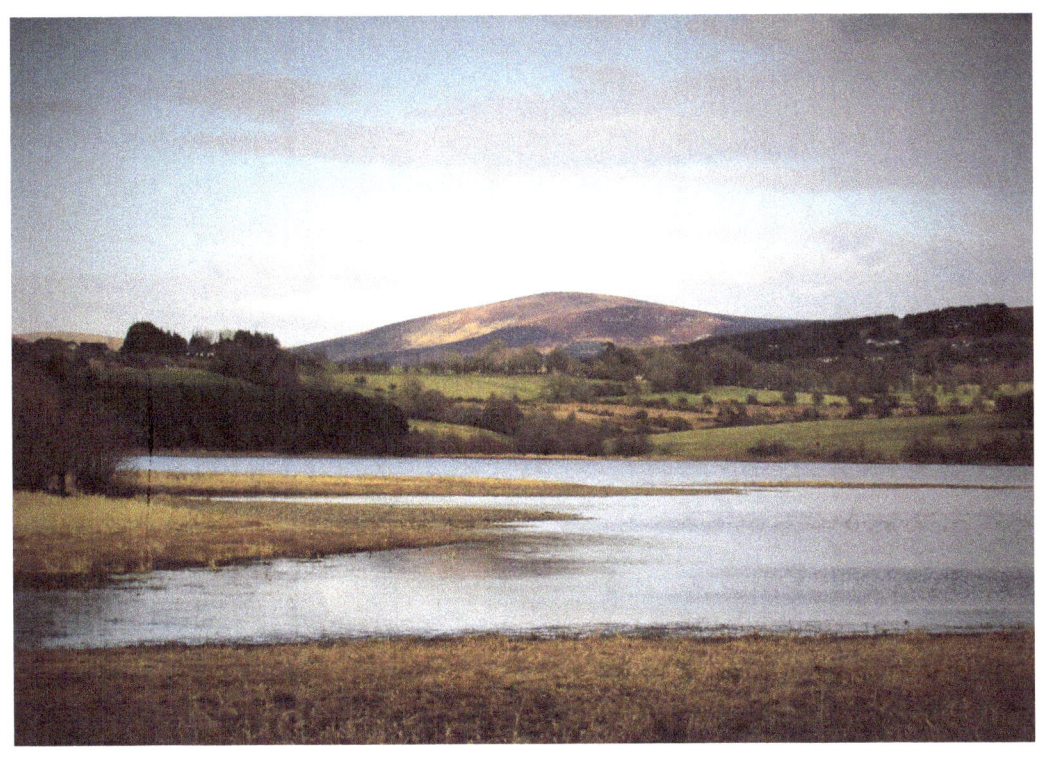

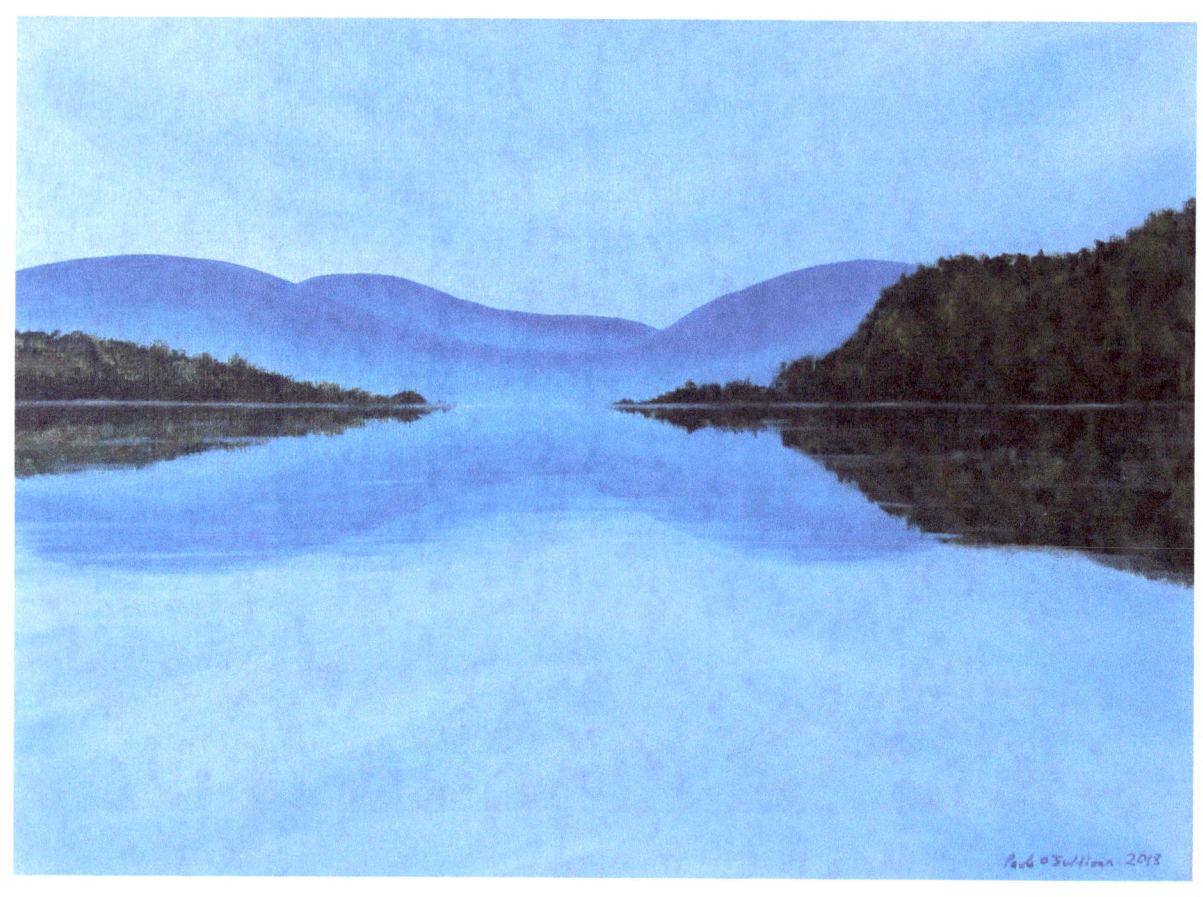

Blessington Lakes viewed from Burgage shoreline - artwork top and my photo below

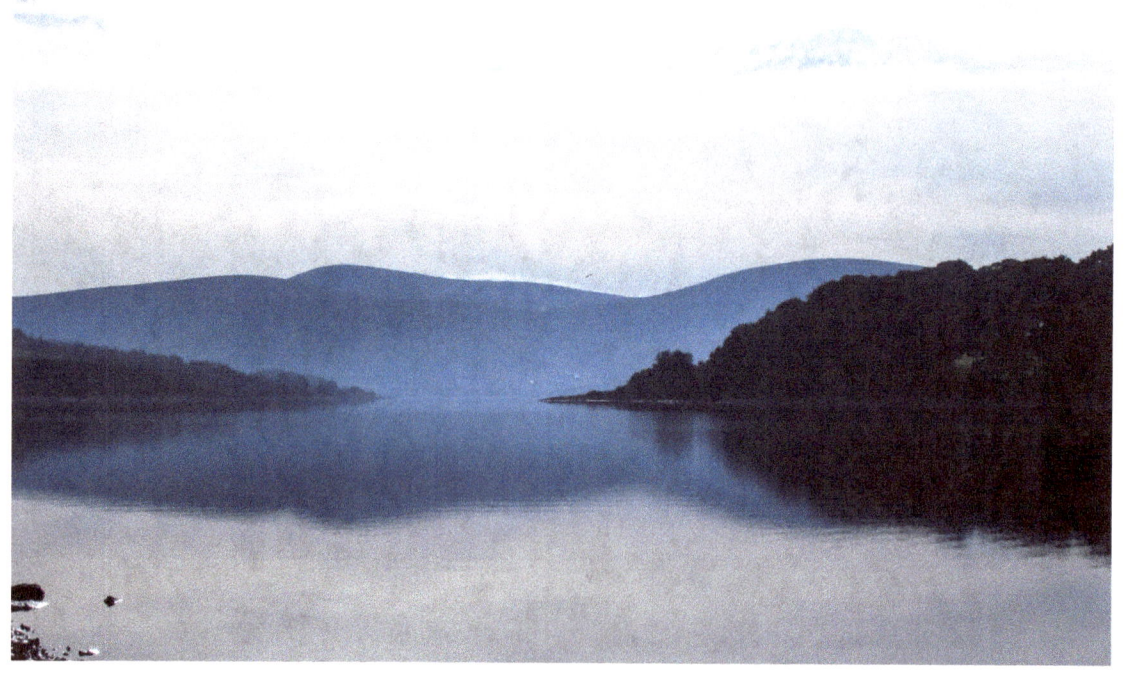

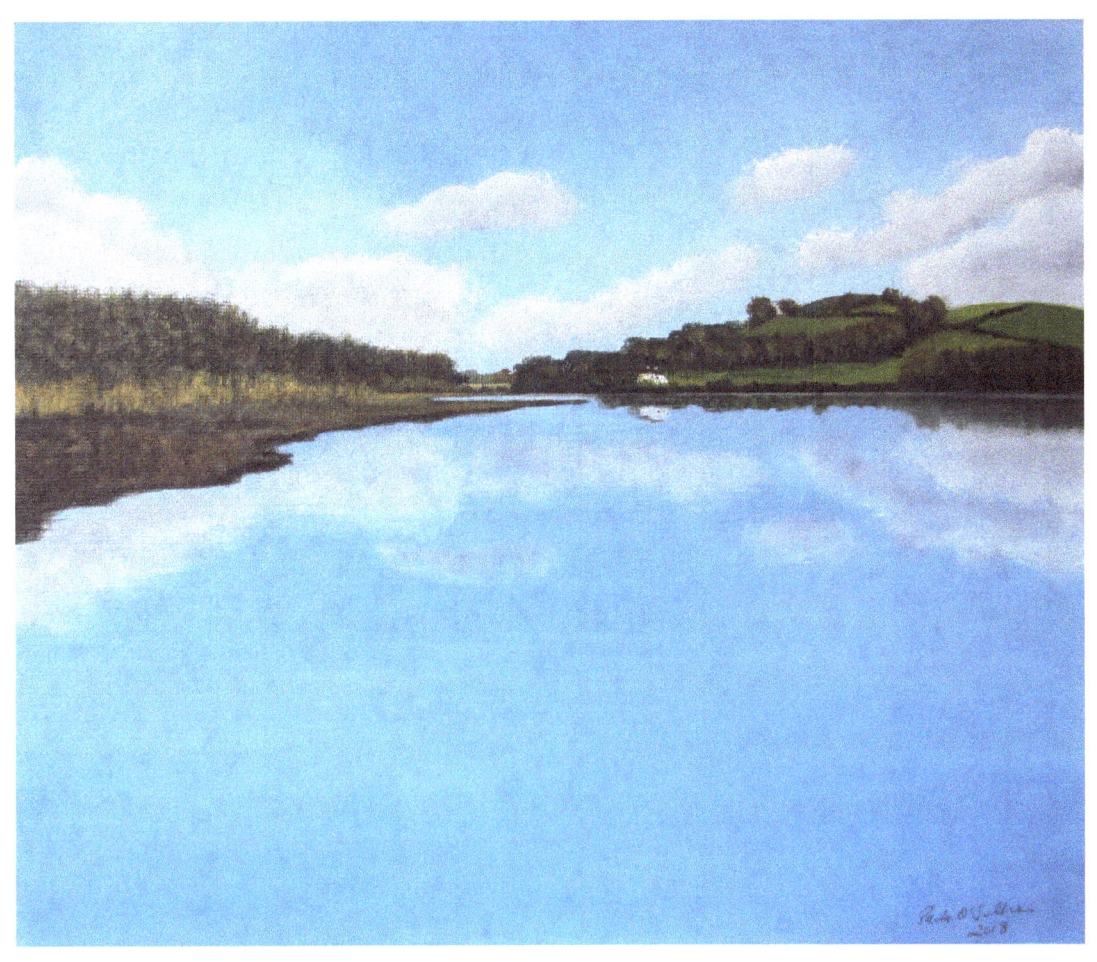

Blessington Lakes and Baltyboys House - artwork top and my photo below

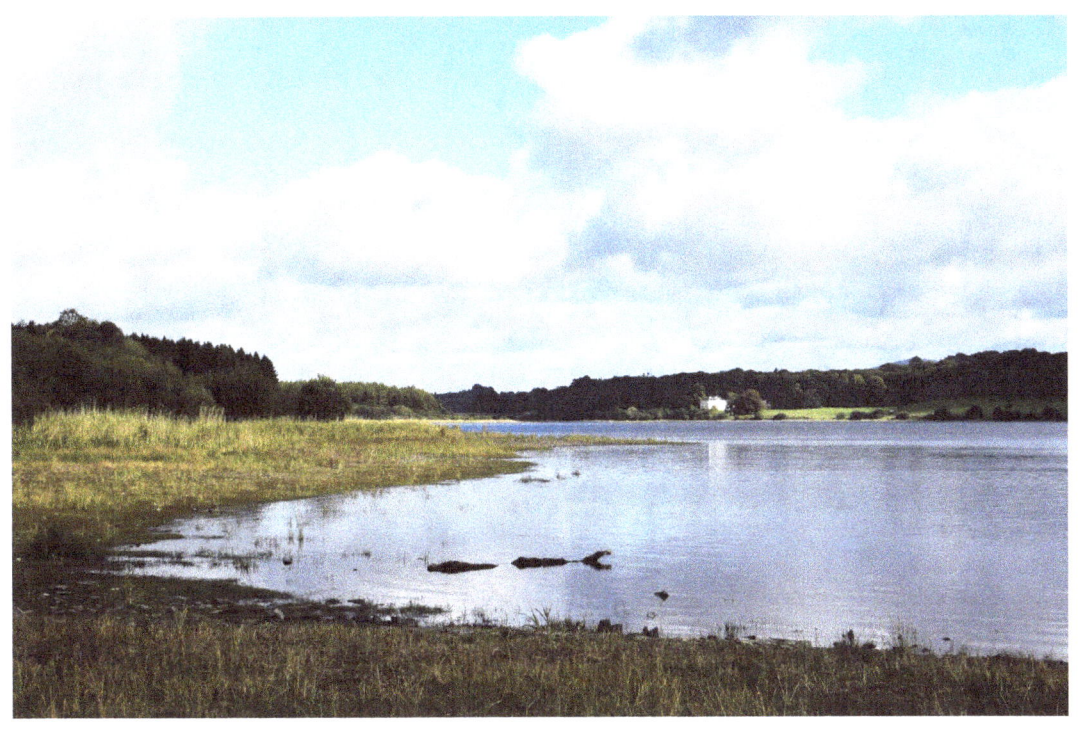

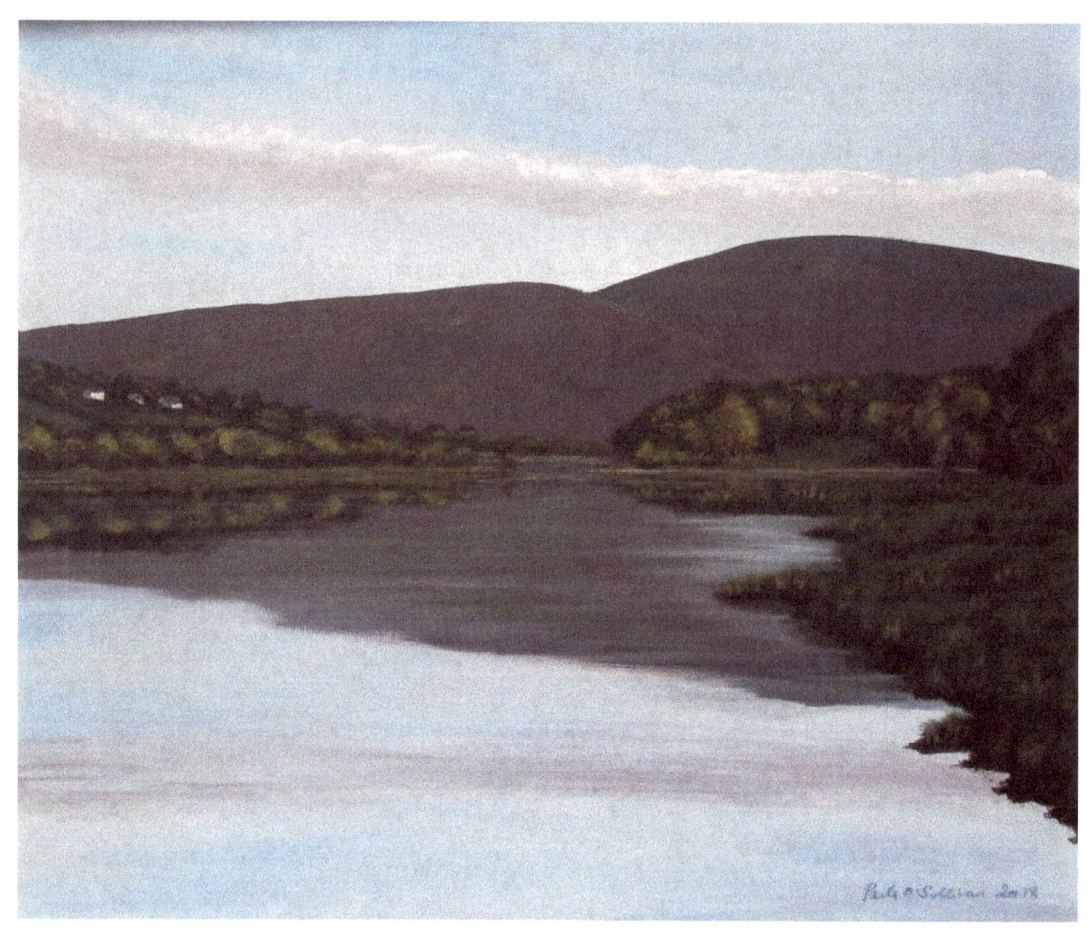

Blessington Lakes from N81 - My artwork top and my photo below

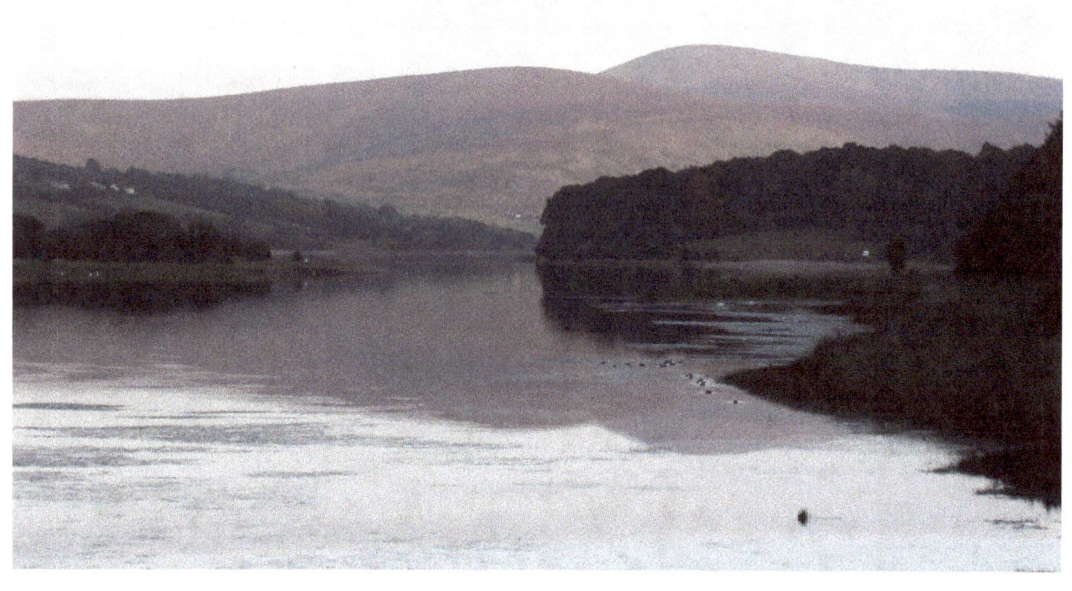

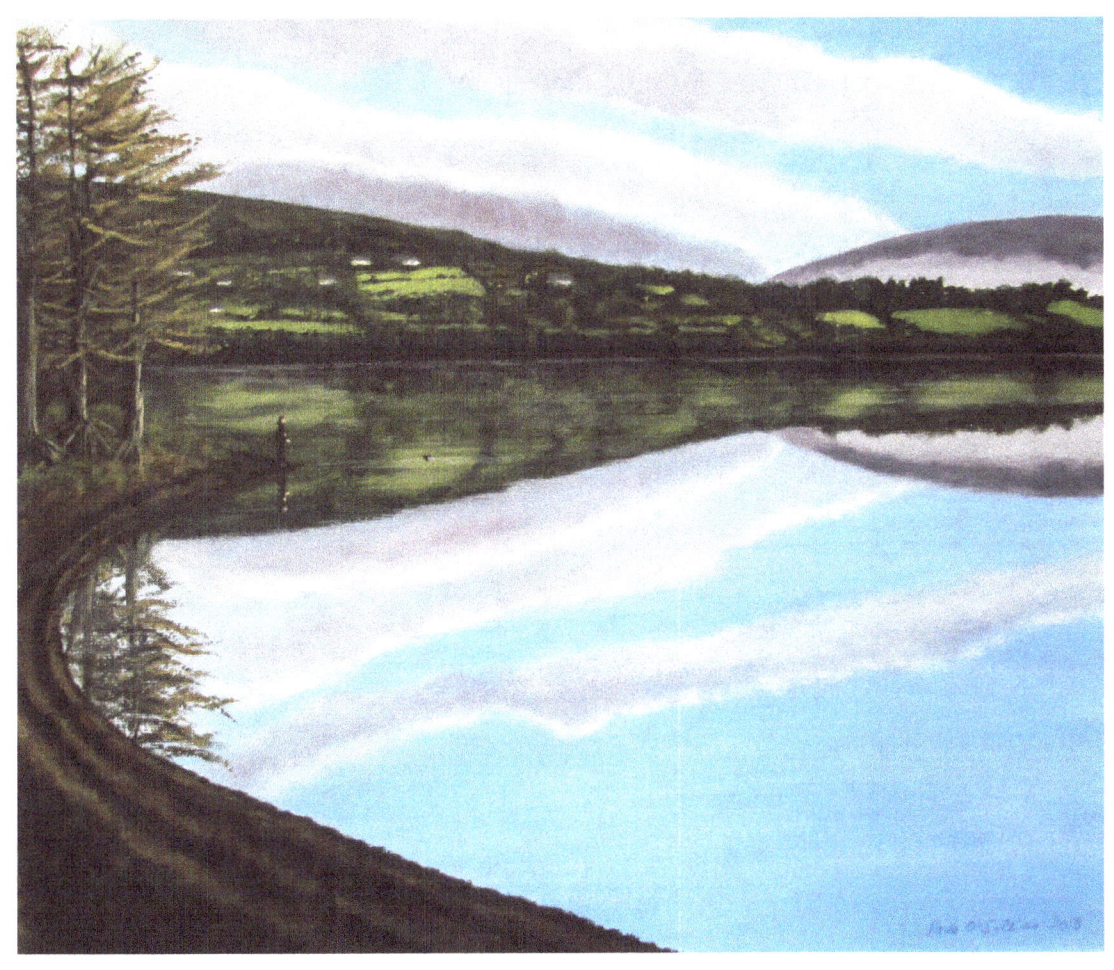

Blessington Lakes viewed from Burgage shoreline - My artwork top and my photo below

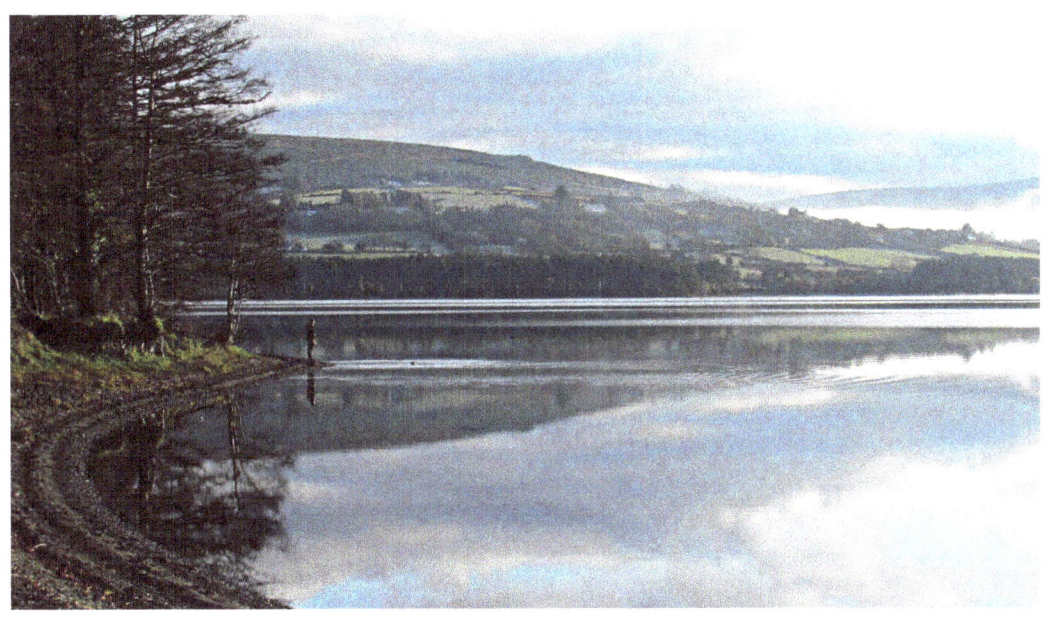

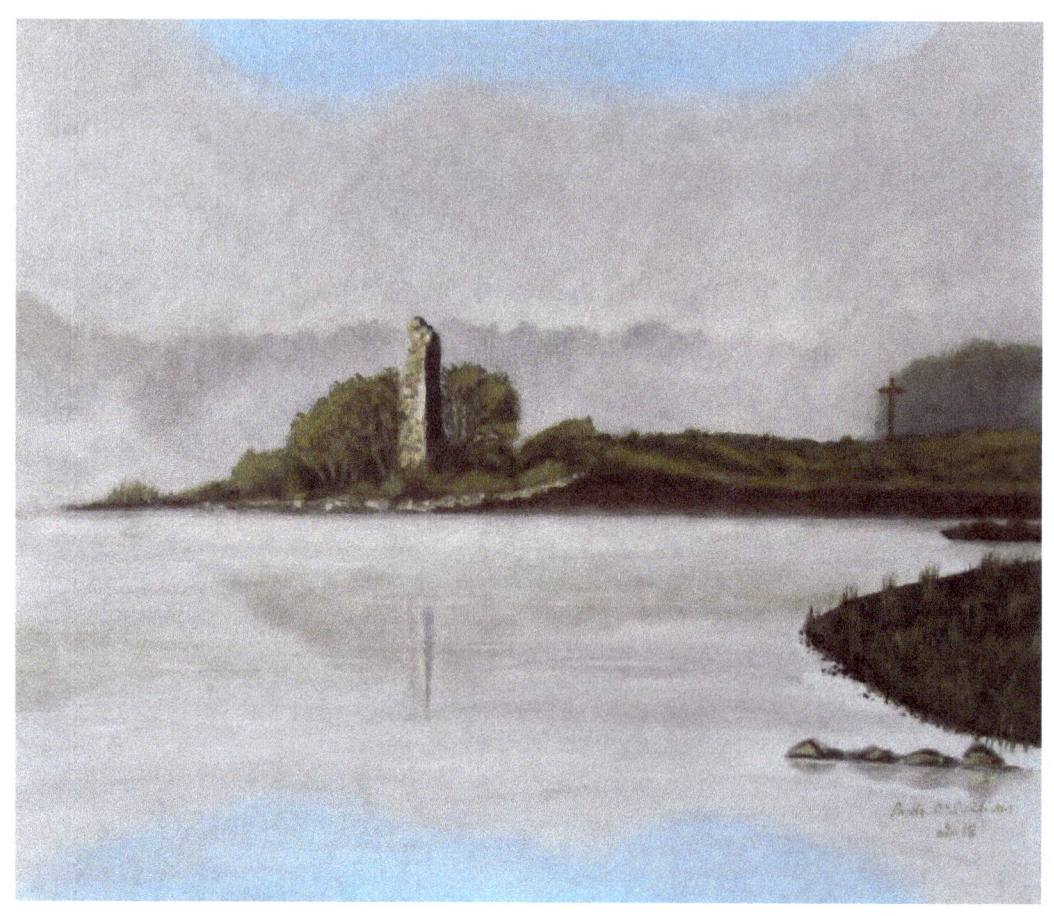

Burgage Tower - My artwork top and my photo below

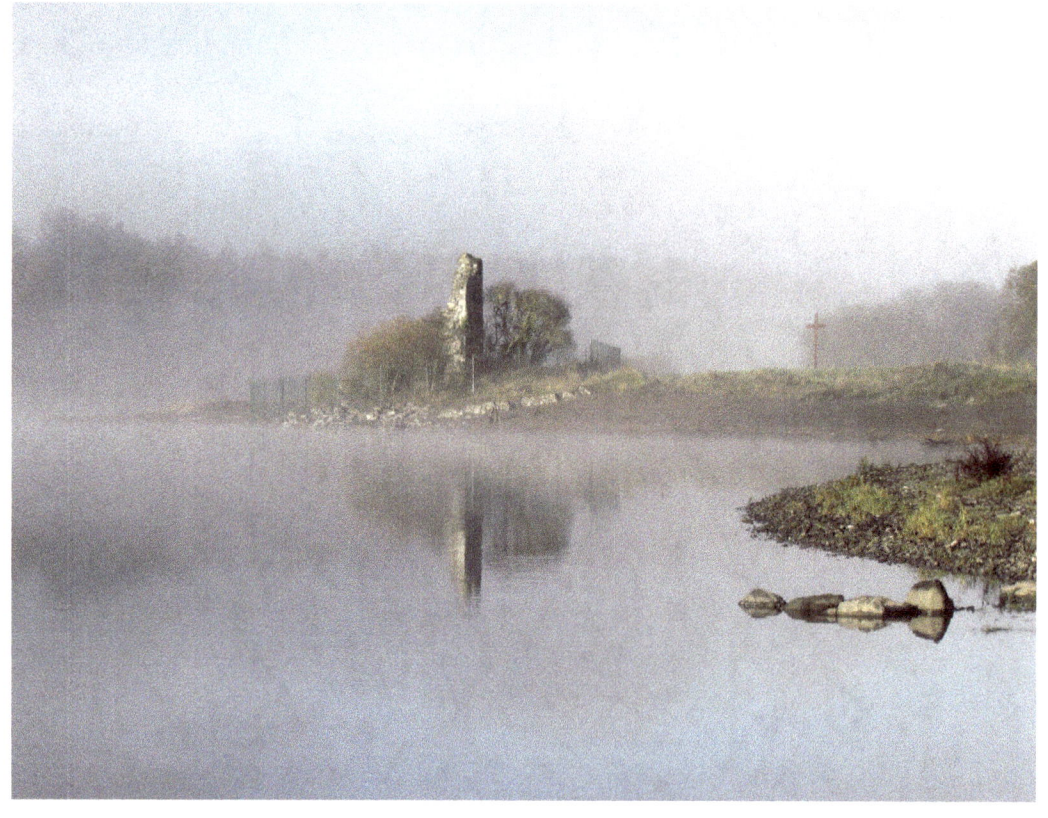

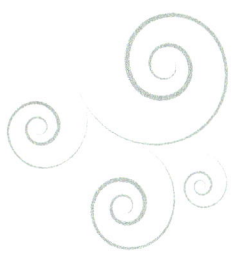

Blessington Lakes viewed from Burgage shoreline - My artwork top and my photo below

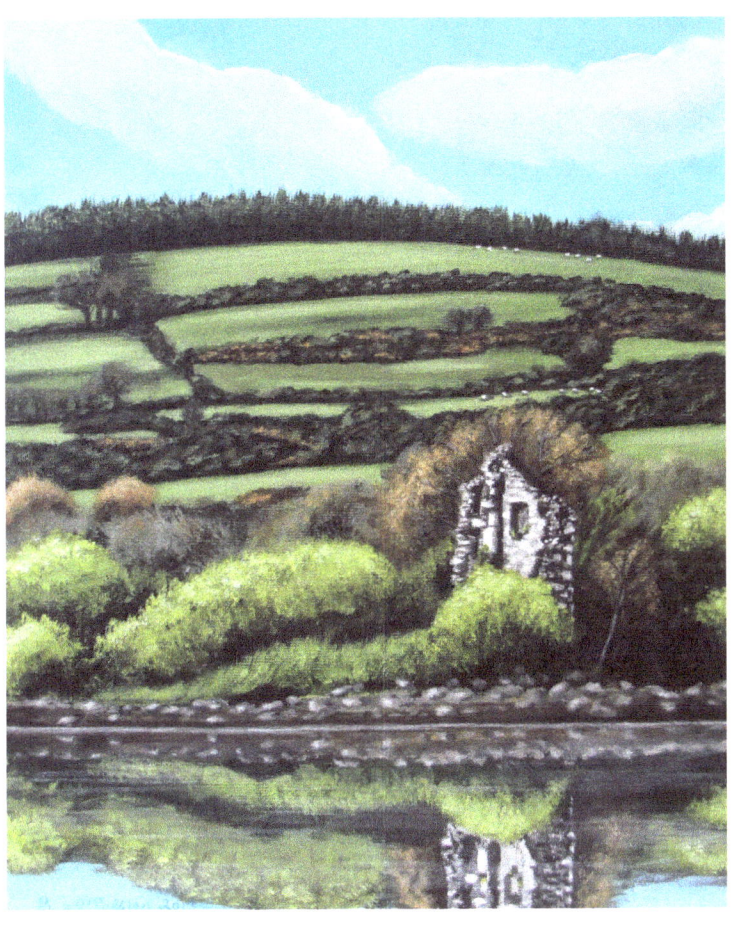

Sometimes I like to add a blue sky or some reflections in my painting, just to make it a little different.

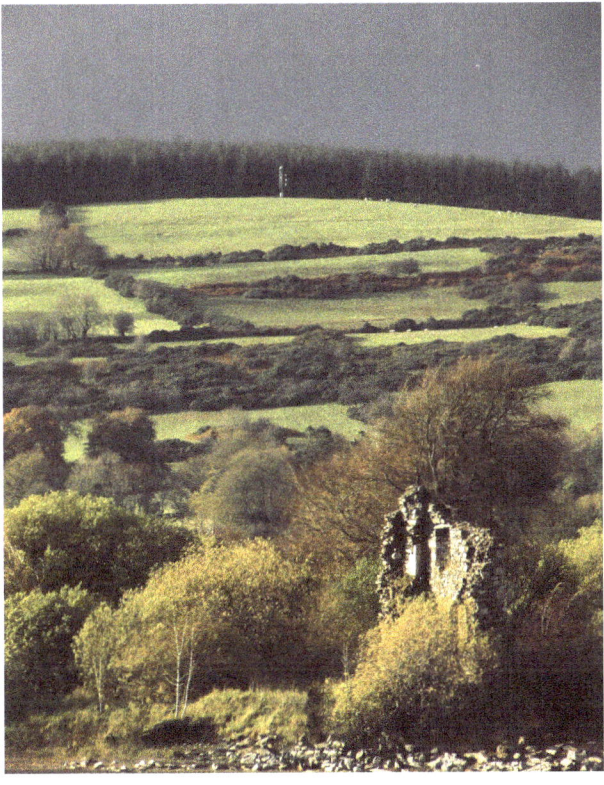

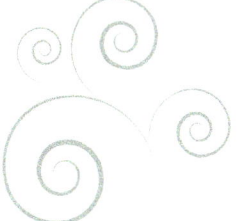

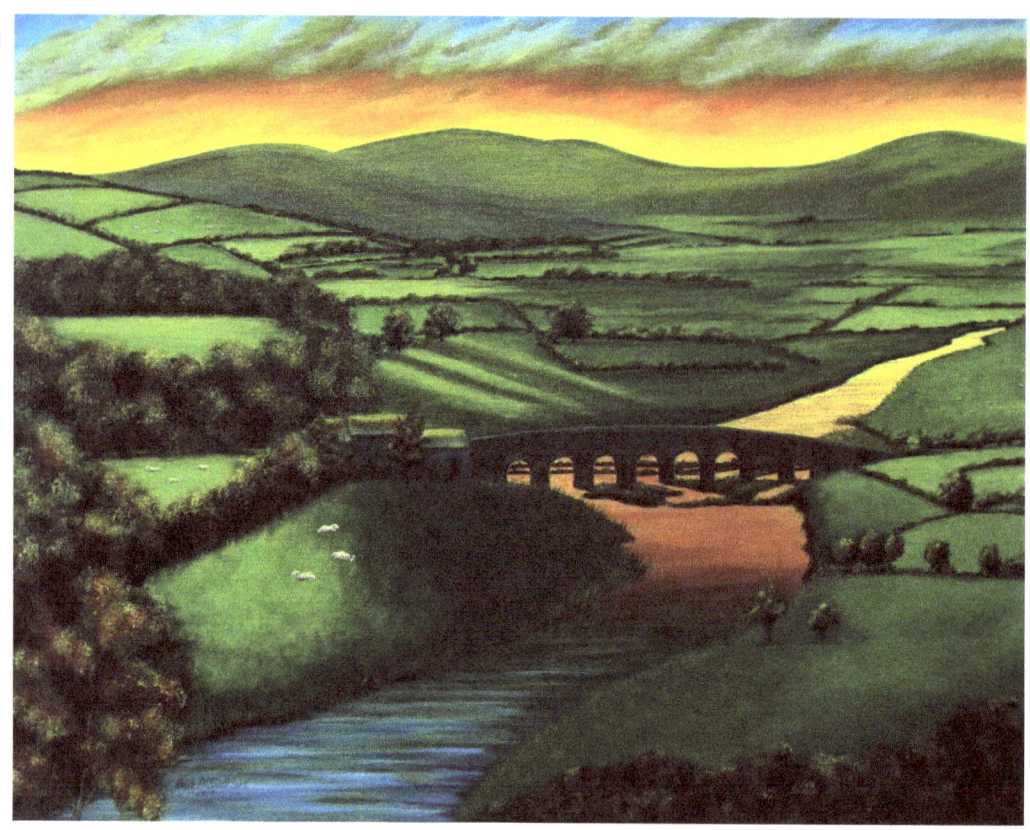

Before the Lakes - My artwork top and the original photo below. The photo appears on the South Dublin Libraries Archive pages, it is thought to be one of Valentine's photos, and I sought their permission to put in this book, which they kindly gave.

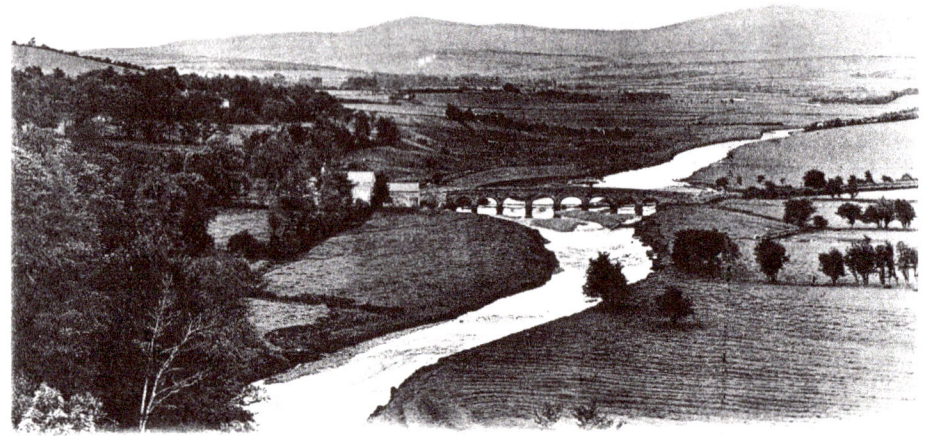

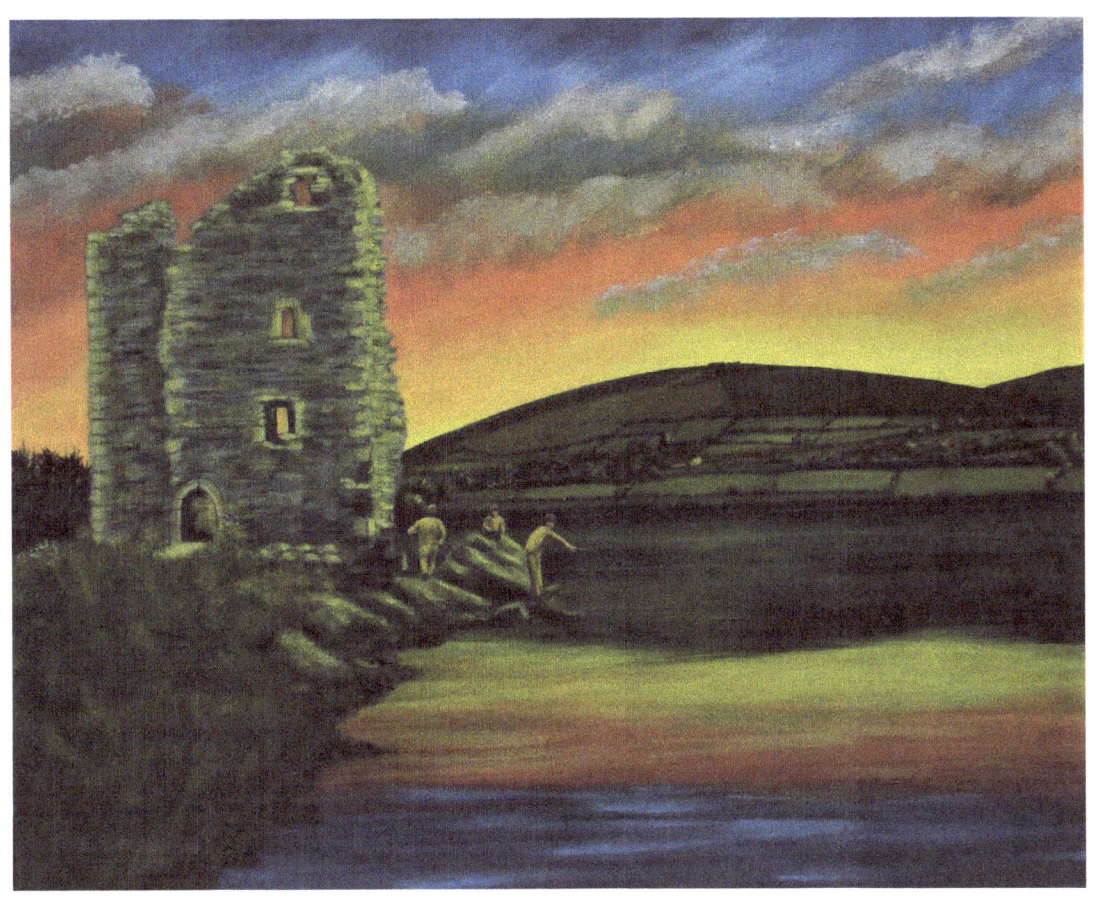

Burgage Tower in the 1980's - My artwork top and the original photo below. The Photo was taken by Patrick Healy in 1985, appears on the South Dublin Libraries Archive pages, and I sought their permission to put in this book, which they kindly gave.

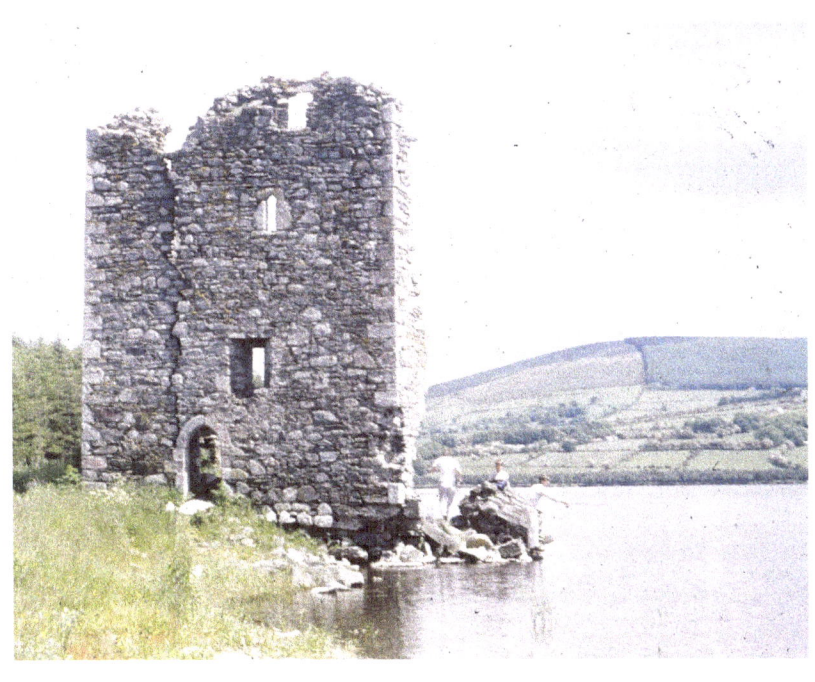

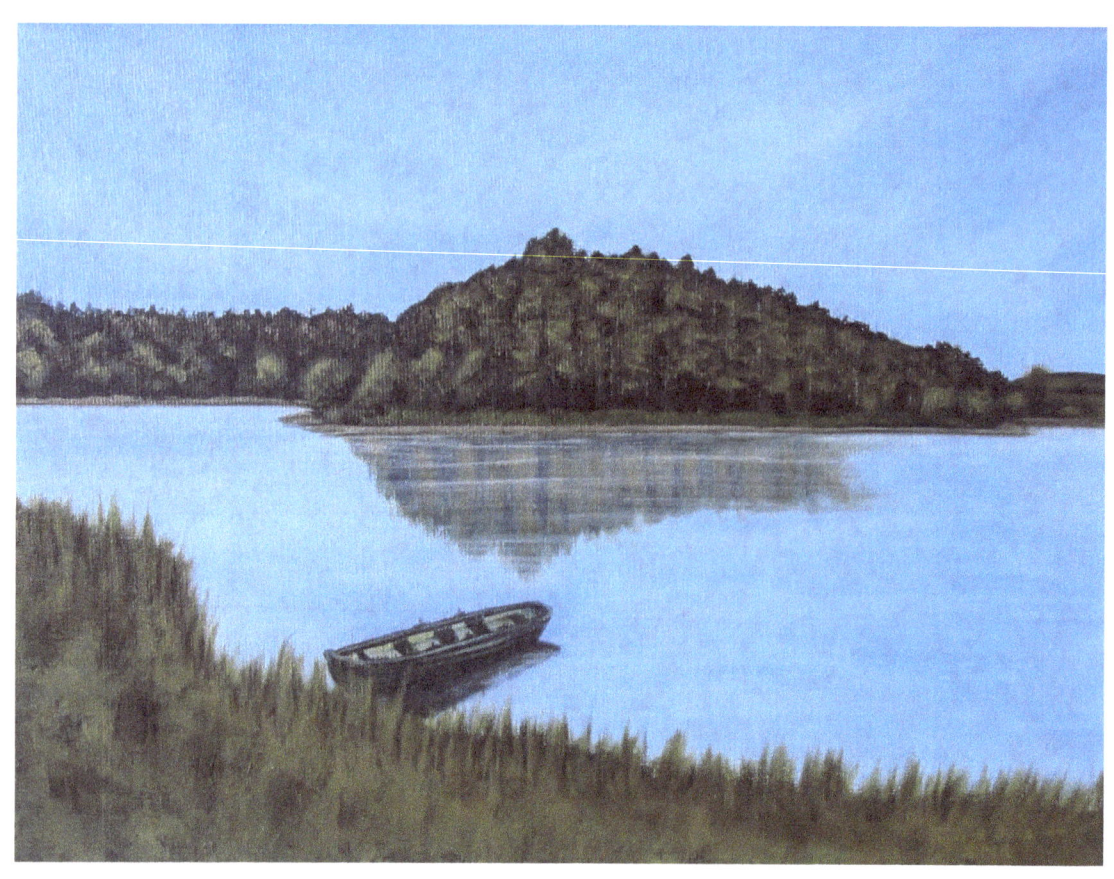

Russellstown Blessington Lakes - My artwork top and my photo below.

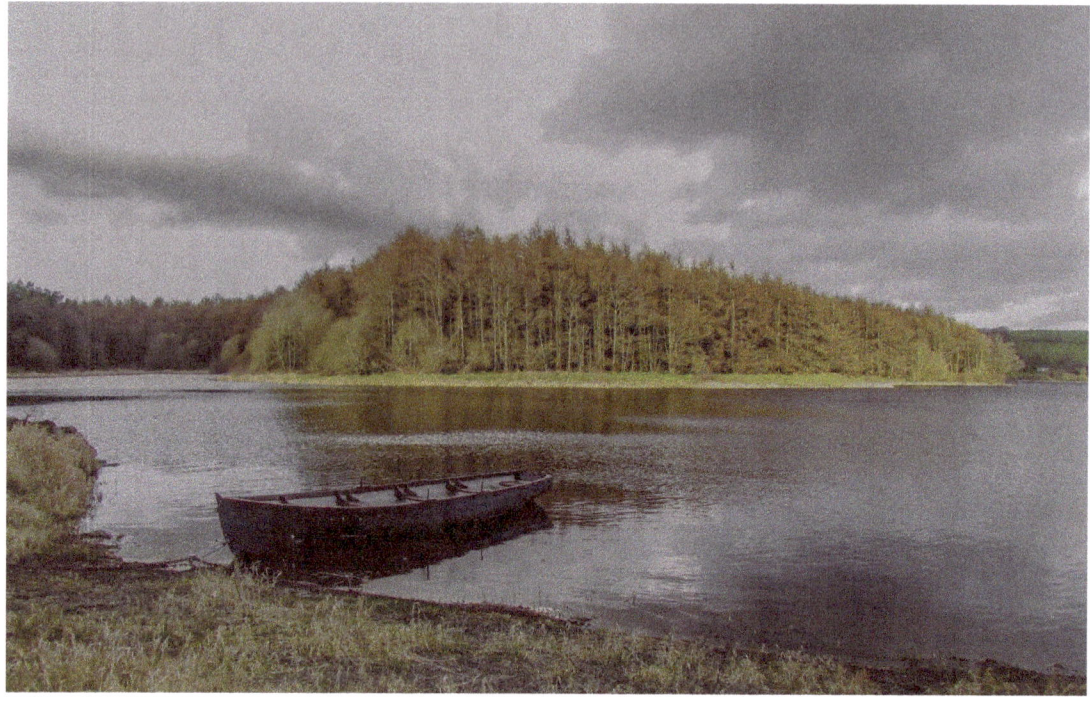

RECOMMENDED READING

In the course of my research for some of the interesting historical facts that I wanted to include in this book. I came across a massive amount of material that was fascinating. There are many books written that have great stories and historical facts in them.

Books with local interest

Journal of Blessington - Lakeside Heritage Group 2013
Blessington Now and Then, Here and There - Members of The Blessington Local & Family History Society
Blessington Estate 1667 - 1908 - Kathy Trant
Tales from a Drowned Land - Journal of West Wicklow Historical Society 1 (1983-4), 14)
The Wicklow World of Elizabeth Smith 1840 - 1850 - Dermot James (Editor), Seamas O Maitiu (Editor)
Memories of the Liffey Valley - Alice (ed) Griffin (Author)

There are more available from Blessington Tourist Office, Co. Wicklow
and also from this website https://irishlocalhistorybooks.com/books/ (formerly Blessington Book Store)

Website References

https://www.tulfarrishotel.com/blog/a-short-history-of-blessington-lakes

https://www.irishtimes.com/life-and-style/motors/haunting-tales-of-submerged-villages-and-steam-trams-in-the-ghost-s-hole-1.735367

https://www.independent.ie/regionals/wicklowpeople/localnotes/memories-come-flooding-back-35872128.html

www.visitwicklow.ie

https://en.wikipedia.org/wiki/Blessington

http://irelandinruins.blogspot.com/2011/09/burgage-castle-co-wicklow.html

https://www.duchas.ie/en/src?q=burgage+Castle&t=CbesTranscript

https://visitwicklow.ie/item/st-marks-cross/?category=426

https://blessington.ie/heritage-trail/credit-union-house/

https://heritage.wicklowheritage.org/places/blessington/blessington_heritage_trail

Website References continued

https://www.christiaancorlett.com/the-liffey-scheme-and-the-poulaphuca-reservoir-part-1

https://www.christiaancorlett.com/the-liffey-scheme-and-the-poulaphuca-reservoir-part-2

https://www.oireachtas.ie/en/debates/debate/dail/1936-11-04/50/

https://heritage.wicklowheritage.org/places/river_liffey_heritage_project-2/burgage_more

http://irelandinruins.blogspot.com/2011/09/burgage-castle-co-wicklow.html

https://heritage.wicklowheritage.org/places/river_liffey_heritage_project-2/threecastles

https://www.igs.ie/conservation/project/russborough-house

Also check out https://blessingtonhistorysociety.com/blog/

Grateful Thanks to the following

Aidan Cruise - Historian - who supplied some historical information

John Horan - Chairperson Blessington Town Team - who supplied historical information on Greenway

Dave Power - South Dublin Libraries - who gave permission to use archived photos

Jason Mulhall - Blessington Tidy Towns - who helped me with my query

And to all the people who are involved locally with making Blessington a better place. All the people who were and are involved with the Greenway project, the Heritage Trail, the Planning and new layouts for pedestrian areas. All the lovely staff in The Blessington Credit Union, and all the lovely staff in The Blessington Tourist Office. To everyone at Texaco Garage, The Office Shop, Harvest Fair, and Janet from Blessington Bookstore, now unfortunately closed, but the link for her online store is included under the section, books of local interest, who helped me sell my various books over the years. To Mark Wright who runs The Valleymount Country Fair, to Ged, Johnny, Kathleen, Marie and all the volunteers, to Pat Tiernan who runs the Craft Collective. To all my fellow crafters who are friendly and supportive, thanks so much! Blessington is a really lovely place to live in because of you all. You really make my day brighter!

www.ingramcontent.com/pod-product-compliance
Lightning Source LLC
Chambersburg PA
CBHW062355220526
45472CB00008B/1811